RELIGION IN RECENT ART

‘Art is man’s nature.’—*Burke*

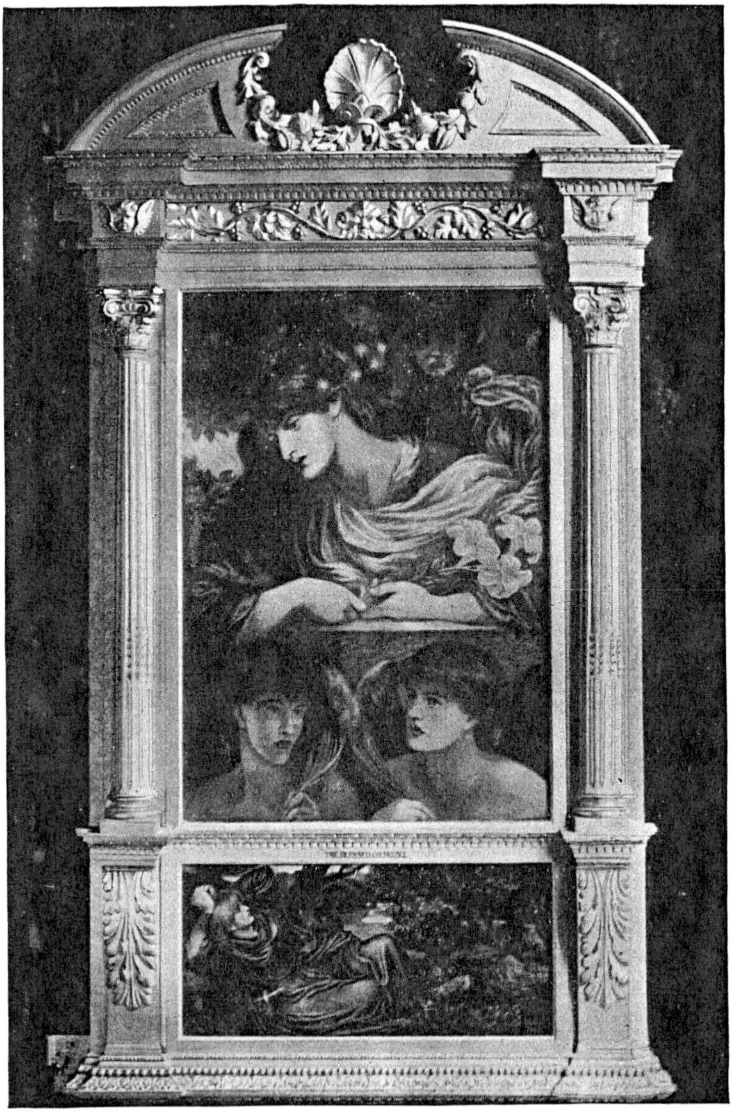

Dante Gabriel Rossetti. *Caswell Smith, Photo, Oxford St., W.*

THE BLESSED DAMOZEL.

RELIGION IN RECENT ART

EXPOSITORY LECTURES ON

ROSSETTI, BURNE JONES WATTS, HOLMAN HUNT AND WAGNER

BY

P. T. FORSYTH

WITH EIGHT ILLUSTRATIONS

Wipf & Stock
PUBLISHERS
Eugene, Oregon

Wipf and Stock Publishers
199 W 8th Ave, Suite 3
Eugene, OR 97401

Religion in Recent Art
Expository Lectures on Rosetti, burne Jones Watts, Holman Hunt and Wagner
By Forsyth, P.T.
ISBN: 1-57910-017-1
Publication date 11/10/2004
Previously published by Hodder and Stoughton, 1901

MATRI

PRIMOGENITUS

MEAS LITERARUM PRIMITIAS

D. D. D.

PREFACE

It may account for several features, and especially for the style, of the following pages if it be explained that, with the exception of the Sixth Lecture, they were written for a promiscuous audience, to whom they were also, in the simpler parts, spoken. The discourses on the painters arose out of a desire much less ambitious than publication, which was not originally contemplated. They sprang from a desire to lend some help to those whom it was the writer's business to teach in spiritual things, and who were much more likely to be grateful for fragments of assistance than critical of blunders on which the clergy of Art might be severe. They were lay sermons.

To students and experts in Art, as such, the book (be it humbly and sincerely said) is of no worth. It has what would be described in another connection as no scientific value. Its purpose is popular, though not in the extreme sense of the word. Nothing has more to do with that public genius of ours for hideousness which Art Congresses deplore than a vague but deep conviction on the part of the public that Art is for the artists chiefly or alone, and that it is out of vital relation to our most serious interests and beliefs. Art is a spiritual product; and it is fatal to every spiritual product that its church should exist for the sake of its clergy. An effort was here made, *faute de mieux*, to bring home to a small section of the lay mind that spiritual interest in the great subject-matter of Art which must in the long-run constitute the basis of its appeal to mankind at large. It was sought to familiarise people who do not claim to be considered artistic at all with a true way, which for them is the truest, of viewing pictures; while at the same time the writer makes no claim to be correct in every particular interpretation. Some of his interpretations he offers with much more diffidence than may appear from the text. It is believed, however, that there is room and need for more *expository* criticism than we possess either in Art or Literature. Nowhere is this so much the case as in Music. When shall the Ruskin of that art arise? A vast number of people are willing to be helped to see. And a growing number, on the other hand, who have neither the faculty nor the courage for criticism which becomes itself a classic, may yet be able to afford some useful help and lasting pleasure by handing their own magnifier to visitors to the galleries. Expository preaching is coming back into fashion and use, and it need not be confined to scriptural texts, nor to that order of Inspiration alone which marks the Bible.

There is one leading principle of Art which it has in common with the most spiritual religion, and which is made much of here. The content of Art, being in the nature of Inspiration, must not be limited to the direct and conscious horizon of the artist. It is of no private interpretation—even when the artist himself expounds. We must indeed avoid and reprobate interpretations which are as alien to his intention as the chief baker's three baskets are to the doctrine of the Trinity, or the 'badgers' skins dyed red,' in Exodus, are to the Atonement. But while we refuse to do violence to the text, we must equally refuse to go no further than itself on its own road. Mere textualism of this sort really is violence to the text at last, and the Bible has almost been ruined for the public by it. And we shall never get the true taste for Art afloat as a social power till we can set people free from the paralysing fear of going a jot beyond the direct and immediate consciousness of the artist at his work. We must feel ourselves free to find in a picture any suggestion which is really and reasonably congruous with its central idea, whether deliberately meant by the painter or no. The great spiritual products of an age or a civilisation reflect something much more than their artist or even their art. And painter, singer, and poet are alike, as Shelley says, 'the hierophants of an unapprehended inspiration.'

The perusal of a few pages will readily show that the writer has in view chiefly the religious significance of our contemporary Art; that he prizes Art chiefly as it can speak to the soul; and that he hopes for much to religion from it, unless it aspire to oust Religion, and drive itself the chariot of the sun. Æsthetic culture has become to many but a piece of slang; but the large culture of the imagination won from Art may be of essential use in defending us from the dangers to Religion of our national type of mind. Far more than half of the religious difficulties which torment people in a day like this are due to the hard, inelastic, and unsympathetic order of mind which they bring to bear upon subjects the most subtle, genial, and flexible of all.

And, furthermore, a true understanding of the message of Art might prevent some from seeking there an immunity from that malady of thought which they dread in Religion. If men can be convinced that the greatest Art is fullest of thought (in due artistic form), it will be the more easy to assure them that the greatest Religion cannot do without it; and so the escape from sentimentalism in one direction will do much to help us clear of it in the other. It will be useless to seek in Art the calm which was destroyed by Theology in Religion, or to think to evade the moral taxation by Faith in an easy seclusion with Beauty. It is not an absolutely certain sign of largeness of mind to turn into artistic tastes the energies that could find no scope in piety. If devotion be poor and intelligence low in a community, the Art will not be rich or high which is adopted instead. Bald devotion and trivial art are alike symptoms of that spiritual poverty which underlies the hard-featured piety of our pushing Christian type.

The theological passages will by some be deemed an impertinence in such a connection.

To the writer they are very far otherwise; but he feels that the *Zeitgeist* is not with him here. He trusts much to the ability of the skilful reader to skip.

CONTENTS

PAGE

ROSSETTI; OR, THE RELIGION OF NATURAL PASSION. I. TO VII., ... 1

BURNE JONES; OR, THE RELIGION OF PRÆTER-NATURAL IMAGINATION. I. TO IV., ... 40

WATTS; OR, THE RELIGION OF SUPERNATURAL HOPE. I. TO III., ... 86

HOLMAN HUNT; OR, THE RELIGION OF SPIRITUAL FAITH. PART I., ... 141

HOLMAN HUNT; OR, THE RELIGION OF SPIRITUAL FAITH. PART II., ... 174

RICHARD WAGNER AND PESSIMISM. I TO VII., . 209

WAGNER'S 'PARSIFAL.' I. TO IV., ... 252

ILLUSTRATIONS

THE BLESSED DAMOZEL (ROSSETTI), . . *Frontispiece.*

PROSERPINA (ROSSETTI), ... *to face page* 13

MARY MAGDALENE (ROSSETTI), . . . „ 26

CUPID AND PSYCHE (BURNE JONES), . . „ 66

CHANT D'AMOUR (BURNE JONES), . . „ 68

THE RESURRECTION (BURNE JONES), . . „ 77

HOPE (WATTS), ... „ 107

THE SCAPEGOAT (HOLMAN HUNT), . . „ 180

ROSSETTI

OR, THE RELIGION OF NATURAL PASSION

I

THERE was a time in the history of Christendom when Art and Piety went hand in hand, and Religion and Imagination were almost co-equal powers. It was in the wonderful Middle Age, the age of Dante and Thomas Aquinas, of St. Francis, and the great artists Flemish and Italian. And it was the second time the same spectacle had been seen in Europe. Once before, in the golden age of historic Greece, Art and Religion had gone side by side, and men's worship and their fantasy were in full and fine accord.

But how different the two ages really were. Neither, indeed, was permanent. In Greece, as in Catholic Europe, it was impossible to stand still. The fine balance of powers could be maintained but for a moment, as it were. In neither case was the human spirit yet mature. A vaster and wiser Spirit impelled it. A more unearthly heaven allured man to brighter worlds and led the way. The House Beautiful of this earthly tabernacle was dissolved. Sense and soul fell apart, and a new spirit rose from between. Faith and Fantasy went to war for a new realm, and the vexed spirit had to sound its perilous way through new and greater problems to conquests and discoveries on higher seas. But mark the difference between the two dissolutions, between the break-up of the harmony in Pagan Greece and in Christian Europe. In Greece it was Art that destroyed Religion; in Europe it was Religion that destroyed Art. In Greece, the people, in the name of Beauty, ceased to believe; in Christendom, the people, in the name of Truth, ceased to delight and enjoy. In Greece, Faith sank as taste spread; in Christian Europe, Faith rose and taste decayed. In Greece there came that social weakness and internecine strife which laid the country at the feet, first of Alexander, then of Rome, while the philosophic sects were frittering away both Faith and Thought. In later Europe there came also the wars of the nations, the quarrels of the sects among themselves, and of them all with the Church. But in this case it was a healthy strife, it was the ferment of life, it was the break-up of the old historic sward by a resurrection. It was not dissolution by decay, but reconstruction by the Spirit of a larger life. It was the pulling down of old barns for the building of greater. It was the spirit of God in man taking fresh flight into a new heaven, and shattering its old eggshell into temporary chaos by the sudden spreading of its eager wings. The break-up of Greek art came with the decay of Greece. The very fact that artists went on imitating the old proved the lack of fresh and original life. They had skill without power, law but no gospel. But the break-up of

Mediæval Art came with the new birth of Europe. And the very absence of imitation, while it betrays the slumber of the religious imagination, is due, not to the decay of human power, but just to its violent escape in a new direction more needful for the hour.

In Greece, then, the Art slew the Religion; in Christian Europe the Religion slew the Art. In Greece the Imagination destroyed the Conscience, in Europe the Conscience paralysed the Imagination. But again mark a difference. Art cannot revive Religion; Religion can revive and regenerate Art. Art may be the *vehicle* of the Spirit; Religion is the *power* of the Spirit. Art is a particular utterance of that Spiritual power which Religion alone is able to create. The organ cannot produce the life; the life can produce the organ; as thought produces language. Give us power in the Spirit, and then Art will come; but the taste for Art will not arrest the decay of the Spirit. The culture of later Greece did more to enervate Rome than to quicken humanity. But the religious quickening of humanity gave a new and unexampled impulse to culture. It did so when Christianity entered Europe, revolutionised Paganism, and in the fulness of time sent Art forth on a new and prodigious career. It has done so again now that the Reformation has purified Religion, enlarged the Soul, and made possible the birth of real Science; now that time again fills to the hope of a new and grander triumph of an Art more various still. Nothing has ever been done in the world like the landscape art of Protestantism and

Protestant lands. And the great revolutionary movement known as Pre-Raphaelitism is but the overture to an artistic performance which our children only will see at its height. But we must not lose sight of the point that it all depends on our fidelity to the conscience on the largest and holiest scale. It depends on our reverence for nature's truth, and God's glory therein. I repeat, Art will not make men religious. It is not meant to do so. It should not be used or expected to do so. It can only express, educate, refine, and exalt in certain directions what religion we have. Art does not create Religion, but Religion does create Art. I do not mean that piety will make this or that man an artist, or a lover of Art. But I am speaking of the human spirit at large. And I mean that religion, which handles the most commanding realities, and affects the whole soul, must kindle also in due time its imaginative side. It will open hidden glories, and, what is of most moment for the best artistic purposes, teach men habitually to believe in them. It will create not only Art, but the soil and climate in which Art grows.

The immediate sequel of the Reformation was such that the sympathies of men had to turn away from the gentler agencies of imagination, and flow towards the more militant tasks which the social condition of Europe prescribed. Religious thought had to be reconstructed, and that led to absorption in theology. The moral condition of Europe also had to be reformed; that led to a needful protest against the unchartered imagination which had brought about much of the mischief, and to an extreme protest against the religious use of the imagination altogether. The social and political state of Europe had to be changed, and the change, in most lands, is not yet complete; but it led and leads to over-engrossment with public and practical affairs. Now, although it may seem otherwise at first sight, for the proper conduct, even of movements like these, much imagination is required, and such demands have accordingly been made upon the higher practical energy and constructive power that the field of religion has been denuded of imagination for the time. But now that, in this country at least, we are in a position of something like social and political freedom, we are beginning to feel how wretched, and blind, and naked our religious soul is. We begin, after our outward successes, to be just a little less absorbed in our doing, and in our self; and as we look within for something not ourselves, something to dignify and bless ourselves, we feel poor and helpless. We feel a schism and a drought in our own souls, and not only an incongruity in our philosophy. We are made to realise, not only the sufferings of Art by its detachment from the spirit of religion, but—what most of us should, and many of us do feel much more—the sufferings of religion by its severance from the imagination. Our religion is too often a starveling, pinched, inhuman, and unholy thing. And it is so because it has lost in inspiration far more than it has gained in currency and correctness. It has lost in that aspect and function of it which is kindred to the imagination. It has become harsh, strident, and unlovely, something to be stoutly asserted, blindly defended, and tenaciously held, rather than absolutely trusted, winsomely worshipped, nobly evidenced, and beautifully beloved. Our God has become in many quarters but our Palladium, and our Christ but a crutch or a badge. As a result many of the choicest spirits are repelled from our religion, and are sent back to the huge, exhausting, and, to some, fatal task of building, from the foundations of individual feeling and perception, a new and more commanding, or at least attractive, creed. But on many sides, on almost every side (except, perhaps, among the savage Protestantism in direct collision with Rome) there is rising evidence of a better, larger, and humaner spirit in religion. The improvement is, to a great extent, sentimental, it is true, but as thought returns to theology it will become really imaginative; and we shall be in a position not only to inspire a new art, but to benefit from the teachings of all art, to be more hospitable to its revelation, and to recognise that it can say for us what we cannot say for ourselves, but what our love to man and nature in Jesus Christ is bursting to say.

II

THE mutual relations between Art and Religion—why not at once say Art and Christ?—form a very wide field of thought. How interesting it would be to dwell upon the singular anomaly that the greatest art of the world has risen in connection with a religion whose sacred book is quite Puritan in this respect, and flatly proclaims its antagonism to plastic art by forbidding graven images and declaring that the Lord delighteth not in the limbs of a man. How fascinating to go on and illustrate the Art-Spirit, which, for all that, in prophet and psalmist, would not be denied, but broke out in poetry as it was repressed in the arts of form. But to do this is not my desire or purpose at present. I wish to say something about certain specimens of art which represent our achievements in this kind during the last half century; and of these, I confine myself only to such as are religious in their spirit and bearing. I avoid landscape, not because it is not religious in its principle, but because the religion in it is not direct enough, or powerful enough. I avoid also, for the most part, pictures dealing with expressly religious themes. It is not in these that we best find the religion of the age's art. Indeed, I avoid much in so rich and varied a field, and I confine myself chiefly to the products of that movement whose great feature it is to pursue Art, not merely in an artistic, but in a religious spirit; and which sets forth, consciously or unconsciously, some presentment of the religious and moral soul of the time. I mean the Pre-Raphaelite movement. Whatever may be thought of the technique of these artists, they are distinct and peculiar in this—that they are prophets as well as painters, and to no small extent apostles and martyrs. They body forth the spiritual fashion of the time, and hold the mirror to the better nature of the age. They escape the artist's vice of caring for nothing but their art—often, indeed, for nothing but their colour. They are in the thick of the age's current, and at the imaginative centres of its force. They do not cruise in the secluded lakes of artistic repose, nor dally in the still waters of mere æsthetic content. But they are caught by the riddle of the painful earth. Their sorrow is not the sorrow of this man or that, but of mankind, and of the heart. And their brightness, their charm, their promise, is more than the gleam upon their own single souls; it is part of the light which is our human hope, which lightens every soul, and brightens the general fate. They have a 'public mind.' Some pictures, we feel, may fitly enough belong to private owners. They have not a universal significance. They represent some phase of sectional or personal interest. They are not painted eye to eye with human fate. But there are others that we feel should be public property, because their interest is human and not particular; because they not only touch our hearts, but stir our spirit; because they represent the soul, and not merely an individual experience; because they breathe of the region which is not only free to all, but the destiny of all. They have the stamp of a universal imagination, and the echo of that religion which is neither selfish nor sentimental, but human in its instinct, imaginative in its range, and infinite in its significance. An artist who fulfils these conditions is a Master, and may be a Great Master. And the school of our time, which at least feels they should be fulfilled by Art, and strives to fulfil them, is the Pre-Raphaelite school. And it is because Mr. Watts, who is technically not a Pre-Raphaelite, is akin to them here, that I include his pictures, among those of which I would speak, as being not only of pictorial, but prophetic, worth.

III

Let me invite you at once, then, leaving a thousand things unsaid and criticisms unmet, to come to the pictures of Dante Gabriel Rossetti. How strange is the atmosphere we are in! How utterly alien to our common air! There is a sultry tropical feeling around, the heavy opulence of lands not ours, and passions to which our common lives are strange. We feel all the bewildering associations of the wizard's chamber. Our senses misgive us. We are oppressed, the room seems laden. We are ready for magic. In mirrors are glimpses of solemn beauty. In globes are vistas of hopeless tragedy. The world-sorrow sings through the world-soul. These gorgeous hues are like the sunset of glowing hope. We seem to stand on a loam-field, and wade among poppies to the knees. These strange faces are lovely opiates. These unusual attitudes are like the contortions of rocks—the relics of volcanic passion, and then still death.

The religion of Rossetti's art lies certainly in its spirit rather than in its particular subjects. It is above all things, as Mr. Ruskin says, 'romantic' art, as distinct from classical art like Leighton's or

Poynter's. And the romantic spirit is the specially Christian element in Art. It is the element of depth and wealth. Its vehicle is colour rather than form. It glories more in richness of harmony than severity of melody. Its fulness of chords bespeaks its wealth of love, and if it is sometimes too careless of drawing, that only means that in gospel it has forgotten law, and its power for the moment has outrun measure. The transparent fulness and abyss of colour make a temple for that Christian infinitude of spirit which ever transcends the limits of any finest line we draw. Such art pertains to the soul rather than to the taste. It is beauty deepened by contact with blight, and love at issue with seeming death. It represents a moral conflict in the artist's own soul. Such painters are not only artists, but men, and men in earnest—men who are of the elect of love and grief, who are in the army of mankind's holy war, and who not only reflect upon us a palpable beauty, but reveal a beauty in the grim heart of woe, put us almost in love with sorrow, and show us the budding morrow in all midnight. Sad as is this art of Rossetti, its sadness is not its all. It is clothed, nay, steeped in beauty, but it is also jewelled with hope. We might describe Rossetti's spiritual attitude as broken-hearted hope.

Let us look at one or two of these pictures. I confess I cannot bring myself to like or learn from the 'Blue Bower,' and I never found anybody that could, except from the colourist's point of view. The large picture of 'Dante's Dream,' splendid as it is from the purely artistic standpoint, does not contain much that bears on my present purpose. We may note, however, the fine conception of Love himself so much in love with the dead Beatrice that he must kiss her ere he brings Dante forward to her side. Let us pass on to 'Fiametta.' Fortunately, here Rossetti the poet comes in aid of Rossetti the painter. Some say the one art in him injured the other. That is a large question. But we may say, at any rate, that the one helps ordinary people greatly to understand the other. You should carefully read the sonnet on the frame of the painting. Here it is:—

> Behold Fiametta, shown in vision here,
> Gloom-girt, 'mid spring-flushed apple-growth she stands,
> And as she sways the branches with her hands,
> Along her arm the sundered bloom falls sheer,
> In separate petals shed, each like a tear;
> While from the quivering bough the bird expands
> His wings. And lo! my spirit understands
> Life shaken, and showered, and flown, and death drawn near.
> All stirs with change. Her garments beat the air,
> The angel circling round her aureole,
> Shimmers in flight against the tree's grey bole;
> While she, with reassuring eyes most fair,
> A presage and a promise stands; as 'twere
> On death's dark storm the rainbow of the soul.

What is this noble form then, so glorious in its apparel of beauty? There is nothing morbid about such a figure. It is one of the artist's healthiest, happiest inspirations. It would be a healthy, shapely Englishwoman but for the solemn soul that speaks through the face's tender force. It is the spirit which overcomes Death—serious as becomes the conflict, glorious as fits the victory, full of tremulous sensibility, many-hued passion and sympathetic response, else how should she be the 'Rainbow of the Soul'? She is as it were the soul of the soul, the self to which self dies to live indeed, the self we hope to be. She has pushed her way through the gloom, the stir, and change of death into a higher, but not more shadowy life. The mere natural life and its beauty are represented by the apple-blossom of the Spring. The falling petals set forth its tearful and swift decay. Life flies as the bird flies from the tree. Mark how fond Rossetti is of a red bird for life or spirit. That is to express how full-blooded, rich, and passionate a thing life essentially is, not a pale, passionless, inhuman thing. The background represents the gloom of Death, the lady represents the glory of Death. She is at once a presage and a promise, a boding and a hope, the rainbow of the soul. She is born from Death's dark cloud, but her father is an Eternal Sun. The flight of the red life and the lady's advance betoken that the passing of life is the birth of the true soul; which is to the life bygone as the solemn brimming sensibility of this face is to the hard plumage of the bird. The path of the soul is amid the gloom, but what matters it if heaven's light shine not only *on* her face but *through* it, if heaven's angels play in the very glory of her hair, and heaven's infinite resource in the undying wonder of her great blue eyes. I wish Rossetti had painted more pictures like this. There is nothing dismal in it, nothing wan, but there is beauty of the most luminous and noble sort.

It is otherwise with 'Proserpina.' And yet this is

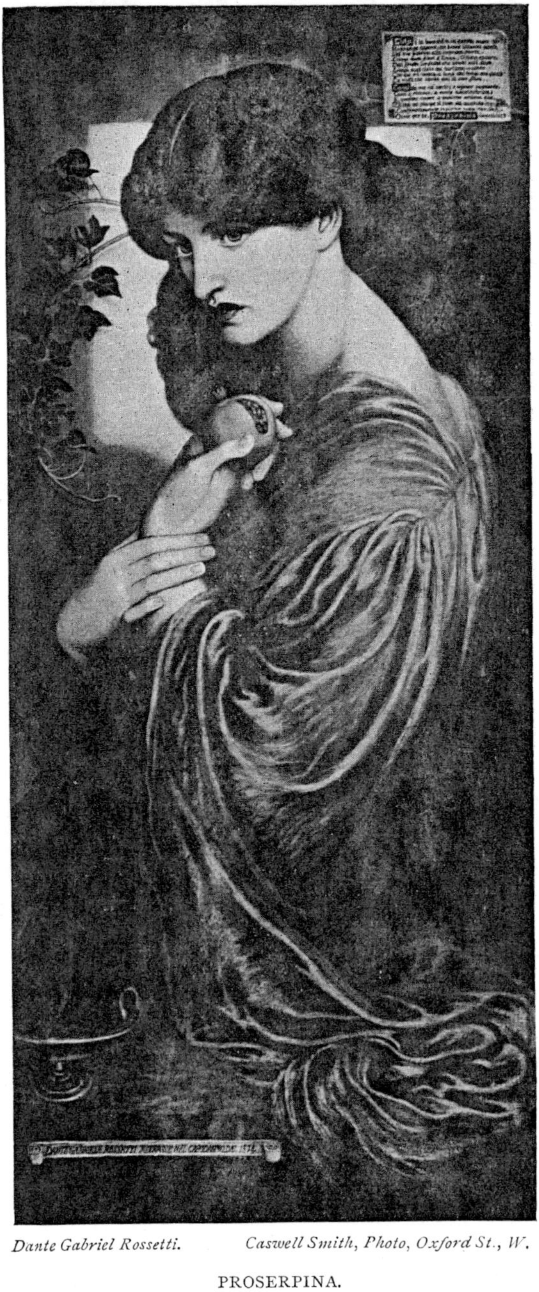

Dante Gabriel Rossetti. *Caswell Smith, Photo, Oxford St., W.*

PROSERPINA.

> And still some heart unto some soul doth pine
> (Whose sounds mine inner sense is fain to bring
> Continually together, murmuring),
> 'Woe 's me for thee, unhappy Proserpine!'

I think the expression of soul dreariness, both in picture and poem, is admirable. There is no wild burst of passion, but a settled frame of regret more obdurate than any fury of remorse. Proserpina is strange to herself; her true self is far away; her thought is in strange ways—ways alien to the nature of her soul. She is the empty queen of a lower world; she, whose birthplace was among the immortals, and whose home is on high. The light that reaches her here is cold—the very skies are chill, and her soul is bare. She has eaten, and her wistful eyes are open to a new light, and she knows now that she is starved and blind. Would Rossetti have complained if one found here a picture of the age's soul? We have eaten of the Tree of Knowledge, and we live in the light of science. But we find it a dreary dwelling when the soul's true self remembers its home, and craves for the old faith which has now dwindled into a faint and sombre hope. How can a soul, a daughter of the living God, and native of a warm and radiant love—how can that soul but feel bare and chilled and miserable in a world of rigid sequence and loveless law, if it awake to any feeling at all? Must not its natural passion be benumbed, thus stranded upon the rocks of a passionless, loveless, irresponsive world? Must it not sink into a wan hysteric melancholy, a blue cold dream?

It is, perhaps, of little matter whether the artist intended this or not. It is quite congenial to his habit of thought. We know that he sympathised with none of the scientific negations of the age. We do him no real wrong when we see painted here the serious agnosticism of the day, its settled sadness, its not infrequent grace, its twilight tones, its restless intuition of a higher creed, its dim discernment of a larger light, its fond surmise of possible pity, and its wistful irresolute memory of better days, which were days of faith and settled hope. Then the soul had less command of the lower earth, but more power in heaven; the fruit of knowledge had not yet dimmed the sense of a present God, nor been bought by the loss of a living love.

Such a genius as that of Rossetti could not paint even his own sorrow, without painting, in some way, the sorrow of his race and age.

Is there beyond the grave a living love and a passion of patient pity, a sweet remembrance of old affections, and a wonder-smitten waiting for the knitting up of severed hearts? Who does not find it easier to believe that after looking at the picture of the Blessed Damozel? Again, I remind you that you must surmount the mannerisms of the painter; you must surmount the strangeness, the extravagance of his new and original style. Above all, you must try to banish from your memory the follies of those feeble imitators, who have taken æsthetic aspects of life for moral principles, and striven to order their conduct by the visions of art. Forget also the laughable parodies which have been called forth by the extravagance of that school. I much enjoy both the satire of *Punch*, and the banter of *Patience*. But I think they have taken an undue hold of the public mind. They arose to rebuke a race of imitators, and they are having their imitators in turn. There is a flippant style of talk and allusion, after a fashion set by Gilbert's and Du Maurier's exquisite fooling, a style which is much more foolish than exquisite, and which destroys our power to receive the real gifts of touching and unearthly beauty which this art can bring. Of course we may ridicule languishing attitudes, and stalky necks, and faces hungry, and eyes intense. Any dunce can do that. But it is only poverty or vulgarity of feeling that dismisses the whole school in that fashion. Depend upon it, if we see nothing more than absurdity in a picture like this Blessed Damozel, it is no compliment to the healthiness of our feeling, but rather a confession of its inadequacy. If we dismiss the whole thing as morbid, we should remember that there is such a thing as being 'morbidly robust'; and we are buying our amusement at the cost of some of our heart, if we enjoy the parodies of æstheticism till we cease to find emotion and delight in the abused art itself. The abuse of anything by fools does not destroy the liberty to use it of the wise.

Now, both the poem and the picture of the Blessed Damozel seem to me of the most moving sort. There is passion in them, and music, which linger in the memory not only as visions of beauty, but as spiritual possessions, and furniture of the soul itself. The situation is quite simple, and needs no explanation. There is no abstruse depth of allegory. The only depth is the depth of sorrow, and the distant dawn of joy in store. Few people whose grief and loss do not fall away like water from them, need more than their own memory to place them where that widowed man lies, long forlorn, in the weird tree-shadow of the autumn eve. Life's rest and charm are gone away, as it might be on the bosom of that cold blue stream, which winds slowly and afar beneath the dim green shade. You call him sentimental and unreal, perhaps. But that is only because we seldom or never are allowed to see the strong man when this hour is upon him. When we come to occupy his place, we certainly do not know how he looks. We can safely and decently see him only by the aid of art of this kind. His loss is ten years old, but his grief is still near and young. The yellow leaves drop around him, and play about his worn face. In his mood of dreamy abstraction and reminiscence, they seem to him like the touch of long-gone golden hair, and the breath of a presence, far, far away. So far and yet so near. The upper part of the picture represents the vision which these suggestions wake in his rapt spirit. It is one of those dreams in the strength of which a man awakes, and goes without other heart-food forty nights and forty days, and indeed all the days of his life, till he come himself to the Mount of God. You can see at a glance that all these reunited lovers in the rear make a promise of one more re-union in its time. But you will not see at a glance, you must wait a little and pay some court, and then you will see the soul of the picture in the central face. You will see the wonder of the new realm, that has not yet died away from her eyes, nor ever by any familiarity will die, in a world where all things are made for ever new. You may see the fathomless pity for him who is left behind, pity subdued to patience by the sight of redeeming power, and longing chastened by faith into watchful waiting over the sufferer in the fitful fever of life. Beatrice looked from Paradise upon Dante like that;

> 'Whereupon she, after a pitying sigh
> Her eyes directed towards me with that look
> A mother casts on a delirious child.'
>
> PAR. I., 100.

This is no pale angel to whom patience is needless, and radiance a birthright, without struggle or pain. But the love that watches and pities yonder, is of a piece with all the sad realism of life here. It is an angel, yet a woman too. It is memory redeemed, not enfeebled. It is earth glorified, not erased. It is the old affection taught to wait, and content to wait—not to help; for its patience comes of the sure faith that the help is in perfectly competent hands. The love that waits in wonder and trust, helps us enough by allowing itself only to be seen. The sight of one that has loved us, and overcome, and loves us unto the end, is perhaps all the help we really need—all that is good for us. It is the help we crave the most. Few Christian souls can stand before that picture without feeling afresh that there is waiting for us, and watching over us, a love, a wonder, a pity, and a patience which, if we knew them, would make any life tolerable, and any endurance brief. Life's Providence is kind like this. And we may well pray for moments when, in our weariness, we may have these glimpses to leave us less forlorn, and, in the long hours between, a faith to preserve us from the slow perdition of a habitual and passionless despair.

I am not sure that we have the right to call this a religious picture, or a spiritual work in the highest sense of the words. It may be that we have here, severely speaking, but the finest ensoulment of natural passion. But one does not care to raise these distinctions in its presence. And the religious spirit placed before it will not hesitate to make eternal and universal the lovely and touching suggestions it conveys, or to see in the deathless love of two high hearts, the symbol and promise of a love that is to rule, unite, and satisfy all hearts. No picture will give us the faith which makes a victory of life; but to a latent faith, and the wish to believe, art may afford the spirit many a foothold, many a kindling, many a gleam.

IV

It is not really difficult, with sensibility and docility, to overcome Rossetti's mannerisms. It is true you do not see such women as these often. But it is equally true that if you did see such a woman you would not be very able or willing to forget her. I fear the great example of Raphael has fixed our imagination down to a type of female beauty which has become at last a bondage. Rossetti has made a strong if not violent protest. He has gone back to another type, represented, perhaps, by that strange Jeremiah of the Renaissance, Botticelli. And not before time. Women have no greater, but they have other interests than sweet maternity; and it might be made out that the Raphael type of Madonna has been a considerable influence in retarding the development of female intelligence. I do not mean intellect. I mean the kind of spiritual intelligence which best befits womankind. We may call it soul, if by soul is understood the intelligence of the heart—not the mere sweetness of the affections, but the sensibility and divination of them, their power, not only to respond but to perceive—and to perceive not by the rude methods of the understanding, but by the fine skill of the sympathies, and the subtle insight of pure passion. Soul is as alien to mere sentiment as to mere thought. It is mind and not sheer mobility, but it is mind like music breathing from the face. Now women have been so long glorified by our great artists as ideal mothers that they have in some cases taken a rebound into the opposite extreme of eager intellects. They have been religious devotees, and they threaten to become religious sceptics by way of protest. What they are like to miss, meanwhile, is the religious intelligence of the soul. Now, I do not say that Rossetti's women are women of lofty intelligence; but they are not Madonnas, at least of the usual type. They interest us. Madonnas are often not interesting. And they are not interesting because, though they have affection, they have not soul; their affection has in it no note of distinction; it may carry consolation, but it does not touch us where those powers touch us which inspire. We may here, perhaps, find one reason why so many of Rossetti's pictures are of women. He paints the religion of noble natural passion, or of the soul. His work is the ensoulment of passion, and not its mere portrayal. Now the soul is just that part and level of us which covers the relation between man and woman. The higher region of the *spirit* brings us face to face with God. But the *soul* is the sphere of all those influences which are gathered and typified in the central relation of man and woman. A man of soul is a man sensitive to the distinctive influence of womankind. A woman of soul is a woman capable of responding to the most distinguished and characteristic features of men. The art, which may most truly be called art of the soul, is deeply engrossed with the relations of man and woman, with the fine passion and drear tragedy of hearts. And if divine relations are handled, they are handled by the medium of those relations. His female ideal is the measure not, indeed, of a man's spirit, but certainly of his soul. And you may, farther, now guess why so many of these faces are sorrowful. It is because in most cases it is sorrow that ennobles affection, gives passion the air of refinement and distinction, and changes a heart into a soul. The noblest intelligence of the heart, the birth of the soul, comes not but by sorrow, loss, and the cross's gain. You must not think of Rossetti as merely a painter of a certain type of pretty women. Any clever sketcher can fill the printshop windows with pretty faces in bewitching hats. Rossetti worshipped beauty, and he gave himself up to portraying the most potent kind of beauty he knew, the beauty of living and ensouled flesh. And remembering that Rossetti has been a very great force in our Victorian art—perhaps the greatest single force, while we allow for the influence of his wife, there is some presumption, perhaps, that there may have been an intuition of genius in his selection. I mean, that he may, by the prophetic instinct of genius, have been led to select, first as wife and then as type, an order of beauty which is destined to become more powerful than ever in the future history of the human soul. Man is much greater than nature. A face can convey more than a landscape. The beauty of woman is much more influential than that of nature. But it is so, just in so far as she rises above her merely natural beauty, and discloses the fascination of intelligent and sympathetic soul. On all sides the influence of women is growing greater and greater on male society. More and more must the true and feminine woman be taken into account, and recognised as a power—of her own order. More and more, too, women are taking to the practice of art. Rossetti's instinct was probably prophetic in indicating that more and more they will become the subjects of art, in the sense that female beauty will more and more engross the artist's pencil. There are signs that the great battle of society will be fought round the position of women, and their relation to men. And as Art will be more and more in touch with the social condition, Art must feel this and utter it in its own way. And who can doubt that it is the Christian spirit which is thus moving society and affecting Art? As surely as the worship and the painting of the Madonna were allied, so must the more Christian idea of woman, which is fighting the pagan idea in current society, take its artistic shape, and determine the themes of Art.

V

But you will mark that the painting, like the poetry, of Rossetti, has a very strong grasp of the material base and vehicle of the soul. These are no pale or emaciated ascetics that he paints. If consumed, they are consumed with the fire of passion cherished, and not repressed. There is depth of colour—none of our painters has such colour. And there is some roundness of form. The perfection of the soul does not come by despite and mortification to the beauty and passion of which God has compounded human nature. Rossetti believed strongly in the divinity of the material and physical. But he was not a materialist. On the contrary, his art shows more affinity with those Pantheistic tendencies which are being forced upon the science of our day, and which lead some to a worship, not of nature, but of the spiritual ground of nature. He claimed a sanctity for the material because he felt that it was essentially spiritual. It had its right in the name of spirit, and its law was the law of final love. Do we not insist on that as part of the New Testament teaching? The laws of the material world have their right in the last resort, as expressions of the spirit of God, and agents of the love of God. That amazing depth and brilliancy of colour, which you see in Rossetti's pictures, is not simply luminous matter. It is transfigured matter. There is a spell about such light and depth which is the play of spirit, the radiance of unearthly lustre, the transparency of matter which is but spirit congealed on the top with the eternal current flowing strong beneath. Nature and natural passion are in their place divine. True, there is a something higher. But it is not higher in any sense which would destroy the innocency and divinity of that earlier natural stage. Art, here, is surely the handmaid of that true faith which delivers us from the curse laid by superstition upon the beauty and affection of nature, as if intense passion were lawless passion, and the love of the body were no more than the lust of the flesh.

Rossetti does not paint character so much as sensibility. He paints, so far as form goes, abstract visions and types of beauty. But he paints, as to the spirit of it, with great sincerity, with a genuine reality of passion, and a firm grasp of the essential truth. We let the mere unfamiliarity of his manner mislead us if we think he was a moonstruck dreamer. Love for him was no abstraction. It could exist only in living concrete form, as some loving person and loving life. As his poetic Bible, Dante's *Vita Nuova*, says, so he firmly held

> They are the same, love and the gentle heart;
> Nor can they more abide from each apart,
> Than reason parted from the reasoning soul.

He grasps material reality; there is reality also in his passion; and he had a power of facing sternly some realities of life which most people have neither the purity nor the courage to handle. This art of his is pure to the quick. And all pure art which handles themes convertible to impurity does a service to religion. To handle impurity purely is surely the very manner of Christ. The purpose of religion is to purify, not to ignore the passions and realities of life. How little of our painting is real in this courageous, and almost religious sense. There are many artists far more conventional than Rossetti, who are far more unreal in their spirit. They never face the realities of life in the way a strong, pure soul alone can do. He began with a strong dramatic faculty. He did not always paint female faces. It is unfair to forget that he could paint such a picture as that where Mary Magdalene, passing along the street in a band of gay companions, is suddenly arrested and changed, as the Saviour looks on her from a window. Nor must we forget the most powerful and terrible of all his pictures, entitled 'Found,' where, in the shimmer of the dawn, a countryman, coming to market, meets, on Blackfriars Bridge, a woman in gay attire, and grasps by the wrist to the horror of both, her who long ago, in a green

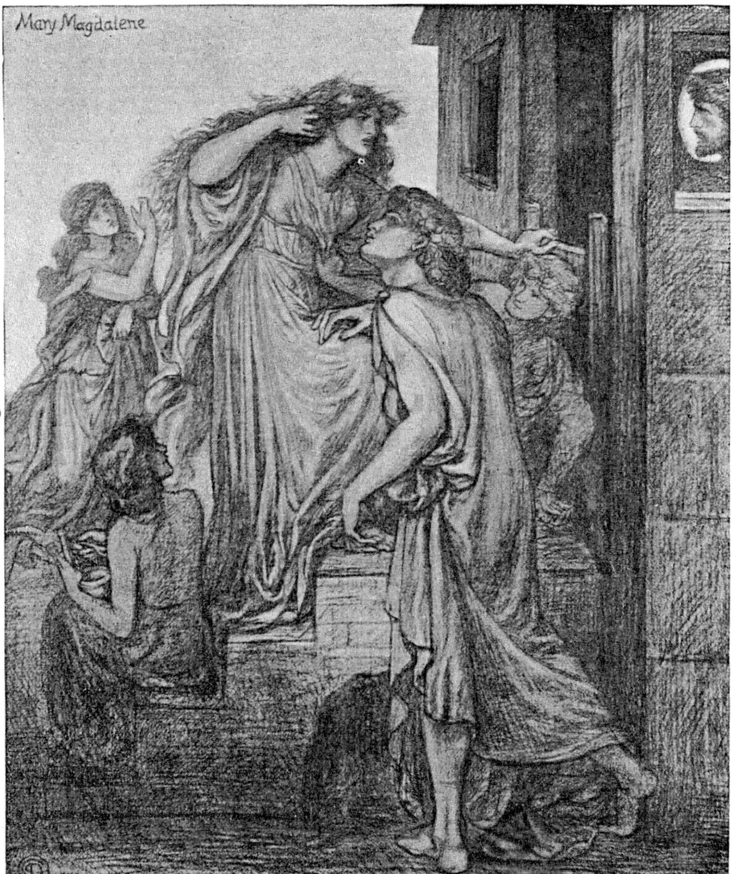

Dante Gabriel Rossetti. *Caswell Smith, Photo, Oxford St., W.*

MARY MAGDALENE.

art back upon nature's reality, and deepen the harmonies that had become so classic, correct, and thin. This he and his friends had to do, amid neglect, misunderstanding, and even coarse vituperation. Then came the death of his wife after a very brief wedlock, his utter prostration, his slow suicide, and the development of those weaknesses of character which a happier career and a warmer welcome would have probably overcome. It is a dreadful fate when a man whose vocation is keenly and finely to feel has also to fight like an apostle, and suffer like a martyr; when fate crushes his one personal passion, and men shoot poisoned arrows into his raw flesh. From the time of Rossetti's great loss it is always the one face, and not merely the one type, that appears and reappears in his art. His affections get the better of his genius. He had a spiritual principle of beauty, but he had not a spiritual principle of life. And for lack of that the victorious spirituality of his beauty faltered. Love seemed to him like a power which loads and depresses life. Death and Love went hand in hand everywhere. The very richness of passion became the source of its decay. Its wealth became like a miser's misery. The mood of Shakespere's 64th Sonnet became chronic with him:

> 'Ruin hath taught me thus to ruminate,
> That Time will come and take my love away.
> This thought is as a death, which cannot choose
> But weep to have that which it fears to lose.'

He was familiar with the Angel of Death; but he

did not see the Angel of the Resurrection ever close behind. The Bible and its gospel was a beautiful and moving tale; but not in practical effect much more than a tale. Love, with its appetite for the infinite, found too little of infinite beauty to feed on. When the finite reached its end a blight fell upon Love, which was rooted in no deepness of Faith, but only dallied with a dreamy and seductive hope, or cherished a beautiful and fleeting surmise. Genius, at least, was meant for something more than wife-worship, or, indeed, the worship of any beauty which can be gathered up in one visible face.

Still we must remark that, though his natural passion was blighted, and beauty henceforward infected with despair, passion remained beautiful, and did not become bitter. It was sicklied o'er, but did not turn to an utter lie. Dreary it was, sometimes with a sad longing, sometimes with a settled vain regret, a dismal acquiescence, and 'cold commemorative eyes'; but it was not bitter or diabolic. The sad beauty of the soul was still for him nobler than the heartless, selfish beauty of the body alone. *That* was diabolic, that was the true curse—worse than the death curse. Look at his picture of his wife after death, as the dead Beatrice, *Beata Beatrix.* What sweet and utter resignation —'her features wore such an aspect of humility, that they seemed to say, "Now do I behold the beginning of peace."' What a cool and placid atmosphere of eventide behind, where love stands pointing to Dante the contrast with his own glowing heart.

In this picture the low twilight beauty is unspeakably sweet. You may compare it with a similar dawn in Burne Jones's 'Song of Love.' Now, by contrast, look at his water-colour, 'Lady Lilith'; that is his type of healthy, heartless, proud, selfish, inhuman beauty, the idol of men, and the slayer of men. 'Not a drop of her blood was human,' he says. Here is his sonnet on her. He calls it 'Body's Beauty':

> Of Adam's first wife, Lilith, it is told,
>   (The witch he loved before the gift of Eve)
>   That, ere the snake's, her sweet tongue could deceive,
> And her enchanted hair was the first gold.
> And still she sits, young while the earth is old,
>   And, subtly of herself contemplative,
>   Dares men to watch the bright web she can weave,
> Till heart, and body, and life are in its hold.
> The rose and poppy are her flowers; for where
>   Is he not found, O Lilith, whom shed scent
> And soft-shed kisses and soft sleep shall snare?
>   Lo! as that youth's eyes burned at thine, so went
>   Thy spell through him, and left his straight neck bent,
> And round his heart one strangling golden hair.

Here, too, is the companion sonnet, entitled 'Soul's Beauty.' It was intended for one of his most healthy and pleasing pictures, 'Sibylla Palmifera':

> Under the arch of Life, where love and death,
>   Terror and mystery guard her shrine, I saw
>   Beauty enthroned; and, though her gaze struck awe,
> I drew it in as simply as my breath.
> Hers are the eyes which, over and beneath,
>   The sky and sea bend on thee,—which can draw,
>   By sea or sky or woman, to one law,
> The allotted bondman of her palm and wreath.
> This is that Lady Beauty, in whose praise
>   Thy voice and hand shake still—long known to thee

> By flying hair and fluttering hem—the beat
> Following her daily of thy heart and feet,
> How passionately and irretrievably,
> In what fond flight, how many ways and days!

I quote those two sonnets, the first to show what Rossetti felt devilish, the second to show what he thought divine. That second is a confession of faith, of almost all the faith he had. What he worshipped was Beauty—Beauty which rose to awe and solemnity, though not sublimity—Beauty which was a soul in nature, and a soul so intense that nature broke down and died in the effort to express it; just as his own soul was always behind in the effort to attain it. That is the source of the melancholy in his art. It rose from the solemn intensity of his passion, the inadequacy of any earthly form to utter, to meet, or to retain it, and the absence of a real spiritual world to receive it. Beauty was in its physical vehicle, much what the burden of the Lord was in Jeremiah. It was too much. It broke him, tore him to pieces. How Italian! Old Dante tells us the sight of Beatrice in the street made him shake like an ague. So it seemed to Rossetti that the Beauty which strove to utter itself in the loveliest things was not only a presence, but a power. Nay, for him it was *the* power, the passion, and the shaking of the world. It was a power which, in the effort to express itself, brought such torrent and strain to bear upon the physical world that the latter became simply disorganised and collapsed. The Beauty of the world had every power, except the power fully to reveal itself, and so give peace.

Soul burst body in the struggle. Therefore, there was another power warring against this soul of Beauty, and blighting it like a curse. It was Death. Rossetti never rose above that to the highest conception of the spiritual in his art. I say nothing of his personal religion, I speak of his art. If we are body, soul, and spirit, his art was far more than that of the body. It was the art of the body ensouled. But it was not the art of the body spiritualised. It was a Transfiguration, but it had not attained to the full Revelation and the Resurrection of the Dead. And it needs much religion to carry this load of Beauty and Passion. It is one of the miseries of our age that its science has not left enough faith to sustain the intense sensibility of its art; and culture constantly tends to a pessimism, either furious like Byron's, sublime like Wagner's, systematic like Schopenhauer's, cynical like Carlyle's, melancholy like Rossetti's, or affected in the style of any of them by the few youths of the period who are still above some form of the average natural man.

We must not despise Rossetti for this intoxication of beauty. Nor must we despise ourselves, if it is a foreign tongue to us. We must just recognise that there are souls dowered with this fatal gift of pursuing the fine gold of beauty with a passion more keen than the money-maker's for *his* gold, and that such souls belong to man's high aristocracy. We must let them teach us what they can, but we must not go to them to look for a creed, a principle, a guide of life. I do not envy the man who is not by Rossetti made ashamed of himself, and the poor low quality of his love. I think the better of the man who confesses under his spell, that he has, times and ways without number, done despite to love in its noblest shapes, and missed, both for himself and those he loves, chances of soul-beauty which he will yet have bitterly to repent, and sadly to regain. But I advise nobody to seek in art like this, or indeed in any art, the real power of spiritual beauty, or the true help to make the heavenly best of love. For that can only come from the love of the Eternal Heart; and poor folk, who are not geniuses, need for the due safe culture of beauty, a double portion of reverence for the beauty of holiness. An immortal spirit, with the promise and potency of infinity in it, can be at peace in no beauty which becomes withered and wan as its earthly tenement decays. It was because beauty was worshipped by Rossetti for beauty's sake, that it suffered the fate of every idol; it lost in beauty, and it injured the worshipping soul. It contained no revelation. It spoke only of itself. It was revealed everywhere, but it revealed nothing in which its colours were fixed and its spell eternalised. Its own wealth ruined it, as a man's wealth may ruin him in various kinds. And what an immitigable grief it was that this artist's love of beauty brought him, what a dislocation of the world, what a chaos of life! Still he felt what we should be better were we able to feel more. He makes us recognise that there is a whole world of splendour about us which we are too blind to see, and of sorrow deeper than we have heart to feel. And even when his world is sicklied o'er, there are healthy intervals and higher hopes.

> 'What of the heart of love,
> That bleeds in thy breast, O man?
> Thy kisses snatched 'neath the ban
> Of fangs that mock them above;
> Thy bells prolonged into knells,
> Thy hope that a breath dispels,
> Thy bitter forlorn farewells,
> And the empty echoes thereof?'

But he goes on—

> 'Still we say as we go,
> "Strange to think by the way,
> Whatever there is to know
> That shall we know one day."'

He relapses into miserable self-distrust—

> 'The sky leans dumb on the sea,
> Aweary with all its wings;
> And oh! the song the sea sings
> Is dark everlastingly.
> Our past is clean forgot,
> Our present is and is not,
> Our future's a sealed seed plot,
> And what betwixt them are we?'

But he winds up after all—

> 'We who say as we go,
> "Strange to think by the way,
> Whatever there is to know,
> That shall we know one day."'

And here is a specimen of the way in which the needs of his life cast him for his hope, in his deepest and most desperate hours, beyond the soul of Beauty, or the helps of Art.

From child to youth; from youth to arduous man;
  From lethargy to fever of the heart;
  From faithful life to dream-dowered days apart;
From trust to doubt; from doubt to brink of ban;—
Thus much of change in one swift cycle ran
  Till now. Alas, the soul!—how soon must she
  Accept her primal immortality—
The flesh resume its dust whence it began?
O Lord of work and peace! O Lord of Life!
  O Lord, the awful Lord of will! though late,
  Even yet renew this soul with duteous breath;
That, when the peace is garnered in from strife,
  The work retrieved, the will regenerate,
  This soul may see Thy face, O Lord of Death!

There is one part of man, and it is the one part needful, which Art does not do much to cultivate or brace. It is the will, the conscience, and the habitual faith that overcome the world in the great, great peace. Art may give calm, but 'calm is not all, though calm is well.' But, at least, we may learn this from Art. The keenest seers of earth's beauty feel that the earth is too poor for the beauty they surmise. And the loveliest devotees of natural passion feel the world all too small for the true dimensions of love in an immortal soul.

VII

I WILL, by way of contrast, close with two sonnets by a greater artist than Rossetti, and a greater Christian than many saints—Michael Angelo.

Yes! Hope may with my strong desire keep pace,
  And I be undeluded, unbetrayed.
For if of our affections none find grace
In sight of Heaven, then wherefore hath God made

> The world which we inhabit? Better plea
> Love cannot have, than that in loving thee
> Glory to that eternal peace is paid,
> Who such divinity to thee imparts
> As hallows and makes pure all gentle hearts.
> His hope is treacherous only whose love dies
> With beauty which is varying every hour.
> But in chaste hearts, uninfluenced by the power
> Of outward change, there blooms a deathless flower
> That breathes on earth the air of paradise.

The following was written in prospect of death—

> Now hath my life across a stormy sea,
> Like a frail bark, reached that wide port where all
> Are bidden, ere the final reckoning fall
> Of good and evil for eternity.
> Now know I well how that fond fantasy
> Which made my soul the worshipper and thrall
> Of earthly art, is vain ; how criminal
> Is that which all men seek unwillingly.
> Those amorous thoughts which were so lightly dressed,
> What are they when the double death is nigh?
> The one I know for sure, the other dread.
> Painting nor sculpture now can lull to rest
> My soul that turns to His great love on high,
> Whose arms to clasp us on the cross were spread.

Yes; and is it forced if I say that the power of the Cross was the chief thing needed to have made Rossetti the greatest painter that this country has ever produced. He knew the bruise, he hinted at the balm. He knew the love that makes earth's worst sorrow. He had gleams of the sorrow which works heavenliest love. But hints and gleams are not power. His problems were not intellectual; they were rather of the heart, and its experience. And the power we need to cope with such is the faith and power of the Cross, the healthful word of Jesus Christ. It is in Him that we not only perceive love's unspeakable loveliness, but share love's eternal power. There is the love which not only does not dread death, but demands it, is made perfect by suffering and enriched by all loss. There we cease to speak of vain desires and vain regrets, fruitless sorrow, and pitiless fate. We are unhinged no more by the spectacle of those who are slain in war, or crushed and ground in peace. The world's sorrow is there indeed, but the world's love is there too. It is a love that lavishes upon the sorrowful world a power of redemptive passion but faintly imaged in the poet's wild affection, or grieving fury, a consolation sweeter than his sweetest pity, a new birth more wonderful than his loveliest creations, and a solemn fear holier than beauty's most breathless awe. We are too prone, perhaps, to separate beauty and sorrow. Our gladness is too far apart from our grief, our salvation too independent of the Cross. We demand, with unreasonable levity, that those who delight us shall never remind us of our sorrow, that grace shall be severed from woe instead of entirely victorious over it, and that the power of faith shall be ours without the gymnastic of conflict, without doubt conquered, and

> Kept quiet like the snake 'neath Michael's foot,
> Who stands calm just because he feels it writhe.

Our religion and art alike are prone to dwell upon a happiness which is all sunshine and no shade, and we seek our rest by refusing to think, instead of pushing on to thought's all-seeing victory. It is indeed a world where to begin to think is to be full of sorrow; but, by the grace and cross of Christ, to go on to think is to approach the invincible joy. An artist like Rossetti teaches us, what the Catholic movement sought to impress on the desiccated Church half a century ago, that the very shadows of life have their colour too—that shade is not wholly dark, that beauty does not cease to dwell with death, and be upon it the halo and promise of a trembling hope. Truly it is not Art that, amid the burden of the world, gives power to the faint, and to them that have no might increaseth strength. It is not by waiting on Beauty that we renew our strength, mount up with wings as eagles, run and are not weary, walk and are not faint. The unearthly calm of Art is not the mighty peace of God. But there is even in Art, and in these days it is quite a power in some art, the grace and mystery of the Cross; and Beauty quivers like the Resurrection dawn upon the very forehead of doom and death. Through the tremulous, fleeting, and fiery aurora of our human passion, there gleam the quiet eternal stars of another world, where after all these losses there is peace. This is the Eternal Gospel of the Passion of the Cross.

Once to find the gain of loss,
  Take the sweetness out of pain,
Feel the uplifting of the cross,
  Is to know all fear is vain.

And thy heart to thee shall prove,
  When its own reproaches cease,
That the heart of all is love,
  And the end of all is peace.

BURNE JONES

OR, THE RELIGION OF PRÆTERNATURAL IMAGINATION

I

IT is a source of much more than regret to observe how far the great interests of the Spirit have become separated from the interests of a lofty and humane culture in our general religion. I suppose, were one to take a dozen Christians at random, while six would stand for the vigour and rigour of what they call the Gospel, five of them might be found to admit that it was quite innocent to devote a little interest to music, painting, or poetry, and take such passing pleasure as these could give; but it would never cross their minds that the principles underlying the inspiration of Art have any real and vital connection with those which rule the inspiration of religion. They would admit, and think they were liberal in admitting, that religion permitted Art, and allowed a certain neutral region of the mind to be harmlessly occupied by the claims of the imagination. But they would set you down as an extravagant, not to say profane and dangerous person, if you maintained that religion not only permitted art but demanded it. They would ask you for your text in proof. While from the opposite and artists' quarter might come the charge that it was nothing less than sectarian to assert that the same principles which make religion possible, and are therefore its theology, are those which underlie Art, and even form the inspiration of its most imposing themes.

Still, I venture to make the assertion. And the text of proof would be found written in the book of European history, and illuminated, indeed, upon the open scroll of the Universal Church. It is most hard to get people to realise how truly the Christian regeneration permeates the whole of human nature, renews it in its total aspect like a fresh creation, and quickens to divine vitality every noble faculty that man owns. It is hard to impress upon our modern and Protestant individualism the unity and totality of the human soul, and to make people see that the rational principle which renovates its very centre is the same principle that is carried by the spiritual circulation to nourish every member, joint, and limb. The soul is not a section of human nature, but its unity. And the unity of the soul is in its religion, which is at once its bond and its freedom. Nothing impresses that truth upon us more than the study of the religious history of the human spirit. The tale of Christendom alone is the Bible itself writ large and practical. The triumphs of the imagination under the near or remote influences of Christian culture are unique in the world's record. And the very principles which make Pagan art so great are principles which only the Spirit of Christ has fully revealed to the self-knowledge of the soul. Our modern Christian mind understands the principles of Greek art better than the Greeks ever did, just as we know and understand the Old Testament better than did the Jews.

We English have suffered from the defects of our great qualities. As a nation we take a foremost place in practical energy, and in the development of the practical applications of Christianity. But on the other hand we are apt to let our practical bias, even in our Christianity, rob us of our sympathetic and receptive soul. We grieve the Spirit by our hard absorption in affairs; we seal our souls, without knowing or meaning it, against His finer revelations. And when we wake up occasionally to the fact, we have to confess, like the prophet of old, 'As thy servant was busy here and there He was gone.' Then again, as Protestants, we helped to deliver Europe from the Church into the Bible. But, as a set off, we thrust upon the Bible a wrong and bad kind of pre-eminence. And now our great need is to be delivered from our Bible—from ours back into God's. We must incessantly, as Mr. Browning says:

> 'Correct the portrait by the living face,
> Man's God by God's God in the mind of man.'

We gave the book its true place among books, but we did not apply to it the true principles of interpretation. And we are even now suffering from a literalism and a dogmatism in the treatment of the Bible, which are death to that spiritual imagination in which the Bible was conceived. We have been overtaken by that pinched and strenuous worldliness, and that sectional water-tight-compartment habit of mind, which are the ruin both of noble Art and of pure religion.

The consequence of this is that the larger and more generous imagination of mankind has been repelled from the associations of the religious, and the camp of culture has in many cases assumed an antagonism to the Church no less intense than that of the army of science. Genius has gone to Pagan sources for its inspiration. In some instances it has even striven to force life back to the Pagan principles which the great world has so long outgrown. But in many more cases that has been felt impossible. Even Schiller could not do it, and wise Goethe did not seriously try. The very genius which falls in love with Greek or Norse antiquity has been a genius inspired by centuries of hereditary Christian idealism, and reared in a society troubled, amid all its Paganism, with the presence of the Christian dream. And so, when a Greek tale or a Scandinavian hero has become the object of modern art, the treatment has been such as neither Greek nor Norseman could have attained or relished. The old tales and characters have become the vehicles of new ideas, passions and inspirations, which to the old days were impossible. And when our modern poets sing, or our modern painters paint, the stories of these times, they fill them with another spirit than of old, and make them speak the language of the human heart, not exactly as it was two thousand years ago, but as it is in the passion and vision of to-day.

How, it may be asked, is that possible? Is it true that we have no right so to treat the old myths? In doing it are we 'emasculating a fresh strenuous Paganism by our modern emotionalism?' It is possible, because in these old myths and tales we have the deep religion of humanity, which is ever at heart the same, and only waits to be revealed and explained. It is expressed in forms lent by the ages when religion and a præternatural imagination went hand in hand. But it is inspired with thoughts which go on like living spirits, or the moving masses of the clouds, or the rolling stream, changing their shape, but never losing their identity, wearing form after form, but still witnessing to the same soul in the midst of the same warfare, and in presence of the same fate. The riddle of the painful earth is substantially the same now as it was ages and ages ago—as its Answer is the same yesterday, to-day, and for ever. It is the same soul that lives on with the same fears, the same powers, the same weaknesses, the same forebodings, the same joys, griefs, and thirsts as before. Nature is the same to the soul now as it was then, whatever it may now be to the scientific intelligence. It stirs the like questions, breathes the like balm, kindles the like delight, inspires the like fear, and presents the like imposing and imaginative hopes. Women are still to men the spell they were as soon as each to the other grew cherished and dear. And men are to women now substantially the same power they were when the only prowess was the valour of war. And over the same soul is the same God. ''Tis the same, same self, same love, same God; ay, what was shall be.' Beneath our modern spirit, as under the ancient, is the Spirit of the Eternal. All this is a region of things where we are sustained by the power of the changeless, rather than refreshed by the wonder of change. And the old myths have in them a perennial power as expressions of living and undying Spirit, whose passions and principles are in their nature permanent, though the fashion of its countenance alters from age to age. These are the passions and questions, about which all religion moves. They brood and they storm about the portal of the unseen. They essay to body forth the great invisible presence. They strive to forecast the soul's future and invisible destiny. These are the questions which, by the proper treatment of them, raise a book into a Bible, and give to *the* Bible its most commanding and invincible significance for the general heart.

A strange revenge has overtaken that dull and dismal literalism which idolised instead of revering the Bible. The injured and dethroned spirit of imagination rose in a desperate revolt. The poetry of the soul, which always revives with its true religion, made a violent protest against the dullards who would reduce Scripture to mere record, religion to theology, and piety to matter of fact. A school arose that turned into myth the most sacred parts of Scripture history—those Gospels about which the Christian imagination will always so affectionately and inquisitively play. They were declared to be no actual history, or to have but a slender basis of such. They were products of popular imagination, and their central figure, instead of creating the Church by his inspiration, was mainly created by the inspiration of the Church. The miracles had been so abused to produce faith, that, in violent reaction, faith was asserted to have produced the miracles, on the principle that *Das Wunder ist des Glaubens höchstes Kind.* Do you not see how sure are the laws of the soul, how impossible it is to defraud the heart for ever of its due, how you may drive the imagination out at the door but it will always re-enter by the window. Reduce your Bible to a mere theological history and your piety to humdrum, and depend on it the insulted spirit of imagination will find means to make you regret your mistake. Banish imagination from your religion, and Art will be forced to invent a religion of its own, to the loss of many souls, and the peril of more. If you feel any resentment against those who reduced the gospel history to myth, it will be juster and wiser to transfer it to those who first reduced the whole Bible to a dumb wooden idol, which must be carried because it could not go, and the piercing word to a theologian's lathen sword. The 'old gospel' laid hold of Europe not by its antiquity, but by its novelty. It came teeming with life and possibility. It transfigured existence, and made all things new. And it is mere cant to revile the public taste for novelty as a source of religious danger. It is the cant of piety which is half conscious of having lost its own renovating power, and has ceased to regard the world as a standing wonder, or the soul as its living key. It is the severance of religion from spiritual imagination which is at the root of that hard conservatism and consecrated ignorance which make a palladium of a book, and a bogey of 'modern thought.' And it is the same divorce which encourages our most eager and vehement modernism to treat our positive religion as a creed outworn. Modern Christianity has largely lost that note of vitalising freedom by which it conquered, and must hold the West. The 'torpor of assurance' has deadened the nerve of spiritual enterprise, and faith walks no more with the air of the freeborn. It is too unused to spiritual conflict. It lacks either the tonic element in doubt, or the courage which masters the weakness of doubt and puts it down into its useful place. It fears that which is high. In some cases, it is even dead to the true imaginative grandeur of its own ancestral theologies. It has no spring in its gait, and no breeze in its hair, no gleam in its eye, no large utterance in its speech, and no fresh pæans on its lips. It is winning the manner of charity, thank God, but its charity has not the manner of a faith which sees life steadily because it sees it whole.

But, on the other hand, what has enabled the present age to go back and find unsuspected spiritual treasures in the old mythology, is the Christian spirit. It is the sympathy, the largeness, the flexibility of the spirit dominating the Bible, which have given us the eye to see, and the soul to feel her own infancy in imaginative antiquity.

The same heart longs in the ancient myths as is now fed by the verities of Christian faith. It might be well to face and answer this question. What would have been the results to the world, to our treatment of its past, our view of its present, and our attitude to its future, if Christ had been a person of no imagination? The state of our religion may be measured by the uneasiness of many, when they are asked to think of the imagination of Christ. And yet it is true, as Shelley somewhere says, that the highest goodness is not possible without the highest imaginative power. Imagination is not faith, but faith is not possible without imagination; and it is all the imagination some have, or by their nature can have. If the greatest dream that ever the soul entertained was the redemption of the soul, what must have been the imaginative compass of that soul which conceived it, and so conceived it as to fulfil it to the end? How can we wonder that the greatest triumphs of pictorial imagination are still among those great mediæval painters who made the Redemption their theme, and brought their universe in symbol round the Cross. And how can we wonder that the sympathetic spirit of Christian imagination should now go back into the remote ages of history, and out into the shy and secret silence of nature, to draw gently forth the living soul of beauty there, and present it to us with some modern echo of the eternal meaning in its voice.

II

Sir Edward Burne Jones is distinguished by two great imaginative features—the power of mythic interpretation* or the fine treatment of the soul, and the power of poetic beauty or the fine treatment of nature; and I venture to describe the religion in his work as the religion of the præternatural imagination, because, while his beauty is unearthly in its exquisite excess, it is still not pure heavenly in its spiritual strength. He depicts the nature within nature, and the soul's ethereal soul. He is præternatural so far. But he is not caught up into the seventh heaven, and set by the throne of God for ever above nature. He is not supernatural. His delicacy is greater than his power. He does not threaten ever to burst the very limits of Art in the expression of the holy things he sees.

First of all Burne Jones is a mythologist of genius. He not only reads the writing, but the interpretation thereof. He not only replaces before us the ancient forms with ancient beauty, but he invests them with an abiding spiritual significance. This significance is conveyed to us in our own tongue, in the speech of this nineteenth century, even in its spiritual dialect. The severity of the antique soul is tempered by the sympathy of the modern spirit, and the old problems are set in a new, deeper, and lovelier light. We are familiar with Sir Lewis Morris's 'Epic of Hades.' In that charming poem

* Ruskin.

he tells once more the oft-told tales of mythic Greece. But he tells them as no Greek could have told them. He tells them with a reference to problems, moods, and passions to which the Greek spirit had not yet awaked. He clothes Olympus with the light, the mist, the movement, the colour, the shadow of a far later and richer time—a time, too, more sad, and more vexed than was old Greece with the great gulf between the mind's power of putting questions and of answering them. In the same way William Morris has treated the Scandinavian legends. And it is the happy tendency of our age altogether to view antiquity with kinder and more intelligent eyes than the old schools of scholarship used to turn upon it. Archæology has become much more than archaic. It is something else than antiquarianism, something humaner than a polished study, or a pedant's hobby. The past even of Greece and Rome is becoming more a portion of the present than it was when the only liberal education was in Latin and Greek. 'More and more the dead rule us,' as Comte says. They repay our fresher, humaner interpretation of them by interpreting us to ourselves. We thread the ancient maze with a modern clue, and we come at last on a magic mirror in which we see our own ghostly destiny. Rossetti has a fine picture, in which he represents two lovers wandering in a dim wood, and being met by their own ghosts. What weird romance! Well, that is a symbol of the way in which, lovingly wandering in the dim tangle of the past, we come upon these old tales, and find ourselves confronted with our own inner selves. And this romantic treatment of the old classic legends is too profitable and too beautiful to be arrested by the severe protest of those who will have no 'reading in' of our modern moods there. We are not so much reading in modern experience as spelling out ancient though unconscious prophecy. We are making explicit in our modern statements, what is implicit in the ancient fact. It is man's soul, now aged, going back and finding its ripe experience latent in the child which was the father of the man. Our days and those days are bound each to each in a natural piety. Ruskin has worked out this vein with all his unique insight in his 'Queen of the Air.' And Burne Jones has done it in pictorial art. He can charm the eternal soul from an ancient tale, as no other painter can, except, perhaps, Mr. Watts. And he can clothe it in the fashion of the contemporary mind. And it is no small feat of imaginative thought to do that—apart altogether from the skill of his particular art of line and colour. Burne Jones is not only a painter, but a seer, and a penetrative poet. If Rossetti is the most pictorial of all our poets, Burne Jones is the most poetic of all our painters. He is so in his treatment of nature; but, apart from that, he is so in his insight into the great mythic poetry of the past. He does for mythology what it is so hard to do for Scripture. He makes it, without fanciful application, or fatal violence, speak in the tones and to the needs of the hour. He plucks the heart from the old mysteries, and lo! it is red, warm, and vital like our own. The ancient spirit bled like our own when fate pierced it, and the blood is after all but little colder and no paler than ours. Just so we say, and say truly, that the Old Gospel is not too old for any age; that its spirit does not lose, but gain by being fitted to the needs of any special time; that its eternal significance for successive generations is but the drawing forth, from an endless storehouse, of treasures new and old; and that the many changes of form it has undergone, and must still undergo, need never be deadly to its central, plastic, and abiding power. There we have the principle for the treatment, not only of Christian antiquity, but of all antiquity. It is a wise principle and a great one, to treat Scripture like any other book. It carries with it the farther maxim that we shall treat all records of the past, not with the same reverence, but with a like reverence to that which we give to the records of one special race. And particularly must we read them with their own spirit, and try the records of the soul by the soul its peer. As we make the Bible a book for every age, not by reading into it, but by reading more deeply out of it; and as we do no violence to the Bible by such a course, but only treat it more and more as a message of soul to soul; so with the tales of classic imagination it is neither rude to hail them from our shores of young romance, nor cruel from the shipwreck of their letter to snatch the spiritual cargo and the living souls aboard. The true treatment of the Christian past is the

Christian treatment of the whole past. It is the treatment of love and insight. What we mete out to the messages of the Holy Spirit let us bestow also on the relics of past imagination—adequate and appropriate sympathy to each in its kind. Let us bring to the imagination of the past imagination from the present, to the soul of the past the soul of the present, just as to the Spirit of God in Scripture we bring the holiest spirit of to-day, and retire discovered unto ourselves beyond all we have ever discovered by ourselves. As religion must be interpreted by religion, so art must be interpreted by art. And, as the saintliest men in the thick of ages past are best interpreted by the saintliest men in the thick of the age to-day, so the imaginations that uttered a bygone generation's soul, are to be best expounded by artists who feel beating in their blood the very pulse and passion of the generation that now is. No man can deal fairly with the past, especially with the imaginative past, unless he is a living citizen of his own present. And the man who is a channel and an organ for his own age's soul will find often no better and truer means of interpreting his brethren to themselves than by duly using the imaginative remnants of otherwise forgotten days. Anybody can turn a legend to fanciful account, but it needs genius so to seize its living thought as to transplant it uninjured, and acclimatise it in the soil of a very distant and foreign time. We need only compare with the works I have mentioned, the very far-fetched, modern, and incongruous applications of mythology in Bacon's *Wisdom of the Ancients*, to realise what is meant here. We used to hear somewhat of the craze that Bacon wrote the plays we ascribe to Shakespere. We may be quite sure that nobody would have had the heart to treat mythology with the laborious and scientific ingenuity of the philosopher, if he had the power to treat it as it is treated by the imagination of the poet.

III

Mr. Burne Jones's second feature is his exquisite power of poetic beauty in the fine treatment of nature. Exquisite is not here a piece of vague slang. We pass from the luscious opulence of Rossetti, to a region of rarer spirit and more ethereal grace. There is more of ancient Greece than of modern Italy, in the type of Burne Jones's beauty. His drawing is more faultless than Rossetti's, and his colour more limpid. His joy of beauty almost rises to the intensity of pain, and its heart seems to palpitate with a certain surcharged ache, like the faces of his women in the small picture called 'Green Summer.' In all his work there is more delicate spirituality than we find in Rossetti, more sweet *naïveté*, more of slender charm, and of the *χάρις ἀθικτῶν ἱερῶν*, the grace of sanctities intangible and inviolate. The painter's own sensibility to beauty, one would think, must be a pain to him in a world like this. He cannot be called a representative of the masculine order of art. But he has access to regions which are closed to the foot of man, and where feminine sensibility alone may tread. Nature has her virginal hours and her conventual solitudes. There are shy places and sweet solemn hours, like the beginnings of dawn, *otia dia*, abodes of unearthly calm and præternatural grace. And Burne Jones is their confessor, whose tongue may be sealed, for he is no poet like Rossetti, but whose hand is not held. What he puts before us is not nature, nor is it what is above nature, so much as what might be called the astral body of nature. 'Move along these shades' he says—

> 'In gentleness of heart; with gentle hand
> Touch; for there is a spirit in the woods.'

It is that spirit he paints, 'the quintessence of nature where nature is loveliest.' He has magic; but it is the magic of the imagination, not of the fancy. It is not the magic which sees fairies in nature, but goddesses. Only not Heré, not even Aphrodité. His goddess of beauty rises neither from the sea nor from its foam, but from the spirit of the foam, from the rainbow hues in its innumerable bubbles, and their fugitive gleam. It is what Aphrodité would have been, had the Greeks been a colour people instead of a people of form, had their abstractions had blood or even ichor in their fine veins, and their hearts had love as the grace of all grace; had their weariness sprung from too much love instead of no love at all, and their beauty found a home in the shade as well as in the sun.

It is not so much in his power of composition

that Burne Jones excels, as in his power of expression. He has not the dramatic force, the realism, the noble materialism which are so striking in Rossetti. But in the expression of soul, especially through the face, Burne Jones can rise to a height of charm which was much beyond Rossetti. If the latter paints the ensoulment of passion, the former paints the passion of the soul. This is most noticeable in the faces of his women. It is true, his range is not wide. Like Rossetti, he is dominated by a type; but how much sweeter a type, how much less weighed upon with the load of mortality. If we can with any truth call Rossetti a successor of Botticelli, with the like truth may we discern in Burne Jones the spirit of Luini, though with much less than Luini's heartfelt peace. Still these women of Burne Jones's are no more eligible Englishwomen than Rossetti's are. You can no more think of the one set playing lawn tennis or nursing children than the other. Both artists seem equally sick of the usual Madonna type. For both the placidity of maternity, actual or possible, has fled from the female soul. Both are denizens of an age when, for better or for worse, another *métier* than motherhood is being claimed by and for womankind, an age troubled about the 'decay of domesticity.' The sex is asserting itself on the one hand socially and politically, and striving to become a direct force after a fashion which offers nothing to art, and promises peril even to nature. And, on the other hand, woman is properly claiming an education which shall develop her soul after its own proper kind, and raise her to an influence of the more spiritual sort, by making her intelligently sympathetic in the issues of spiritual problems which man for the most part has felt alone. She may not realise these issues exactly as men will; she may entertain them in a form of her own. But she will entertain them, and probably contribute to their solution, especially if she refuse to sacrifice charm to championship, and if she let alone men's forcible action and direct pressure, and devote herself to that spiritual action and influence which both religion and nature assign as her true sphere. The bulk of women must always be most occupied with the rearing of children. And it is only desired in the main that they shall not cease to influence them after they have grown to men; that the woman of the future shall have a heart devoted to her offspring, and, without the competitive intellect, an intelligent soul to understand and help the causes for which men and women most worthily live and die.

But a change of this kind brings its own risks and drawbacks. What is the result of bringing face to face with the problems of life a sweet and simple soul, untaught by any severity of mental discipline to handle them, and unblest with any competent guidance to follow them out? Inevitably an oppression, a sadness, a certain blight upon the freshness of beauty, a weariness in the aspect of affection, and a pressure of sensibility too vehement for the available ballast of reason or of faith. A subtle languor takes possession of the soul, a refined fatigue, an eagerness which is constantly haunted by probable disappointment, an intensity which is more sure of its power to love than of satisfaction in love. Now I should say that this is the type betrayed, if not expressed, in many of Burne Jones's female faces—excessive sensibility to the shadow of issues which they hardly grasp in substance, and are unqualified to cope with. These women, of course, have not been to Girton, but they have been touched, wittingly or unwittingly, by the spirit of the age and the riddle of the earth. They have taken the epidemic form of *Weltschmertz* in some mild way. The heart in them has been catholicised by culture into soul. But of religion they know nothing as a power which has anything to do with the mastery of life's sorrow or the consecration of earth's love. Perhaps the only religion they have ever known has been confined to attendance at some suburban church, and a taste of æsthetic pessimism from promising youths. But the shadow of great questions has fallen on them (from Mudie's, it may be), and some cloud is about their beautiful hearts. They are just awakening to some sense of what a world we live in, and the joy of earth is dashed with the presentiment that the heart is mostly greater than its fate, man than his place, the spirit than its own self-knowledge, and that the beauty of dreams is holier than the pleasures of life. They are the descendants of those paradisal beings who, in our artist's 'Banquet of Peleus,' are troubled by the intrusion of Discord, and who utter so beautifully and dramatically their love's horror and sorrow at the presence of strife in the heavenly world.

Not all Burne Jones's women are victims of this trouble, but all witness to its presence or possibility. The dream of fair women which he has painted in 'The Golden Stair,' shows rather its relics than its presence, but it has been there and still may come. He does not paint the thoughtless, self-satisfied, narrow-minded beauty who is perfect in all her trivial social duties, and the death of any better soul to which she is bound. He is as far from mild conventionality in his type as he is from an equally fatal hardness of intellect. The trail of the serpent may be there in his beauty, but, whatever be the fall, there is also a rise. The soul has begun to awake, as may be seen by comparing those exquisite faces in 'The Golden Stair' with the mindless beauties that athletic young tennis-players delight to contemplate in plenty of more popular work one need not name.

What we have, then, in Burne Jones is beauty wounded with its own keen grace, and sensibility saddened with the abundance of lovely revelation. One is tempted to say that while Rossetti's trouble was that love is not enough, Burne Jones's is that love is too much. Both testify that beauty is not always the bringer of joy, and that another strength than its own is needful to sustain it, and preserve it from its latent sentence of decay. There is a weariness in pure bliss, and a weakness in sheer loveliness, which are foreign to the complete ideal of life, and, taken by themselves, fatal to the health of the soul. Beauty, we are in so many ways taught, is not enough for the health and growth of the spirit of man. Art is not life, nor has it the key and secret of life. It is sufficient if it present us with its own aspect of life, and play its own part in it. And here is the grand moral difference between the old paganism and the modern soul. Here is where the modern mythologist has to recast the old myths, and pour into them a new spirit. The great pagan times did not feel this inadequacy of beauty or of art. The soul has yawned inward on itself since then to an unapprehended depth. It feels a new hunger, it aches with other needs. Love has come to know the passion of infinity and immortality. The world even of beauty is insufficient for it, and the vaster our earthly world the greater is our unrest if that world be all. The soul which has won the power to see a huger universe has grown also in the power to feel its inadequacy. And so we have the nineteenth-century weariness, amounting in cases to despair, pessimism, nihilism, and reckless revolt. It is this weariness that we see just shadowed on these lovely faces of Burne Jones's. It is pagan beauty suffused with modern, nay recent, melancholy. It is the very loveliness of the soul's lassitude, the fine wistfulness which marks a time when the old creeds are dead and the new ones not of age; when the general faith is no more uncritical and strong, but anxious or paralysed amid the success of science and unexampled wealth. We feel more than we did, and we believe less. We are more busy, but perhaps we achieve less, as achievement has been known to go. Our excess of passion is subdued to a tear of melancholy or a sigh of regret, and we dare hardly pray to feel, lest we should only have to weep our inability to weep. There are, of course, thousands who do not realise things in that way, and who still possess a vigorous working faith; but they will seldom be found among those who are alive to the finer sensibilities or wider sympathies of the time. To some such the voice comes 'Art still has peace, seek refuge there,' and they become either like Burne Jones, painters of the present, who regret the past; or like Rossetti, painters of the past, who ignore the present.

IV

I WILL go to the pictures and at once illustrate what I have been saying by the beautiful large water-colour, 'Love among the Ruins.' It is not for me to speak of the wondrous harmony of blues and greys, or the skilful interchange of light, shade, and gloom; though such beauties are the first that must be expressed by any one who has anything to say in paint. And I am very diffident about ascribing ulterior intention to the artist in this picture. But I seem to see there the ruins of those old systems of belief that once formed such a splendid tenement of thought to house the loving soul. Portions of the structure are not so far gone as the rest, and sunlight lingers upon the outer courts. But love still haunts the penetralia of decay, and sits with silent harp, as Judah sat by the confusion of old Babel's streams. A darker gloom fills the background, as if the end were not yet, and the worst were still to come. But what could be worse? Worse would be the ruin and death of love itself. The gloom in the rear is reflected in trouble upon these lovers' faces, whose love is too much if faith is tottering to its fall, and if there is nothing in love itself to overcome or re-create, or do more than decorate the world. How different from Mr. Browning's poem of 'Love among the Ruins,' full of the delight of two hearts amid decayed empire, and their 'paradisal laugh at fate.' The picture is a fine illustration of Tennyson's line about 'love, half dead to know that it shall die.' When love loses faith in its own eternity, then its passion is too much for its own peace. And if the Eternal and the Unshakeable be not love, then love becomes the great tormentor of life, and, instead of a relic of bliss, the chief source of the agony that makes death a curse. If the systems fall only as a presage of utter gloom, and not to make room for new systems as habitations of a larger love, then love is a bane indeed, and we should be happier, with all our beauty, if we loved no more.

What has dissolved the systems and troubled our love, put the canker of doubt in the heart of faith, and the suspicion of mortality in the soul of beauty? For the present, it is the disproportionate growth of the inferior knowledge. We have eaten of the tree of knowledge, and our guileless Eden is no more glad and gay. Look at another picture, 'The Hesperides.' These, in the old fable, were maidens, who dwelt on an isle of light and bliss in the Western Ocean, and along with the wise serpent, Ladon, guarded the tree with the apples of gold. That might be an allegory of the daughters of England, the weathy, and wise, and girt with the dragon of the sea. And these we see here are no Grecian maids; they are English, maids of our later west. And the sadness in these faces surely never troubled the ancient women whose island lay so near the island of the Blest. Why, as they dance, are they sad? That trouble is surely one of our later gains, and there is some grim irony in this picture. Can a fruit-laden tree with a serpent in it suggest anything for us, now that the Hebrew story is more familiar than the Greek, but the tree of knowledge, with its fair seduction and its lurking peril to the soul? Will it be said that knowledge has no dangers for soul? Has not our modern soul in the increase of its knowledge increased its sorrow, and troubled, nay, lost its faith? And, as our daughters gather about the tree, and are welcomed to eat of its fruit, is there no risk to their spiritual womanhood, and that gladness which is the birthright of their purity? I know that purity is not a thing of ignorance; nevertheless, knowledge alone does not bring happiness, and it preserves neither purity nor power; everything turns upon how and what we know, and especially upon *whom* we know. And for the most part in man's experience, however it may be with women, the wisdom of the serpent has been gained at the cost of the purity of the dove, and the fruits of knowledge have been written in sorrow on the face of experience. Let knowledge grow and bring to the mind its own delight and power. But I ask to know what equal provision is being made, or precaution taken, for the power and joy of the greater soul, the finer insight, and the nobler heart. And I speak not only of the soul of a sex, but of the soul of the age. We may pretend to rejoice; we may dance about our tree of science, and revel in our material sway. But there is in our hearts a hunger, and a trouble in our face, which all our progress cannot satisfy or soothe. For the soul is still unfed and its truths are still unsure.

Poor, beautiful soul of man! How naked and how unequipped she comes upon the earthly scene; how void of experience; how credulous, simple, and timid in her thoughts! She emerges into nature almost as a part of nature—nature's ruler beginning as nature's child—with a beauty sweeter and a nobler form than nature wears, yet meek and lowly, unwitting of her own dignity, destiny, and power. And how does nature receive her? Why, look in that little picture of 'Pan and Psyche' and you will see. Pan and Psyche are nature and the soul. See with what kindly concern, and rude, reverent simplicity the timid soul is welcomed by nature in his rocky solitude. Mark how he pities her in her lonely fate, born into a world which she little understands as yet, and which will never really understand her. His very compassion, kindly as it is, is unintelligent. She is filled with a great surprise, a beseeching meekness; he, with a concern which will one day become a worshipping devotion to her as the superior being, more to be loved than understood, at least by him. Yes, nature is a rare and kindly tutor to the first stages of the soul. Wordsworth anywhere will teach us that, especially in such lines as begin 'Three years she grew in sun and shower.' It is when the inevitable hour comes that the soul must pass beyond nature and be taught by soul, when men begin their methods of education, and bungle on to instruct the soul to her own self-forgetfulness, it is then she discovers how inhospitable to her the world can be made, and how sad the fruits of mere knowledge may be to one who was made for heavenlier lore.

Love is the real tutor of the soul. Science has no food for it, and nature's kind offices go but so far. Pan is a companion only for Psyche's childhood. He is like the kind and simple old forester, full of all woodcraft and nature-lore, who is the beloved companion of some young lord's boyish days. But ere the soul comes to manhood or womanhood it must go to school to noble love, and learn by all love's fears and losses solemn lessons of a deeper awe than nature's hush. As there is awe in beauty and a tragedy in life, so there is fear in love and a high discipline in love's fear. It is love that makes life's worthiest, holiest fear. It is love that lifts the soul into its truest reverence, and clothes beauty with its great solemnity. Love is a great destiny—*magna res est amor, magnum omnino bonum*—and a great destiny stirs much fear. 'Thou shalt fear, and thine heart shall be enlarged.' Mark the fear in the sweet face of the Virgin in Rossetti's

'Annunciation.' You can see it also in the Virgin's faces by Sandro Botticelli and older masters; and if you look at Burne Jones's small water-colour of 'Psyche and Cupid' you will read the same thing there. It is ruddy and winged Love that comes upon the mysterious wind from some far sea, and lifts the soul from its green-girt, darkling, nature-stage to the noble anxieties of the larger life. 'A vaster being brings severer cares.' You will mark the affection in the eyes, and the fear in the mouth, the trembling joined with every great soul-joy, and the solemnity of love's great and credulous surrender. Yes, there is fear in our great loves. They would have no moral quality else. It is only trivial philandering that ignores it. Loss brings it to the surface, but it lies latent in the shape of that reverence which crowns the grave happiness of love's possession; and it rises at moments to awe in those gifted souls who tremble with the very intensity of the beauty they enjoy without seeking to possess. Art must be reverent, for beauty is solemn, and love is girt about with godly fear. Over and above the sadness stirred by the brief life of beauty, we are always to be solemnised by the awe which springs from the mystery of beauty's intensity and love's mastering power.

The thought in the great picture of 'Fortune's Wheel' is plain for all to see. What a curse life would be if down our streets there rolled ceaselessly no more than the wheel of this cold Topsy-turvydom, and we had no more than that vast impassive figure for our Providence. Look how

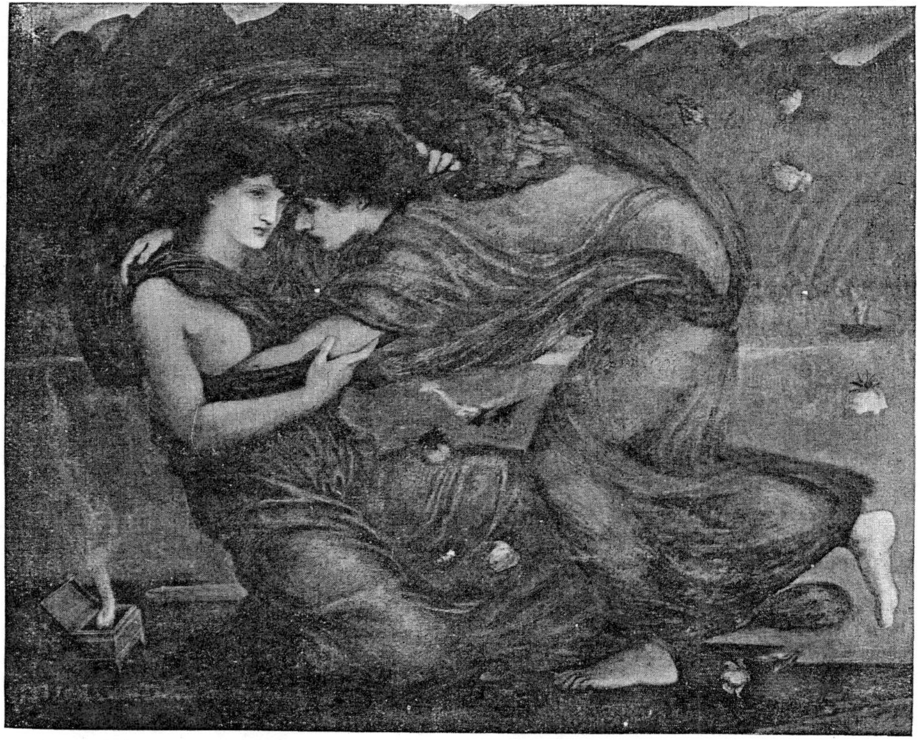

Burne Jones. CUPID AND PSYCHE. *Caswell Smith, Photo, Oxford St., W.*

she broods with utterly careless eyes upon the results of her huge mechanic toil, reckless of the irony which for the moment puts the poet under the heel of the king, and both of them under the foot of the slave, while all are under the load of a power unseen, unknown, unknowable, but vast beyond all proportion to our streets and homes. You can gaze on that tall grey figure till it become quite a terror to you, and the very silence of the night, above the home where you cower, turns to the rumble of this ever-turning, all-erasing wheel. And yet this is the deity and the creed under which the vast mass of people live, and which have been enthroned by the scientific agnosticism of the day. No wonder that there is a blight upon beauty, and a trouble upon art, if this power is the be-all and end-all of human effort and human love, if infinite apathy be life's providence, and if no other meaning than this lie in the words 'that the first shall be last and the last first.' 'The set grey life, the apathetic end.' Can that be the life indeed? Are the vicissitudes of men and nations, dynasties and civilisations, nothing more than such chance and change.

> All passes; nought that has been is;
> Things good and evil have one end.
> Can anything be otherwise,
> Though all men swear all things would mend
> With God to friend?

Let me say plainly that the vice of the day is no such danger to manhood or Christianity at last as such an agnostic, worldly, and acquiescent creed. Vice ruins many souls, though respectable pharisaism ruins more; but such a creed as this means at last ruin of the entire human nature by the cooling down of its central sun, and the slow extinction of its trusting life.

I said that Burne Jones was marked by two chief features in his art. First, his rare and exquisite poetic beauty; second, his interpretative treatment of the myths of the soul. To illustrate the first—the exquisite poetic beauty, I would select the picture called the 'Chant d'Amour.' The idea here is simple in the main. Yet its simplicity is not all of it. Most people probably regard the situation as no more than a variation of Mr. Dicksee's well-known 'Harmony'; but nothing could be more superficial. 'Harmony' is popular because it is well-handled sentimentalism; the 'Love Song' seems strange, because it is suffused with exquisite feeling and solemn thought. 'Harmony' is only innocent; the 'Love Song' is unearthly. The one has the Eden charm of the natural domestic man; the other the apocalyptic spell of the heavenly city and a supernatural grace. In both cases the immediate suggestion is that the music charms because it is love behind that supplies the inspiration. But how ordinary the suggestion is in the one case, how illustrious it is in the other! In the one we have a usual episode in the way of a man with a maid, in the other a poetic representation of the ideal, the spiritual nature of Love. From the one we have familiar pleasure, from the other fresh delight and revelation. One is the work of a painter simply, the other of a true poet and critic of life as well.

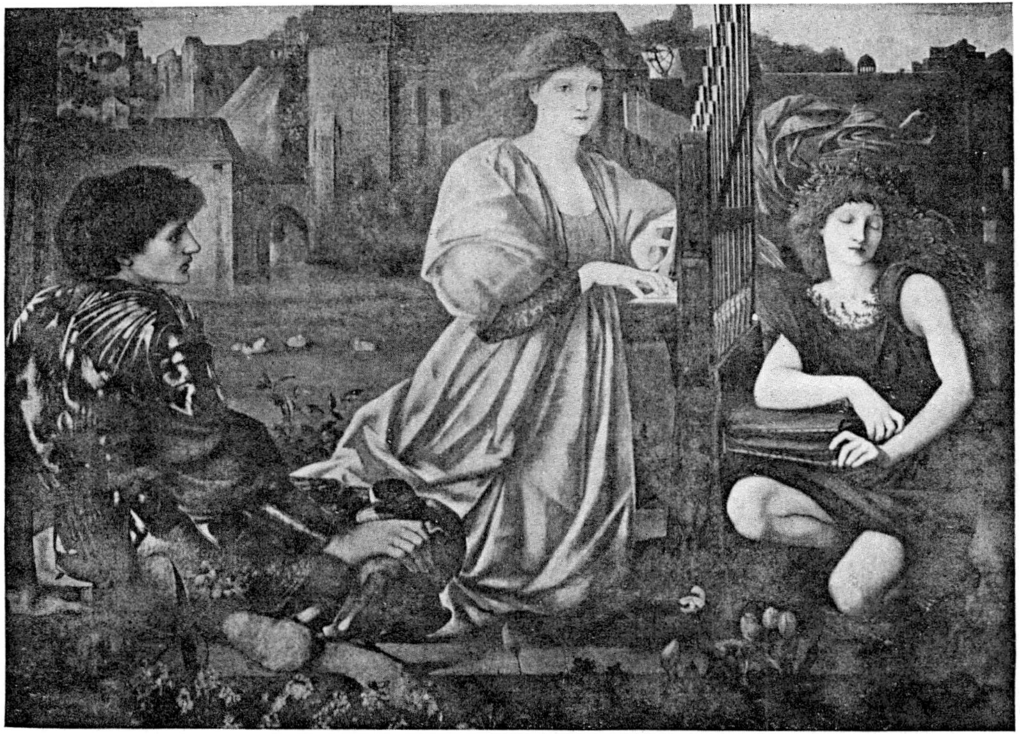

Burne Jones. *Caswell Smith, Photo, Oxford St., W.*

CHANT D'AMOUR.

The main point in the thought of the 'Chant d'Amour' I take to be one of the least obtrusive. It lies in this; love is not heavenly, till it solemnise him whom it has kindled and delighted. It must not merely kindle but capture, nor capture only but consecrate. But the love that consecrates must be touched from heaven; and the knightly heart is only subdued to reverent affection by a power nobler and clearer-eyed than the blind doting that mere passion feeds. Love's purity only reaches the unearthly holiness of the untrodden dawn when its honest ardour is smitten, changed, and uplifted by the finger of God; its choicest mood and subtlest power are in the withdrawn and holy moment when it reconciles us to a 'touch-me-not,' being clothed upon with the sacramental light of a life beyond life, and a grace that breathes at once of worship and reserve. What flows from the singer and enchains the knight is something other and higher than is inspired by the winged figure blowing the organ. That figure is doubtless Love, and the great sweetness of rapture dreaming upon his face corresponds with a rapt expression in the player's. But the eyes of the former are shut, while those of the latter are wide and full. Love, therefore, in the one is blind passion, winged and angelic indeed in beauty, but still servile in function, and careless of right or light. But in the other it is sublimed to a higher mood, it is open-eyed, it has a vision and a conscience and a strain of the love divine. That is what really and finally subdues the strong man armed. And the painter, I surmise, has put this beyond the mere fancy of the spectator by a direct indication. The time is early morning; the mood is virginal and sweet; dawn is just upon the world; it spreads upon the scene a cool, brief, cloistered peace—that tender tremor which is living peace; it streams through the windows of the hoary church to the rear; and a strong shaft of light, *consecrated to more than earthly significance by its passage through the chancel,* is made to fall straight upon the instrument at which the lady sings. This is the touch which converts the blind breath of even noble passion into the luminous inspiration of the heavenly love-song, makes love a holy mystery, and the central figure 'a glorified new Memnon singing in the great God-light.'

But I also invite your notice to this picture because there is nothing to excel or even match it in pure præternatural loveliness. If Keats could have painted he would have painted so, 'these two figures kneeling in the cool sequestered meadow grass, in view of the walls and gables of a little town asleep in the white dusk of dawn.'

How true it is that it is not the hand which makes music but the heart, and soul; that love is the Lord and Giver of life in all the highest kinds; that sometimes most may be done when the hand is stayed and the soul gets room to do her own work without the impertinence of relentless painstaking and laboured conscientiousness. This is the manifold thought in the four pictures of Pygmalion. They afford a good specimen of the artist's treatment of the old myths. We have here classicism quickened by the modern spirit to a more living and loving beauty. I cannot say I feel here the full charm of that exquisite beauty in the execution which marks Burne Jones. There may be some reason for the livid and chalky tones, which I have not seen or heard of. It may have been desired to begin in very low tones, and raise the colour through the series as the idea grew and deepened. The cold hues may be a fit atmosphere for a desire whose first ideal was but sculpturesque beauty. Upon that I will not dwell. I desire to invite you a little way into the moral suggestions developed in the series, and indicated in the lines which form the inscriptions:—

'THE HEART DESIRES.'
'THE HAND REFRAINS.'
'THE GODHEAD FIRES.'
'THE SOUL ATTAINS.'

Everybody knows the legend, but it is not the legend that the painter paints. It is the idea—the moral truth of continence, the spiritual lesson of patience, and the practical value of faith over works.

'The heart desires.' It is not the gay desire of those commonplace girls who, in the garish sunlight out of doors, are discussing with puzzled interest the young idealist whom they cannot fascinate; but the soul's desire, which the sculptor nurses in a dim unrest, to give shape to the dream he loves. He lives in an unreal world of woven shadow and tremulous change. He would put his vague heart into living stone, just as a man of soul might long to wake into his own spiritual life some beloved being who was still in the stage of nature, and unquickened to the passionate issues of the spirit. The sculptor goes to work on his material. He hews and chisels incessantly, and the floor is littered with chips of marble, but still his ideal is unattained. The stone is still cold, the figure fails to live; it is faultless, perhaps, but he feels it is lifeless. Just as many a man meddles with some undeveloped heart that he would train to his own high notions, and while he succeeds in getting a certain obedience, a certain fashion of living, all his tinkering, shaping, and regulation do not raise the new spirit of life. He does not kindle love in the thing he loves and moulds. Some parents treat their children like that; some superior husbands their wives; some teachers their pupils; some preachers their charge; some states their schools. Some men's passion will not bear to let those they love sufficiently alone, and then they wonder that their effort fails and their love flags. They know love's desire; but they do not know that love's patience and love's reserves are as needful as love's efforts for the culture of the soul.

'The hand refrains.' The sculptor stops. He will not work, but think. He will collect himself, examine himself. He has been too busy to succeed. His marble is the victim of overpressure; his meditative soul suffers from underfeeding. He is full of the true artist's dissatisfaction with his work. He will abstain; he will practise a temperance, or a total abstinence, of effort for a time. *Il faut reculer pour mieux sauter*. He will cease to potter at his creation, to correct every excrescence in detail, to press for a shapeliness merely from without. He will revise his procedure. The stoniness, the dulness may be there. At any rate he can do no more along the old lines. In just the same way, if we were wise, we should bring ourselves to book about many of our methods of soul-sculpture. They are too external, too occupied with pairing the raw life to our plans, too critical of this or that excess or defect, too officious, too unsympathetic, too instructional, too sculpturesque. The living is regulated, but the life does not appear, and the spirit may even be broken or killed. We cannot bring soul out of nature by any trimming of it, but only by a treatment far more sympathetic and inward than that. The Dutch gardener is hardly an artist, and we must teach in the artist spirit; in the spirit of inspired sympathy, which moves the true artist at his best. We must learn the educational, creative, spiritual value of holding our hand. We must practise a continence taught by reverence for the true nature of the soul and its love.

'The godhead fires.' While he mused the fire burned. In his abstinence the heart grew fonder. The spirit of true love which had been scared away by bustle returns to whisper, 'Be still, and know that I am God.' The mallet and chisel are laid down, and the goddess of love comes in her clouds and roses and doves. The marble moves, melts, and glows. Love completes what skill resigns. Faith quickens what work left dead. There may be a cant of work and a gospel of letting alone. No toil or vigil by itself kindles life. Not that either can be dispensed with, nor good intentions, nor the fervour of desire; but for the highest purposes of creation and culture these are but 'under-agents in the soul.' They may make symmetry, but they do not create life; it is only inspiration that does so. All the law in the world, or the knowledge of it, will not make a quickening gospel. And we may produce, by our mechanical education, orderly and ordinary lives, but we shall not make free and living souls. The secret of that Redemption is with the divinity of love. Without divine love, with mere intensity of eager passion, we may make idols, but we shall not make living souls. What we make will be neither warm, gentle, nor free; but, like the products of our soulless systems, hard, conventional, and cold.

'The soul attains.' The ideal and love are at one. The ideal is love. It is neither labour nor imagination in the last resort. 'Wisdom is a loving spirit.' Life is not a hymn to the intellectual beauty. The shaping spirit of imagination is perfected by the creative spirit of a less æsthetic love. The heart's desire is not enough, and the labour of the hand must cease and yield, then comes the power of the living God, the touch of the Eternal Spirit, and the trust of the Almighty love. The artist is a lover, a holy and humble man of heart. Then his soul attains what heart desired, and hand toiled for in vain. He has by true love learned reverence and so success.

The question is put ceaselessly by all our art. Amid all our getting, and all our achievement, what and how are we doing in the culture of the human soul? We are pampering the human body, and stocking the human mind; but are even our religions, our churches, and philanthropies really shaping, feeding, quickening what is best worth the name of soul? Our religion becomes a mechanism, and our word is bound; but the word of the Lord is not bound, and His severe, free spirit is abroad, beyond the churches, as well as through them, to rebuke, to quicken, to enlarge, to refine, and over the whole region of the soul to redeem. It will need more, indeed, than an art of præternatural imagination to redeem us at our worst, but the method of redemption surely has an echo in the method of art, the method of inspiration, the method of the soul. And the inspiration of art does its work not only when it calms and refines us, but when it puts beautifully to a people the searching question, 'How is it with your soul? Come from your business, and from your science, and from your churches and schools, and tell me how it is with your soul?' If we had that question forced home, as art has power to force it, we should be appalled at our poverty of reply, and we should demand, and we should receive, from our religion far more for the soul than now we allow it to give.

I am afraid, however, that art alone cannot, any more than science, answer the questions or still the longings it can raise in the heart. There have been men who were at once thinkers and artists, like Schiller, and who had a boundless faith in the regeneration of society by æsthetic culture, who would make culture a religion, and who would readily replace an Established Church by an Established Art, a subsidised stage, and the like. I am quite certain that art might do a great deal more for the quality of our religion than it ever has done. If it only raised the quality of our demands from religion, and taught us to thrust finer questions heavenward, it would do that. But it is more than doubtful if it can safely become a religion for any. The soul is larger than even art can cover. There are many crises in life for which it has no word. Experience does not show that the power of art to satisfy aspiration is quite equal to its power to stir it. Nor does experience say much in favour of art's power to evoke and rear those unselfish affections and principles which are the real cement and salvation of society. And some of the greatest artists who have not lost their *rapport* with society at large, would be the readiest to protest that it was an abuse which could only entail degradation upon art to call upon it for that work. Art is amongst the agencies that redeem; but art is not, in the strict use of words or forces, the Redeemer. And without claiming that Burne Jones reads us that deliberate lesson here, I think he has certainly provoked the suggestion. And I could point to no more striking illustration of art's impotence to satisfy the heart or quicken life than this series of the Pygmalion parable, with its direct incoming

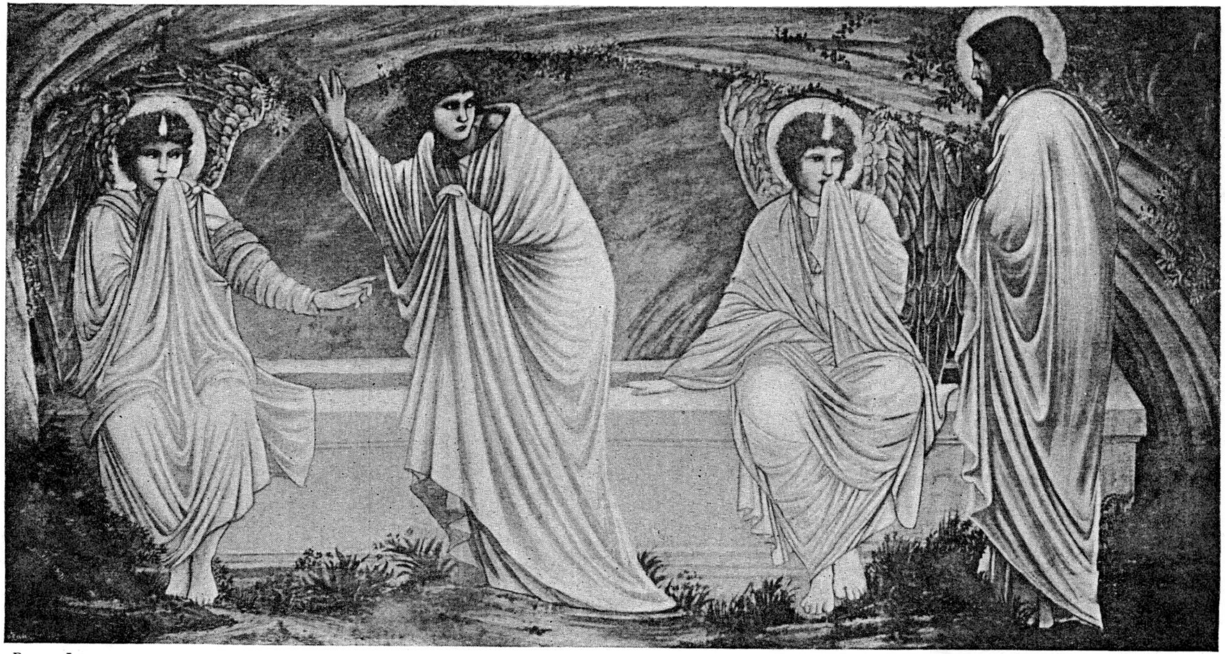

Burne Jones. *F. Hollyer, Photo, 9 Pembroke Grove, W.*

THE RESURRECTION.

of love's deity to bestow a warmth and life for which imagination had toiled in vain.

There is one other picture by this artist which is of special interest—'The Resurrection,' or rather the appearance to Mary after the Resurrection. No more beautiful episode could have been selected, none more congenial to Burne Jones's genius. Here is scope enough for imagination, and need enough. Does Ruskin not tell us that imagination will find its holiest work in the lighting up of the gospels? and do we not feel every week how starved of imagination the gospels have been, to say nothing of our pulpits? Do we not groan under the stiff ecclesiasticism that pervades the narratives of our church windows, and the solemn priggery that stiffens the woodcuts of our illustrated Bibles? The sacred figures and faces with which our memory is stocked by the religious art of our youth, do they not bear crushing witness to the wooden density of dulness to which our religious ideas and affections have sunk? Most of the art which we associate with Scripture narrative only conspires with a thousand other influences to petrify the Bible for us, to turn its dignity into stiffness, its solemnity into pompousness, its sanctity into mere decorum, its beauty into prettiness, its passion into sentiment, its movement into a strut, and its radiance into tinsel. And when we try to escape from such an authorised version we rush into the opposite extreme, and from soulless modernism we rebound into soulless archæology. We reproduce the exact conditions of life in Palestine; but we only get the statue, we do not get the life and soul. We transliterate, but we do not translate. Yet what a field the gospels offer for the concrete imagination, what a familiar nobility of subject, what a variety of situation! Many orders of artistic genius can come and make each its own selection. There is much that is of the happiest in the very selection by Burne Jones of a situation in exact affinity with the quality of his genius for exquisite, poetic, magic, and delicate soul beauty.

But what is the relation of this picture to that other feature of his genius, to his power of interpreting myths? Have we here another case of it, only applied this time to a Christian myth instead of a Greek or a Norse? Has the artist for once stepped into the *rôle* of a historical painter, or has this scene no more historical reality for him than the story of Pygmalion? Who can say? And why should we be too careful to ask? If we regard this event as history we may be glad to take the service and correction which the mythic treatment offers. We have contended for the historical reality of these narratives in such deadly earnest that when people ask us why we so prize the fact, we are not always very able to tell them. We have often picked the history into mere fact and then quarrelled over the bones. We have lost the art of clothing them with living flesh, and restoring by an imagination at once pious and true, the vital colour. A few realise in silent adoration the deep spiritual significance of the facts for the personal soul, but how few even of these realise the concrete power and beauty of the recorded situation. If any man of potent imagination come forward, though he tell us that these things are myths, if he body forth for us the myth in luminous colour, exquisite beauty, and overflowing soul, and if he further body it forth in the thought and spiritual language of our time, why should we not welcome the quickening service his imagination has rendered to our historic facts? Why should we not tell him that while we do not accept his authority on a matter of history, we are glad to profit by his imaginative reconstruction of the scene, and his vitalising of its spirit? Let us have the myth set forth in all imaginative truth, and it will only serve to enrich the fact in its impressiveness, not to displace it in its reality. If I were informed that Burne Jones had no faith in the historic actuality of the event he here depicts, that would not in the least affect *my* belief of it, but his treatment does quicken and enrich my appreciation of it. What has art to do with the historic actuality of events? Its business is so to grasp the soul of the event as it would have been had it been. It is religion and not art that finds it a vital matter to discuss the reality. It is part of our religion to believe that this thing took place. Can this artist, or any other, help us to realise the circumstances, the emotions, the air, and spirit of the hour? He need not go, like Holman Hunt, to copy the exact and literal conditions on unessential points. He may, without offending us, represent the tomb as Burne Jones has here done, as a trough of red stone, instead of a horizontal cavity in the rock, with a millstone rolling on its edge across the opening for a door. But we do ask for the unaffected and exquisite solemnity of the hour, and I think that in no mean degree we here have it. This at any rate is not the mythic version of Renan. It is not in Mary's ecstatic fantasy that the Saviour appears. The two angels are aware who is there before she is. The light falls from the Saviour upon her, not from her upon Him. She has come out in hasty morning attire—a very natural and original thought of the artist; her hair is carelessly gathered round her head; a great cloak has been hurriedly flung about her, and over its dark mass her sweet and wonder-stricken face rises as if itself were issuing from a tomb. She had not recognised Christ; His face is in shadow as the dawn is behind Him. It is the moment when He has just said 'Mary!' She has 'turned herself,' in the words of John. She had had no expectation of seeing a risen Lord, but that tone in a moment made her heart leap, her head turn, and her eyes swim. She totters and clings to the rock for support, as she quickly gazes in His face. How beautiful it is! In a moment she will make to cast herself at His feet with the cry of 'Rabboni.' O, it is very beautiful. What joy to know Him, what shame not to have known Him! Look in that brimming face, all sensibility, in those eyes like round worlds redeemed, and see what the Lord has done for her soul.

But can this stooping figure be the risen Lord? Why not? 'But there is no power, no dignity, nothing commanding.' That is what commonplace art has brought us to,—the sort of art that dresses Mary as if she had been going to a ceremony,—art with no fine original feeling, the art patronised by monumental masons and dull wealth. They need something heroic, something stalwart, something with dimensions to impress them. It was none of these things that impressed Mary. It was the tone whose secret was in its quiet, the look whose power was in its unearthliness. All is quiet crepuscular solemnity here. How fond Burne Jones is of the unearthliness of the dawn! The death poppies that are trodden under foot are not yet opened. The light is sweet and low. All things else are in keeping—the sun creeping into the cave, the dawn of recognition in Mary, the dawn and but the dawn of the risen life in Christ. How coarse a blaze of radiance would be, or a figure standing in dramatic pose with uplifted hand! Where do we get that notion of Christ having issued from the tomb in a blaze of light? In the narrative it was an angel that shone and terrified the keepers. And I suppose people thought that the risen Christ must not be less luminous than an angel, or less striking, and so they made Him rise from the grave in an overwhelming splendour, and clothed Him in every subsequent appearance with a majestic, if not lambent mien. All the accounts point the other way. His disciples usually did not know Him; they were not appalled at first, nor was their tone of ordinary intercourse abashed. The two at Emmaus took Him for a traveller, and entered on traveller's talk. Mary, a moment ago, took Him for the gardener. Only a truly spiritual insight could read His face. The shining angels here, winged with the inferior symbols of a visible heavenliness, yet with faces still more luminous than robes or wings, *they* recognise the Saviour's soul beneath the unassuming mien. Their great eyes have discerned before Mary who it is, and one is lifting a shocked finger to hush her after her address to Him as the gardener. We can mark the pity, the tears, the awe and admiration and joy in their eyes. He was not yet in the glory that abashes pity, and makes the angels veil their faces with their wings. His humiliation was not yet wholly over, and angels could love and pity still; their visible glory and beauty pay prompt and tender if distant homage to His glory spiritual and unseen. They can perceive His visage shine over His lowly mien, like the Spirit of endless life in standing resurrection and ascendency over the body of death. It is all so finely true and just. Even death could not destroy His divine simplicity, nor resurrection impair His majestic humility. It did not change His spiritual into a mere visible splendour. It is a truer glorification of the meekness of Christ to paint it in probable beauty like this than to set Him with gentle face upon a gilded throne, or represent Him in a glare of cloud sailing in ecstasy into the air. He was risen but not yet glorified. It was Pentecost and not the Resurrection that enthroned Him in the majesty which to Christian thought He has inhabited ever since. What progress art has made, both in truth and effect, by discarding the common conventional grandeurs, and relying on the fine piercing power of unassuming veracity and unpretentious fact. How much more religious, more spiritual, is its eloquence upon this line than the grandiloquence of days gone by. How much greater is its promise. For this was exactly the change made by those great first realists Giotto and Cimabue, who began to lift Italian art to its glory from the inanities of Byzantine conventionalism and ecclesiastical pomp.

And what has been the great, slow, total tendency of religion from that day to this? Why, to humanise the unspeakable sanctities, to set the Incarnation forth as a real, concrete, historic principle. Art and religion pursue the like great methods in different kinds. The principle of art is the incarnation of God's eternal beauty; the principle of religion is the incarnation of God's eternal human heart. Neither can do the other's work, yet their work is complementary, and I wish the divorce between them were more nearly healed. I wish the artists felt more of the need which art can never fill; I wish the religious felt more of the need that art alone can fill. I wish the Christian ideal might more speedily rise to its function for the imagination; I wish the artistic imagination would more widely respond to the inspiration of the Christian spirit. I wish those who take up art did not gravitate so often either to no positive religion, or to the sultry piety of Rome; I wish those who profess Protestantism would so largely construe their creed as to offer more food and freedom to the prophets of the imagination. But I am sure such wishes are not vain, and the time is coming when faith will do more than it has done yet to fix the colour of beauty, and beauty more than heretofore to sweeten and soften the vigour of faith. The time is coming, I am sure, when the Christ that is to be shall fascinate the imagination as it was enthralled by the mediæval Christ, and inspire a piety purer, because lovelier, than the one-sided purity of Puritanism. Christian beauty is severe, but it is not inhuman; and true art, however humane, is severe enough. That faith which brings real wealth to the soul cannot bring poverty to the imagination. The soul is not something which dwells in a corner of human nature; it is human nature at its finest, completest, and best. Look how the quickening of the soul kindled the prophets' imagination of a real and righteous earth. Look how it has kindled the dreams of Christendom about a kingdom of God and a paradise of heaven. Look how religion has suffered, and lost its power to command men, by losing its spirit of large and generous imagination. How should religion and art be foes? Saints and artists have before now been one. Will there be no restoration of belief in which they shall be one again? I refuse to believe it. I have grounds for not believing it. The soul in search of a præternatural beauty will not be repelled from the sources of true spiritual beauty. 'Whom He hath justified them hath He also glorified'; and the same power which makes life holy makes it also fair and free. The path of beauty is not *the* way, but it is a way to God; and the temple in the heavens, like the old temple on earth, has a Gate Beautiful. We shall not go far in a true sense of the beauty of holiness without gaining a deeper sense of the holiness of beauty. For the glorious Lord Himself shall be to us a place of broad rivers and pleasant streams, wherein shall go no galley with slavish oars, nor gallant ship with sordid crew pass by. But out of Zion, the perfection of beauty, God shall shine. Jerusalem shall be a quiet habitation; hers shall be the hush and coolness of a soft eternal dawn, filled with the low sweet singing love inspires.

WATTS

OR, THE RELIGION OF SUPERNATURAL HOPE

I

THE most rambling notions are afloat about Nature and Art. A man says: 'Give me Nature, I want 'none of the refinements of Art. As soon as 'you have Art you get the intrusion of the frail 'and fickle human soul into the royal beauty and 'grandeur of Nature. You get human ingenuity 'instead of the divine handiwork. You get the fret 'and strain of human effort instead of the calm of 'Nature's exhaustless process, and the ease of her 'vast and simple beauty. Nature speaks direct to 'the heart. But your artist introduces all manner 'of subtleties; and you have to labour in order to un- 'derstand, and you have to watch and wait in order to 'feel. Give me Nature. All Art is but toiling after 'something which Nature has long since attained. 'Why should we trouble about the imitation if we 'have access to the original. Let us hang bits of 'Nature in paint upon our walls when we cannot go 'to the country; but let us be sure that if we can 'go to the face of Nature, these copies are super- 'fluous and may be left behind.' How many people feel like that! And they believe they can pass no higher compliment on a picture than by saying it is just like Nature, just like life. They give you clearly to know (and they could call Aristotle to their aid) that their notion of Art is simply imitation; that it is not ahead of Nature, but in the rear of Nature; and that if ever we succeed in discovering the secret of photographing in colours, the landscape painter's occupation will be gone. Place such a person before a painting of Turner's, and he moves away with a bewildered contempt. He never saw anything like that in Nature. And if he has seen the locality Turner portrays, he easily discovers and promptly informs you that the artist has been by no means accurate in depicting the features of the place.

No; but the spirit of the place is there. And that is what no photograph and no machine can seize or reveal. The spirit of Nature can be seen only by the spirit of man. Spirit can converse only with spirit. It is not possible even for God to speak to a camera. And Art is a function of the spirit. Its message is a spiritual message. Its camera is the soul. The chambers of its imagery are in the depths of man's most godlike part. Art is not imitation, but interpretation. It is spirit prophesying of spirit. It takes of the things of God and shows them to us. You must paint what you see, to be sure. But whether the result be Art depends on what you see. The cry of the hour is for realism. We have it on the stage in elaborate, accurate, and sumptuous scenery. We have it in a host of novels of actual life, which we are expected to admire for their analytic fidelity, whether they possess deep sympathy and noble insight or not. We have it in the abominations of Zolaism and the Naturalistic School. We have it in the demand that preachers shall be 'practical,' and not tease their hearers out of their daily ruts by the breath of spiritual ideals, which play such ironical pranks among the dead leaves of hourly life. We have it in the myriad productions of painters, whose inspiration comes from no higher than the elbow or the shoulder, and from no deeper than the optic centres. And we have it in the suspicion felt about the sound judgment of any man who stands before a work of real art, and reads out of it messages for the moral imagination and not merely for the eye, or revelations for the soul instead of curiosities for the intelligence. The cry in these—and in many other symptoms one could name—is for realism. But we do not get reality by this sort of realism. We do not get Nature. We certainly do not get Art. No copyist ever got Nature, and they have all certainly missed Art. Nature is original, and only originality attains to Nature, or rises to Art. 'Nature and realism,' says Mr. Watts, 'are very different. Nature we rarely see except in the country where man's hand has not been lifted against the landscape. The men and women we see walking about are no more Nature than a well-ordered garden is Nature. The artist must learn to understand the real form, and endeavour to see Nature *through* it.' As I say, Art is interpretation. It is a branch of sacred hermeneutics. It is commentary, but commentary of the noblest and least pedantic sort, which in due time becomes itself the text. It is epistle upon gospel.

Let natural beauty be what it may, artistic beauty is higher. And why? Because it is spiritual. Because you have in Art the finished product of which Nature is but the initial stage. Nature runs up into the artist. He crowns Nature with the miracle of living, conscious spirit. He reproduces Nature with that spiritual addition which is the priceless thing lacking to mere Nature. As Religion is the true relation between God and the Soul, so Art is the true relation between Nature and the Soul. In every true great picture we have two things. We have Nature and the Artist. It is not Nature we get. We must not look for it. It is nature *plus* the supernatural, viz., the spiritual medium of the artist's soul. That is just the difference between a photograph and a painting. With the colour and the hand we get the soul. We do not see Nature as we should see it on the spot. We see it with eyes more anointed than our own. The artist lends us his. The living lens of his soul is adjusted to ours. And we may go so far as to say that the precious thing in his picture is not Nature, but that which is other than Nature, which is above Nature, without ceasing to be natural. The artist's soul is not a mere mirror, and his gift is not perfect achromatic reflection. He has imagination, and his function is interpretation. Do we not say, theologically, that Creation is but a part of God's self-revelation? It is a phase of His self-interpretation.

Art is the process of Nature prolonged, turned back, and applied to Nature herself. Nature, like the climbing train in the St. Gothard, runs back upon her own course, but on a higher level, which commands the lower curves and a great deal of country besides. It becomes super-nature. The method of Art's teaching is Nature's method spiritualised; and I do not mean by that simply refined, nor yet allegorised. Spirit is more than rarefied Nature; it is Nature regenerated. What we have in Art is not Nature, it has been deeply said, but Nature born again—born of the spirit or soul which is above Nature. It is in a sense a new creation, and at the same time the perfecting of the old. Creation can only be perfected by creation—the process in the lower kinds only completed by the same process in the higher. And Art is to Nature what Salvation is to the soul. As Salvation is the redemption and spiritualising of the natural man; so Art is the redemption of natural things, which then speak not of themselves, but with other tongues as the Spirit gives them utterance. There is no such profound and true account of Art's relation to Nature as in Shakespeare. I wish I might enlarge on the passage. It shows how the Art which is more than Nature is yet the completion of Nature, Nature which has arrived at the true knowledge of itself, Nature which has found itself. It is just as human nature finds itself perfected in the spiritual man, and knows by divine thought its own true nature, which is hidden from the thoughtless natural eye. What Shakespere says is this—

> 'Nature is made better by no mean
> But Nature makes that mean; so that o'er Art
> Which, you say, adds to Nature, is an Art
> That Nature makes. You see, sweet maid, we marry
> A gentler scion to the wildest stock,
> And make conceive a bark of baser kind
> By bud of noble race; this is an Art
> Which does mend Nature—change it rather; but
> The Art itself is Nature.'

The fact, therefore, is that instead of Art being an addition, an intrusion, a sophistication upon Nature, a condescension and accommodation to poor human nature, the fact, I say, is that we never really get Nature till Art has helped us to it. It is not a case of choosing between Nature and the artist's conception of it, but between his conception and ours. And, for my part, if I can get at his, I prefer it to my own, as being probably more nearly right, and certainly more full of significance for my own soul. He can teach me far more than I can teach myself.

And Art follows Nature's method in this also that it is not direct in its teaching. Art does not preach sermons, it only suggests them. It does not din lessons into you, it only waylays you with them, fills the air with them, steals with them into you, saturates you, and changes you before you know you have begun to learn. The greatest Art is full of such lessons, and exists for the sake of these lessons. It does not exist simply to please, but to instruct by pleasing. And it is for the instruction, not of the curiosity, but of the heart, the soul—the large, the universal soul—in us. The Nature it chiefly has to do with is human nature. It rises to its great flights when its subjects are drawn from the moral imagination. It places before us impressively, indelibly, the truths, the powers, the passions, the principles of the spiritual man, of the Nature which rules and raises Nature, governs it and lifts it up for ever. I may have been thought fanciful in interpreting some of the pictures I have taken in hand. Well, I will not say I am right in every point of my explanation. In some points I feel the danger of forcing a meaning. But the artists do not want their students to be correct in every point; and what some of you distrust, perhaps, is not the interpretation of particular points, but this style of interpretation altogether. The greatest trouble of my life as a public teacher is to get English people to believe that there may be anything in holy texts beyond what the 'plain man' may be made to see at once. You think Art does not exist for teaching of the kind I aim at. Well, much Art does not; but I have left that alone. I have only touched the Art which is laden with unforced suggestions for the soul. And I am much comforted and sustained by a passage which I will read you from the man who, of all critics, has best known and taught us what Art means, and for what it should exist. Speaking of the Homeric poems, Mr. Ruskin says:—

'They are not conceived didactically, but they are didactic in their essence, as all good Art is. There is an increasing insensibility to this character, and even an open denial of it, among us, now, which is one of the most curious errors of modernism—the peculiar and judicial blindness of an age which, having long practised Art and Poetry for the sake of pleasure only, has become incapable of reading their language when they were both didactic: and also, having been itself accustomed to a professedly didactic teaching, which yet, for private interests, studiously avoids collision with every prevalent vice of its day (and especially with avarice), has become equally dead to the intensely ethical conceptions of a race which habitually divided all men into two broad classes of worthy or worthless—good, and good for nothing. And even the celebrated passage of Horace about the Iliad is now misread or disbelieved, as if it was impossible that the Iliad could be instructive because it is not like a sermon. Horace does not say that it is like a sermon, and would have been still less likely to say so if he ever had had the advantage of hearing a sermon. "I have been reading that story of Troy again" (thus he writes to a noble youth of Rome whom he cared for) "quietly at Preneste; and truly I think that what is base and what is noble, and what is useful and useless, may be better learned from that than from all Chrysippus' and all Crantor's talk put together." Which is profoundly true, not of the Iliad only, but of all great Art whatsoever; for all pieces of such Art are didactic in the purest way, indirectly and occultly, so that, first, you shall only be bettered by them if you are already hard at work in bettering yourself; and when you are bettered by them, it shall be partly with a general acceptance of their influence, so constant and subtle that you shall be no more conscious of it than of the healthy digestion of food; and partly by a gift of unexpected truth, which you shall only find by slow mining for it;—which is withheld on purpose, and close locked, that you may not get it till you have forged the key of it in a furnace of your own heating. And this withholding of their meaning is continual and confessed in the great poets. . . . None of the greater poets or teachers of any nation or time ever spoke but with intentional reservations; nay, beyond this, there is often a meaning which they themselves cannot interpret—which it may be for ages long after them to interpret—in what they said, so far as it recorded true imaginative vision. For all the greatest myths have been seen by the men who tell them involuntarily and passively—seen by them with as great distinctness (and, in some respects, though not in all, under conditions as far beyond the control of their will) as a dream sent to any of us by night when we dream clearest; and it is this veracity of vision that could not be refused, and of moral that could not be foreseen, which in modern historical inquiry has been left wholly out of account: being indeed the thing which no merely historical investigator can understand or even believe; for it belongs exclusively to the creative or artistic group of men, and can only be interpreted by those of their race, who themselves in some measure also see visions and dream dreams.'

II

THESE remarks may be useful in approaching such writing on the wall as the pictures of Mr. Watts, and essaying the interpretation thereof. The truth in them is not so much fidelity to outward nature as the spiritual truths and destinies of the soul. 'We shall find on examination,' he says, 'that all Art which has been really and permanently successful has been the exponent of some great principle of mind or matter, the illustration of some great truth, the translation of some great paragraph from the Book of Nature.' Not truth only, but the great truths are what he has set himself to convey in the language of beauty and the conditions of Art. He is struck with the fact that the power and solid magnificence of English enterprise are almost entirely without corresponding expression in Art. Our energy and our conceptions are colossal, but our art themes are small in comparison. The source of the disparity is easy to see. Englishmen are in earnest about their commercial and political enterprises, but they are not in earnest about Art.

Those who like it, like it as a relaxation, an amusement; their pictures are like the children of some of them, things to play with when they come home of an evening, or, like their sherry, to toy with as they drowse through a Sunday afternoon. They do not become reflections of such men's largest self, or expressions of the earnestness of which they are really capable. Preachers find a similar state of things. Men of large business faculty, energy, and conception, almost angrily and contemptuously resent it if their preacher asks of them scope for anything on a corresponding scale in matters of the soul. They want to be gently interested in a sermon, or briefly soothed; but it is unsafe to invite them to religious considerations as large in earnestness, thought, and scope as the range of their practical ambitions. It is this temper on the part of some Nonconformists that lends much power and charm to the provision made by an Established Church for securing these larger and calmer interests against the popular clamour for a hand-to-mouth religion, which is satisfied if only pressing and immediate wants are duly served. How else should we describe the anti-theological temper which has taken possession of much of the younger and energetic nonconformity, especially its laity, and which seems to make a present of theological science to the ignorant, obscurantist, and ultra-orthodox schools? These are but using the advantage their opponents give them, when they claim to be the only champions of the large and staying truths of the religious reason, as against the variations of individual religious sentiment, or the 'results' of what is conventionally called 'practical work.' It is this state of things in Art that Mr. Watts has set himself to oppose and remedy. He has a national purpose and enthusiasm in his Art. He believes the English could be made to care for grand and thoughtful artistic forms. He wishes to see these plentifully spread in the decoration of our public places. 'Art,' he says, 'can never take root in England till the people at large grow to care about it, and this they can never do till it is presented to them, habitually.' He thinks the English could be made to care for a congenial kind of Art. 'A people who care more for Handel's music than that of any other composer, would not long be insensible to similar impressions conveyed in a different but very analogous form.' And he feels, most truly, what we are made to feel in respect of religion, that the range, the quality, the temper of Art has suffered all manner of belittlement and degradation by its separation from national interests and national aspirations. Art, like religion, has been dwarfed and sentimentalised by sectarianism and individualism. And, like religion, it needs to be re-established in its national connection (which, I may remark, is a very different thing from the establishment of a church, whether of religion or art). The restoration of this national tone to Art would give it a grandeur and dignity it has largely lost in domestic and trivial prettiness. 'It would bring out that quality and nobility deficient in the English school, but not in the English character.'

And it is interesting to remember that the great apostle and agent of a national Art in Germany, namely Wagner, has much in common with Watts in the profundity of his thought, the beauty of his sentiment, and the colossal grandeur of his conceptions.

We have no Art among us so masculine as Mr. Watts's; none so Miltonic, none so conversant with the vast and dignified simplicities of form, the grandeurs of imagination, and the widest sweeps of noble thought. He is our Michael Angelo. He has schooled himself severely on the example of Phidias, and he has lived himself into the large spirit of our own time. He lays hold of us with a grasp, he does not steal into us like a dream. The contrast with Burne Jones is striking. Watts is more intellectual than that fine spirit. He thinks even more than he feels. He does not paint beauty, or passion, so much as the thought in these. His portraits penetrate, as is frequently said, beyond the expression to the character. He seizes not the external phase, but the dominant thought or motive. His landscapes are distinguished by the largeness of their atmospheric effect, as we see in the 'Mountains of Carrara.' 'I hope,' he says, 'that whatever faults or shortcomings there may be in my works, there is nothing mean or undignified in them.' He views life on a huge scale. He pierces to its broad and central issues. As he paints the character of his sitters, that is, their whole life, so he paints the character, rather than the aspect, of life on the whole. Death has a fascination for him, but it is very different from the fascination it had for Rossetti. There is not a symptom of morbidity in his style; and he is impressed much more with death's grandeur than with its curse. Death is for him the object of noble meditation rather than the blight of devoted passion. It is the obverse of great Life. Like Art itself, Death is one of the great interpreters and expanders of Life. He sees it invading passion, and stalking over affection, but he sees it doing so as the bowed minister of a vaster power, and shone upon by a holier light. Art in Watts serves the noblest uses of the intellect; it is vigorous, it is full of hope, like all the very greatest thought. Beyond Life there is a destiny, above Nature there is a power. Above the darkling world is the luminous sky, which has in it always one star, if but one. More than the spirit of Nature he paints the presence of something ruling both Nature and Life, and something that is not wholly Fate, or pallid Fortune by a grinding wheel, but luminous, grand, stirring to the imagination even while dreadful to the affection, and audible to Hope even when unseen by Faith. He is distinctly a religious painter. He is full of the sense of human impotence, but also of human dependence, not of human insignificance. The power which leads Life to its heights is Love. And I think I am within the mark when I describe his religion as that of Supernatural Hope. Whenever he paints Time he does so with an originality that betokens this vigorous hope. He discards the conventional old man with the scythe, and depicts Time as a noble and fearless youth striding onward ever, even with Death by his side, and Judgment in his wake.

Burne Jones, I have said, is a painter not only of beauty, nor of passion, but of thought. And he paints in beautiful guise the thought of his age—an age which an able critic discussing the Victorian era calls 'an age of growing and inevitable sadness.' No sympathetic thinker can otherwise read the deeper spirit of the time, in spite of endless outward jubilation. To be insensible to that undertone of sadness is to exhibit not masculine vigour but inhuman hardness, and such poverty of imagination as no artist-thinker can be credited with. The easy, breezy spirit is not one that has power to live very deeply into the spirit of an age like this. All these painters I am dealing with feel the soul-weariness which beauty itself cannot resist, and love is powerless to drive clean away. We have seen how it affected Burne Jones, how it coloured his versions of the grand immortal myths which are the flexible and imperishable garments of the soul. Mr. Watts has not escaped the infection, but he has risen above its frailty. And he has for the most part taken another method of conveying his thought than Burne Jones. Burne Jones falls back mainly on the old myths, and issues them in a new light and reading. But it may be an evidence of Watts's greater imaginative vigour that he creates new myths for his purpose. Burne Jones found the modern thought in the ancient forms; Watts provides both the thought and the form. Burne Jones took the forms that were to hand; Mr.

Watts invents new forms, and not only interprets but creates. Burne Jones is a painter of myths; Watts, of allegory.* The myth is a common tradition, out of which is read the unconscious thought; the allegory is an original invention created to embody the conscious thought. Of course, Burne Jones has allegories, and Watts has myths with modern interpretation, like 'Psyche.' But broadly speaking, what Ruskin has said, expresses the distinction between them. The mythic painter takes a story and interprets it, the allegoric makes a story for us to interpret. The didactic aim can never be obtruded in either case, but in the case of the allegory it is more direct than in the myth. It betrays more vehemence of moral purpose, more depth of popular sympathy, more of the spirit of the teacher, bent not only on revealing soul, but shaping soul. These allegories of Mr. Watts are painted parables, the work of an artist who is a prophet too. Accordingly, while in Burne Jones we find a solemnity no less than in Mr. Watts, in the former it is the solemnity of unearthly beauty, in the latter it is the solemnity of superhuman destiny and darkling powerful hope.

I had the boldness to consult Mr. Watts about a point on which I was in doubt, and I had the honour to receive a most kind and ready answer. He was deep in work after a long absence, and the letter was written under his instructions by Mrs. Watts. He generously offers me any help I may desire in the interpretation of his works; and I am

* Ruskin.

going to quote certain passages, for the purpose both of enforcing what I have said, and, especially, of showing any who may be inclined to think I am overdoing the exposition, that I have the highest authority for my design, and am not taking a fanciful liberty with pictures meant primarily not for instruction but delight.

Mrs. Watts says:—

'It was a great pleasure to him to find that you understand what he always considers to be the chief end of Art, and the direction which he would hope to give it by his work. He has wished to raise in the mind of the spectator thoughts religious in the widest sense. For this purpose he has refrained from making use of symbols that might be felt to thrust forward anything specially dogmatic, or even border in the slightest degree upon the didactic. . . . How much he deplores that the importance of Art, as a servant of religion and of the state, has been lost sight of. It has become not much more than an article of luxury, and is no longer seriously regarded.'

That appears to me very true. And probably one great reason for the absence of public seriousness in the treatment of Art is the lack of seriousness on the part of the great mass of artists. Painters are like musicians so often—they know and they care for little outside their own pursuit. They have neither the power, the education, nor the desire to interest themselves in the weightier matters of human law and fate. They have neither part nor lot in the general soul. From their work you get no idea of the heart and pressure of the time, the age's central heat, the nation's mission, the thinker's warfare, or the believer's rest. 'There is a cowardice in modern Art,' as Charles Lamb says in his remarkable essay 'On the barrenness of the imaginative faculty in the productions of modern Art.' It is a phrase much less true to-day than it was in Lamb's time. But it is still too true outside the group of painters I am dealing with. It is not at all true of Mr. Watts. He combines profound insight, intense seriousness, and splendid audacity, with masterly technical skill. He is an artist, a thinker, and a prophet at once. And that is the only sort of man that will make Art a real power with a people like the English. We are a serious people, not to say a grim, and we are not to be moved in any conspicuous degree by the kind of thing that makes raptures at Vienna, Munich, or Paris. It is only an Englishman that can rouse in the English serious care for Art, and belief in it. At present we believe in painters, we do not believe in Art. We admire pictures, we are sceptical about the power of painting. We crowd about Millais, but we owe him little more than delight. We are somewhat disposed to resent it if an artist make a call upon us for sympathetic thought.

III

In speaking of some pictures of Mr. Watts's, I will begin with one which, to most, perhaps, is not very interesting, and to many hardly pleasing. I mean the nude figure of *Psyche*. One of the readiest remarks to be heard on this picture is an expression of distaste for the low tone of colour on the figure.

But is your curiosity not roused about this picture? Is it simply a study in a kind of art about the propriety of which there is a good deal of discussion? Psyche is weeping. Why? She has dropped a lamp which is smouldering on the floor. What is there in that? How come these two feathers there at her feet, one red from the wing, and one downy from the breast? This picture contains a story and a thought. It is an instance not of allegory but of myth—an old imaginative beauty with a ceaseless eloquence for each living age. The story of Cupid and Psyche is one of the most beautiful and familiar in antiquity; no more perishable than any deep true tale of Love and the Soul. Its finest English version will be found in the translation from Apuleius, embodied in Mr. Pater's *Marius the Epicurean.* Psyche was beloved by the son of Venus, who visited her often, and kept her in happy and noble state. But the peace and pleasure was to last only on condition that she should not look upon her lover's face, as Elsa in *Lohengrin* must not ask her lover's name. But the restriction was too much for her curiosity, the secret for her rest. One night, goaded by her own inquisitiveness and her sister's taunts, she brought her lamp, and ventured to look upon Love's sleeping face. She marvelled to find how beautiful he was. But by mischance a drop of hot oil from her lamp fell upon his shoulder, and he awoke to discover her distrust; whereon to her lasting grief he took wing and fled. And so Psyche after fruitless struggle was left to bitter tears, to smouldering dimness of vexation, and to gaze upon those feathers on the floor, poor relics of her lost love and lord. That is the story. And it is so full of thought that it has some counterpart in the myths of most thoughtful lands. Love's mysteries are of love's essence, and the soul for its peace must ever trust a face it cannot see, in the faith of a heart-revealing word it hears. To see all is to lose all. To compass all knowledge would be to part with all joy. Science will increase our sense of power, but it has nothing for the soul's peace, as we are rapidly coming to feel. There is a canker in our modern pageantry of power. It is the insecurity of the soul, its vanished harmony, its discredited creed, its restless seeking for its lost lord—lost by the unchastened haste of its curious quest, and scared by the illumination of scrutiny when he might have been kept by the inspiration of sympathy. Psyche there, sad in heart and dull in tone, is the soul of our time with its ignorant knowledge, its faithless and narcotic energy, its interesting and irreverent inquisitiveness, its sad dissatisfaction and its sense of irretrievable loss amid all its outward beauty. The lamp may stand for the practical energy, the scientific method, the mere power of exploring mind and will, which denying Revelation lights us so often to Soul's dissection and Love's undoing. We push in the door, but it falls and kills the life we pursue. We cut up the face of nature and the body of man, but the soul flies faster than our knife's keen edge. We analyse God, we map out His nature, we display psychology, we chase His goings, we chart the currents of His process, and we think we can keep Him by that near us, or look thus into His veritable face. But nay. Not so do we behold the face of any God that will stay with us and be our peace. Not by the lamp of seeing, but by the heart's vision of trust do we win and hold our soul's lord. And that lamp smouldering on the floor symbolises the failure of these curious methods to hold our salvation or come nearer our one true goal. They have their uses, these methods. Science in its place is as needful as faith, and how can we trust except we know? But the knowledge of the day is by no spiritual methods, and it comes to no spiritual things. Nay, it drives spiritual things, and thoughts, and presences from the soul, it fills us with at best a stoical regret, and lights us only to a shock of impoverished discovery, smouldering discontent, and a distrust even of the great things knowledge in its true use and method can do. We looked that the increase of our power should be the comfort of our soul, and we are left to a long and low lament. The feathers on the floor represent what we have parted with, thrown away, and replaced with our sullen tears. They are the relics of our lost peace, the reminders of a time when we knew less but rejoiced more, when we commanded less of the world but more of ourselves, when we believed more in our own souls and less in the power of things seen to satisfy them. They remind us of a time when love was by us with the homely service of his soaring wings, and we daily trusted the truths of the soul with a broad, imaginative trust. They remind us of a time when the soul of man had an infinite Soul to repose upon, ere yet knowledge had banished from the universe a universal Heart and a soft peace beneath the shadow of His pitiful wing.

I am getting fantastic over this picture, you say; I am tacking religious applications on instead of drawing its natural suggestions out. I suppose by its natural suggestions would be meant the real spirit and intent of the painter. Well, here is another passage from the letter I have mentioned. 'The picture of Psyche he himself,' says Mrs. Watts, 'considers to be less a suggestion of modern ideas than an illustration of the old myth.' If he had meant to put the ideas in the foreground, and the situation in the background, it would have been an allegorical picture and not a mythical. Now mark how the myth is not simply treated for the sake of its pictorial effect. 'At the same time, he wished not too obviously to suggest a thought toward the spirit of the times so unduly absorbed by the desire for the possession of material facts. The lamp serves as a symbol of the means to that end, lighted to define the undefinable, and only revealing nakedness of soul, and the frayed feathers torn from a departed possession, a lost innocence, and a lost joy. This, roughly speaking, is what he felt about the picture; but he begs me to say he would in no way wish to trammel your thoughts as an interpreter of his works by defining too much.'

Yes; those who most deeply think to-day, whether they always confess it or not, have their thoughts more seriously drawn to what we have lost than

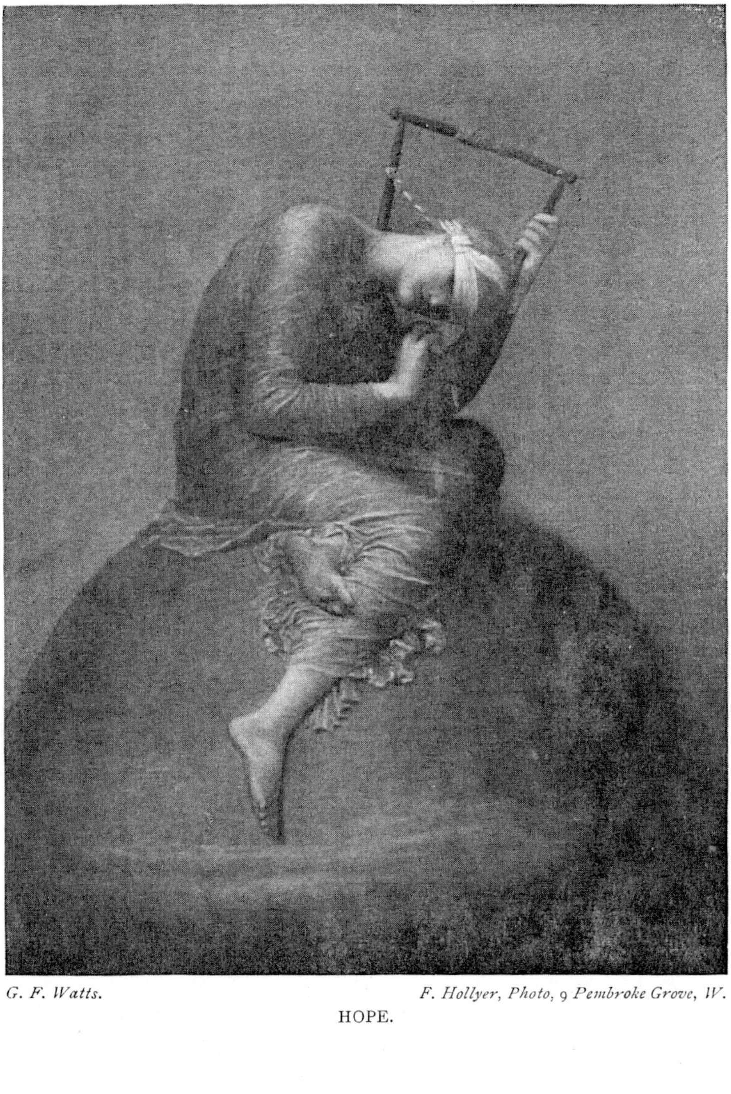

G. F. Watts. *F. Hollyer, Photo, 9 Pembroke Grove, W.*

HOPE.

to all we have gained. And they are disposed to adapt with new and burning significance the old inquiry, 'What shall it profit an age if it gain the whole world and lose its own soul?'

Even Rossetti was no pessimist, far less Mr. Watts, with his vigour, his action, and his noble simplicity. Where there is health there is hope, and Mr. Watts is full of sanity and sober hope. It is not bounding hope, it is not radiant, nor sunny-eyed. The spirit of the age cannot rise to say it greatly believes, and without great belief there is no splendid Hope. Do not think that the loss of Faith develops the strength of Hope. It throws more strain upon Hope alone, and Hope is not infrequently overtasked. Hope was never meant to replace Faith, but to supplement it. An age whose wing of Faith is lamed flies heavily, even when the wing of Hope is left. The Hope of the hour is darkling. We are saved by it, but we are scarcely saved. We faintly trust its larger word. Seated atop of Nature, with the whole of earth's forces at the command of our knowledge, it is yet with difficulty that we hear the harmonies of heaven, and its one star we do not always see. That appears to me the meaning of the allegory entitled *Hope.* Again the figure is the age's soul. The figure itself is not Hope, but that which hopes. It has all the world under its feet. That is a grand height to have reached, a grand conquest to have won. But it is costly. With position gained the soul has lost its music, and its joy. Its lyre is all but unstrung. Its note is thin and low. Every cord has snapped but one. It is the string of Hope. But is there not a commanding view to be had from this height of natural knowledge? Yes, down perhaps. But the figure has turned her back on heaven's light. She, who has seen so much, has lost the power to see what most pertains to strength, and joy, and peace. Her face is turned from it. Ever learning she has never come to the knowledge of the healthful truth, and now, with earth searched and heaven to explore, her gaze is not up but down, her heaven-searching power of faith is quenched. But the thirst to believe is still there. Look how the darkened soul stoops and strains for the one string's note, for the one voice to tell her a gospel that all her achievement has not yet attained, and all the round and mastered world cannot promise. The soul has in its own self and nature a note that Nature has not. But is that note of hope only in the soul? Is it a subjective dream of its own? Is there any promise in the 'not-ourselves'? Is there anything corresponding to aspiration, anything to justify it in the heavens above the earth or the realms above the soul? How blank these look. We have scanned and searched them till they have almost lost their spiritual awe, and beyond our telescope and spectroscope they are still vast, featureless, and expressionless to our agnostic knowledge—'a grey, void, lampless, deep, unpeopled world.' Is there aught there that answers to the one cord, still unlost, that vibrates aching in the soul? Yes, there is one star, though the poor soul sees it not. The painter sees it, and we see it. A star is there, and a dim dawn. 'I will give thee the morning star,' still peals from heaven to earth. You will mark falling on the figure and shimmering in the sky, the light of a dawn which she cannot see. Its source is outside the picture, outside our visible frame. That star, then, is a morning star. Heaven responds to the great, last, indestructible instinct of the soul. Hope's note in the soul might be a subjective delusion, but it is answered by hope's star in the sky. That at least is no dreaming echo of the soul's own self and sound; no music breathed by the soul alone for her own delight, but perhaps also for her own mockery. There is still a star to lead our wise men to their worship, and to cheer them till they find their Christ and King. But she is unconscious in her sweet sadness (observe the mouth, all the pathetic beauty of our modern scepticism is in it), she knows not of this dawn. Her eyes are bandaged, and by herself. Ah! if she had but the courage to look beyond the world she would take knowledge of a light that is not of the world. She would find that there is a knowledge, more than a mere surmise, which kindles hope to faith and fear to love. The bandaged eyes mean much. They mean more than that a man hopes not for the things he sees. They mean more also than that the vision of faith has been unwittingly lost in the gain of material power, or poetry bound, and insight quenched by the network of law. They mean more than that the soul *cannot* see the things that are her true power and peace. They mean that she cannot bear to see the only things she *can* still see. It is that she *dare* not see. Her hands are free; why does she not pluck the napkin away? She has gazed round on a dreary plenitude of lonely sway. She has seen with her immense knowledge so much that is fatal to heart or hope, that she must deliberately bandage her eyes and refuse to look if she is to go on hoping at all. She can be sanguine only if she will not see. She can only believe at the expense of her knowledge. Faith for her only begins where knowledge ends. She must shut her eyes to retain the hope of salvation. To this does mere nature-knowledge bring us. We dare not know all we may. The agnostic is not a coward, but agnosticism is. She turns her mind inward to get cheer. She strains to listen where she is afraid to look—to listen to the dim suggestions of her attenuated soul's last heavenly cord. She has no spiritual objective. Sick of her outward power, she finds more promise in a subjective sentiment which echoes within, and which sounds rather from amid her weakness than her strength. Her broken lyre is become more to her than her clouded throne. She has turned her eyes despairing away from the outward and visible hope of the heavens; and from the perch of her perilous knowledge looking only down, she would fall giddy into the abyss of despair if she did not bandage her eyes, and preserve, by ignorance that will not think, the hope that will not be stilled. Faith can afford with unquailing but solemnised gaze to face the terrors of life, and the more it knows the stronger it grows in trust of the power that overcomes. Faith cannot be based on the weak side of us—our ignorance. But Hope, to live, must forget the horror she cannot overcome, and must keep herself from dizziness, only as they keep the horses from panic in fire, by covering her eyes.

It seems to me we may perhaps read the same thought in another picture, which appears to be only a bit of grand and sombre landscape. Why did it occur to Mr. Watts to paint *Mount Ararat*? Was he only turning some scene of travel to pictorial account? But how many mountains besides Ararat would have given him the like effect. Do we need to go to Asia to see a noble peak stepping out grandly, in flight after flight of massive rock, from the gloomy shadows of earth into the radiance of the nightly heavens? Is not Mr. Watts a painter of myth more than of landscape? Is there not a grand tale hanging round Ararat—a tale of terror, gloom, death, and the flashing again of human life and hope upon the world from its ark-laden summit? Is this picture a modern reading of the old tale? Men disbelieve the tale about the ark on Ararat. Well, but over its summit poise not an ark but a star. That is an image which still may speak hope to the soul with a poetry that is more imperishable than the belief in ancient history. The tale is old, the scene is ever new and eloquent. Every sombre mountain that rises in billows from the glooms of earth into the radiance of heaven may tell us that the summit of this darkling world is still in heaven's light, though it may be but moonlight. And every solemn peak upon whose flanks the darkness clings like subsiding waters, and o'er whose head there hangs a simple star, may be for the soul an Ararat, crowned with an ark, and helmeted with the hope of salvation for a world lost, emergent, and at last sublime.

Hope! And what are we to hope for? For Love, which is more than Hope. Faith is just the power of believing in Love, and so Hope is just the power of looking for Love. And what by Hope do we escape from? From Death, which is less than Hope. Hope does not exhaust Mr. Watts's creed. It does not fill the measure of his moral world. It does not meet the entire grandeur of his spiritual imagination. Life, Death, Love—these are powers that loom larger upon the soul, and stir its passion to intenser heat than Hope. The moonlight of Hope cannot scatter the tough cold mists of Death, and we cannot by Hope alone climb to the summits which Hope gives us to see. We *wait in Hope*, and waiting is all that many souls can do at present. They wait, and listen, and they hope to know. But we *walk by Faith*, by Faith we work, by Faith we climb. And Faith, as I tell you, is just the power of trusting in Love, the faculty of 'lippening,' and knowing that somehow good will be the final goal of ill.

Before I speak about the next picture, I must remind you not to expect the artist to convey in any one picture a theory of life, but only some great or moving aspect of it. You get his philosophy, not from a single work, but from the spirit of the whole series. I give this warning, because in the picture called 'Love and Death' we seem to have an aspect of experience which would be fatal to Love or Hope. It is well known that this picture arose out of the sad and early death of a brilliant young friend of Mr. Watts, whose portrait he painted, and who was dying by inches during the sittings. The situation impressed itself deeply on the painter, who knew the devoted struggles in the young and shadowed home to keep death at bay. But the handling by genius raises the particular case to universal dimensions and general significance. The picture represents, not the calamity of a home, but the great heart's pathetic tragedy of Love, Hope, and Blight. No picture of Mr. Watts's makes me feel more than this that he is a great religious painter, and his Art the art of the deep prophetic soul dreaming of things to come. Pathos and grandeur here meet as in no other picture of the artist. And over all is Hope's great light, and deathless Love's surmise.

The background is the entrance of a house, which is the House of Life. Round the door is trained a blossoming rose—the superscription of happy home and Love's young dream. Stooping and pushing into the doorway, with its back toward us, is a vast figure, draped from head to foot—clearly, the shadow feared of man. Its advance is the effortless, undishevelled, and inexorable gliding of urgent Omnipotence and menacing Fate. Under the shadow, and before the door, is the puny God of Love, barring entrance with a child's passion of protest and frantic entreaty. His wings are broken against the doorpost, and his roses are dashed and strewn upon the ground. We see the hopelessness of the struggle, and its inevitable end. Love will lie bleeding and helpless on the threshold, and the house will be filled with the huge terror and gloom. We see what a trifle, a dream, Love is in the presence of this visitor, how hopeless against it are passion and effort alike. We pity, and we despair; we dread, and we resent the cruel, reckless pressure of that fearful power. We are all on the side of Cupid there; we are all against his foe. The picture seems a solemn rebuke to the Naturalism of the age, with its brief, sweet beauty, and its quavering creed that 'Love is enough.' For the shadow, veiled and speechless, is over all; and the dearest love must one day go down before a vast inscrutable Fate, which blights and erases all. That power, then, that slays Love—has it no word for Love? Does it just kill and say nothing? Is our best passion, our purest happiness, but a fond, foolish child before the coming of that heartless, awful, ageless adult, Death? Has the real sting of Death come to be Love? Then, indeed, has Hope, listening upon the world, snapped her lyre's one string, and lost the last star in her sky.

The great touchstone of a philosophy or a religion is its treatment of death. A man's creed or his soul is to be gauged, not indeed by the way he meets death—for many accidents, foreign to the soul, may interfere in the death hour—but by the way he views death. Every religion or system is to be measured by its interpretation of the cross.

And if what I have said were a complete description of this picture, there would be no trace in it of that supernatural hope which links this life to another, and lights our fate with infinite possibilities. What grandeur would there be about death were it the arch enemy of all that goes to make soul good and great? But Mr. Watts always sees and represents a grandeur about Death—yes, and a tender grandeur too. Nor is it wanting here—though it is not obtruded. It is the undertones, even the whispers, that are loudest for the soul in this great work. I cannot convey to you by any words the solemn eloquence that moves me in the very poise of Death's mighty uplifted arm. It is not mere force, it is not mere menace. It is like the arm of the Lord and the shadow of His wing. That bowed head, too, tells that even Death may be sorry, and the reverent servant of a still higher Might. Little Cupid is too frantic to read the visitor's face. If he did he might possibly see what would make a great calm. But Cupid has never been very quick to recognise his Eternal Father. That great shroud, moreover, is not raiment but disguise. And, chief of all, a great light falls upon the figure's back, and we remember that we never see the dawn upon death till it has gone by, that we get to know our angels when they have left us, and that we mark the sunlight on the graves only when they have well grown green. The source of the light you further mark is not in the picture; and so the hope in our latter end is no ray from within our visible frame of things, but from a life and a world beyond.

Death once gone by is charged with the light of a life beyond life. 'And Death once dead there's no more dying then.' He is a Revealer. He may disappoint our hopes, but he need not quench hope. He lifts it solemnly, tenderly, to heavenly places. This darkness is beautiful, and it is Cupid that is blind. And the great comer who forgets nobody, and spares none, is after all but the old, irresistible kindness, and the Love which loves on to the endless end.

It is the same idea with an added tenderness in the smaller picture called 'The Court of Death.' You might call it, Death the Mother-Queen. How finely the solemn figure cradles in her lap the new-born infant just taken from the mother, who herself fondles up to Death's great knee, and is in sweet rest at last. There is in the babe, death-fondled thus, a symbol also of the new life which death alone can cherish. The lion and his brute force are trampled under the foot of the throne. A book is on the ground, as if learning gave way to a higher knowledge here. The throne itself is a ruin, for the hospitable kindness of Death outlives the works of man. All sorts and conditions and moods of men are gathered by the all-mother's gracious constraint. The man-child plays in the skirt of her robe. The aged crone stoops and worships leaning on her staff. The cripple hobbles up with a gasp of glad relief upon his upturned face, to go softly now for all his endless days. The mailed warrior in his prime with reluctant homage lays his trophy down. And the wise, old, robed King deposits his crown at her feet. 'There must be wisdom with Great Death.' Behind her is a great golden splendour, and two angels are by her side. How beautiful compared with the vulgar skeletons that paganism itself eschewed, or even with the terror on the white horse of the Apocalypse. I am much reminded of Wordsworth's kindred sonnet—

> Methought I saw the footsteps of a throne,
> Which mists and vapours from mine eyes did shroud,
> Nor view of who might sit thereon allowed ;
> But all the steps and ground about were strewn
> With sights the ruefullest that flesh and bone
> Ever put on ; a miserable crowd,
> Sick, hale, old, young, who cried before that cloud
> Thou art our King, O Death ! to thee we groan.
> These steps I climb ; the mists before me gave
> Smooth way ; and I beheld the face of one,
> Sleeping alone within a mossy cave,
> With her face up to heaven ; that seemed to have
> Pleasing remembrance of a thought foregone,
> A lovely Beauty in a summer grave.

It is said that Mr. Watts, himself, thinks much of this fine work, and that it is intended for the Chapel of a Pauper Cemetery. And nothing could be more fit; for death is not so kind to any as to the poor.

Every virtue has its defects, and the strength and grandeur displayed in work like Mr. Watts's have often for an offset a certain brawny and unsympathetic power, which makes heroism untender and inhuman. Your giant intellects miss some potent charms which to babes and sucklings are revealed. Your colossal wills override some gentle rights which are yet in the keeping of the Almighty Will, and whose vindicator ever liveth. Your titanic imagination expands in a solemn pride which is as narrow as it is high, and as harsh as indomitable. The eagle ranges the sky and surveys the world, but he understands not the wisdom which speaks like the dove. There are weak and waiting things in the world whose patience is their power, and whose latent destiny is to outlive and confound the things that are mighty. Life to the Titan becomes all height, courage is exhausted in the idea of fortitude, influence is limited to coercion, and rule resents the conditions of obedience. The type of character becomes Miltonic, and, in its evil form, Satanic. It is heroic and no more, self-sufficient and foursquare, stoical where it suffers, and tyrannical where it acts; 'stern to inflict, and stubborn to endure.' It is strong because impenetrable, and great because it sits solitary. That is the type of pagan nobility, and a time was when it was the highest type that Europe knew. But Christ has changed the spirit of our dream. Goodness since the Cross is something else than stalwart, and life's beauty more than sternly grand. Life is great not by its power to will, to rebel, to endure, and to defy, but by its power to lean, to trust, to adore. No man liveth to himself who is a true man; and no man dieth to himself; he is not self-contained. Faith, not Fortitude, is the ideal of godlike life. And Faith, I remind you again, is the habitual trust of the soul in Love.

This is the teaching of 'Love and Life,' and it shows that Mr. Watts is not the victim of his own vigour, but has the soul to feel the subduing grandeur of the lowlier, holier way. Mrs. Watts tells me that 'this picture is (to Mr. Watts) perhaps his most direct message to the present generation.' I am not quite sure that, artistically, Mr. Watts has the same success in painting pure gentleness and dependence as he has in infusing tenderness into his grandeur. In this very picture it might be said that the manly and pitiful patience of the great figure representing divine love is more successfully portrayed than the utter, helpless, and stumbling trust of the woman who represents the soul. But on such a point I am not well qualified to judge. I think, however, that the feebleness which so many criticise in this figure is not in the art, but in the thing which the art truly represents. The feeble woman is an expression not exaggerated of that dreadful self-distrust deep and secret in the soul of our time, which is so little able to read itself, and so much surer of the message in Nature than of that graven in its own buried and neglected life. Our scientific vigour and rigour is a soft thing enough when it is hit in the heart, and poised in the isolation of grief, between abysses which its plummets cannot sound. And I think few who make a practice of severe self-examination will escape rebuke here if they will let themselves be taught by Art at all, and are prepared to hear in it a word for the conscience as well as for the taste. People, as I say, complain that the figure representing the soul is too weak, that life is a better, stronger thing than that, that it does not tremble so, nor totter so, nor is it so absolutely dependent a thing as is here displayed. But they are not all weaklings who have confessed that life is a vapour, and that it is not in man that walketh to direct his steps. And perhaps most people are too unfamiliar with the divine ideal of life as love to be able to feel how poor and feeble a thing life without love really is, how sorrowful it is, how naked and destitute, how weak is the vigour and rigour of mere force, how mistaken it is to make the forcible person, the merely indomitable person, our manly type, and how impossible it is by any native energy which may be ours to escape life's worst pitfalls, or climb life's purest heights. The mightiest power of life is the power to trust the strength and patience of unweariable love, and I assure you this picture is for us as full of reproof as of beauty. You shall no sooner admire it than you shall ask yourself—'Is that the way that I treat love? Is that the way my love treats the souls with whom I have to do?'

Mr. Watts's message is not unneeded by an age and a people so prone to trust its energy of will and its mastery of material force as we in England are to-day. Would that the professional expositors of things divine had done more to teach us that the soul's one eternal power is, however manifold in form, in its nature Love, and that no other power can lead the soul along life's giddy and rugged edge to sovereign success. Would that we could be impressed with that, not as a poetic truism, but as a religious principle for our moral nature, our practical life, and our experimental consciousness. We hear enough of love as the charm and happiness of life. We do not hear enough of it as the moral principle of life, especially of social life, its guide and clue to the depths, the heights, and the end. We hear plenty about Love as a sentiment or as a passion, but we have not yet practically learned to confess it as our God. Love as a sentiment is beautiful, and it is a great influence in the case of most. But Love as the principle of life and godliness, as the genius and spirit of true religion, as the ideal and standard of eternal and immutable morality, is something which sentimental lovers are not always eager to entertain. Love in the New Testament is not the love of two young people for each other, with its beautiful, but not always redemptive Egotism. What we mostly call love is but divine Love in its infancy and alphabet. We are put in love with each other that we may learn by its expansion through thought, experience, pain, and death, the dearness of a love which by all individual regards is not fettered but freed, which is no mere personal gain, and of no private interpretation, but which blesses all at the expense of none, and is perfect as God's Fatherhood in heaven is perfect.

'I had a little daughter,
And she was given to me
To lead me gently backward
To the Heavenly Father's knee.
That I, by the force of Nature,
Might in some dim wise divine
The depth of his infinite patience
With this wayward heart of mine.'

What is set before us in this picture is not the love which loves this soul or that, but the Love which loves the soul—Love that has wings, not to fly away with us, but to upbear and steady us in the perilous pass, and to climb with us into the heaven of universal blessing and general good. It is not the Love of Paul and Virginia in this noble picture, nor the idyll of Hermann and Dorothea. It is the Love of God in Christ Jesus our Lord.

The imagery of this 'Love and Life' is simple. The woman is the soul. Her helplessness may be emphasised for the sake of impressing us with the intrinsic weakness of the robustest life if it be loveless, viewed from the divining standpoint of Imagination and Eternity. The rocky path is life's arduous and narrow way. On either side yawn the issues of death and destruction. The more we realise their depth and the straitness of our path, the more dizzy and self-distrustful we become. It seems more and more difficult to the soul, as it knows itself and its world, to enter in at the strait gate. Those that really go in are few. We perceive how our very devotion sometimes puts us in danger of hell fire; how our cry of Lord, Lord, may damn us if it lull our conscience to a false security; and we see, with the old pilgrim, that from the very gate of heaven there is a door by which some are carried into hell.

It is a narrow, a weary and a dreadful way to the summit of the far blue hills in the high clear sky. And those gifted spirits to whom heaven is highest and life's heights most beautiful blue, are just those that realise, as the thoughtless do not, the peril and the strain of the present path. It is a gifted imagination that best divines for us the moral earnestness and solemn hazard of common life. But how should we stand if we were every moment to keep our eye upon the path. If we always viewed the peril, and the tension, and the straitness of life, we should lose all power of noble living. If we knew all about life, and trusted nothing, we should be paralysed, we should quail, and fail, and fall. We safely tread the narrow line with our eyes fixed not on our path, nor even on our goal, so much as on some winged power for whom the path has no peril, and whose pinions steady him to sustain our faltering feet. You mark that in the picture the eyes of the Soul are bent upward with devotion on the face of Love, whose eyes see for us, and who makes our progress his tender and fearless care. Observe also that this Love, winged though he be, does not lift the Soul and fly with her over the rocky way. He does not even lift her clear of the loose stones, and the jutting stumbling-blocks. He encourages, he sustains; he does not remove the necessity for walking, he makes walking possible. It is in part the lesson which I said Burne Jones's *Pygmalion* contained. The freedom, the independence, the inbred faculties of the Soul must by true love be respected and developed, not ignored and made superfluous. The object is not merely to place the Soul somewhere, but make her something. And look how little contact there is between the two figures, how gently her hands are just laid on his, as if it were no material support but a mere contagion that Love supplied, a magnetism, an inspiration through the finger-tips. The Soul just needs to know that Love is there.

Such was what seemed the meaning of the picture to me when I received a second and unexpected letter from Mr. Watts. I was much relieved to find myself borne out by these words—

'It is an idea,' he says, 'that can be amplified to any extent, being indeed intended for the Love that Paul preached; the sustaining, guiding, and raising power, impersonal, not the love of any one for another, which may be carnal in its nature, and could not have been represented as winged, the love that brings life—tenderly trusting herself absolutely to him—to a finer atmosphere, and gives it its clearest vision of celestial heights.'

Such is the love of God, if by impersonal, we mean freed from the *limitations* of personality, but not divorced from the *nature* of personality; if we mean that God is no respecter of persons, and is superior to mere individual regards.

Mr. Watts once showed me two pictures in his studio of which a third form and a more complete hangs in the new Tate Gallery at Millbank. A noble female figure, draped, sits by the side of a mountain stream, which laves her feet. There is blood on them, which the brook washes away. On her lap lies a sword, now sheathed, which she fingers in a careless, preoccupied way. You see that it is preoccupation when you look at her face, which has a rapt and absent air, but not a quiet. It is not the rapture of peace, but a startled rapture, as if the glory of some new idea smote her face and troubled her with its joy. A new inner light has broken upon her mind. She is of ideal proportions and mien, and it is a new idea that dawns on her, half fascinating, half unwelcome, a fearful joy, that humiliates while it transfigures, and saves with consternation. One knows these visitations—when a thought rises and a truth goes home which fills you with infinite presentiments and breathless possibilities, but which, if it be true, will fill you with dreadful misgivings. If it means what it seems for the future, you have been making a dreadful mistake in the past. Your life has not been all mistake, and you have pursued amid storm and passion the one true way. But the very truth and fidelity of your past in the hour of revelation makes you feel more keenly the curse your cardinal error has been to truth, and the bane your violence has been to faith. Paul had that vision. 'If *this* be the Christ, what have I been doing? If this be glory, mine is shame. If the cross be the Divine way, what an awful, awful mistake is the sword.' The Church has had that vision. It is hampering parts of the Church to-day with glorious misgivings about her methods in days gone by. And this is Mr. Watts's meaning as he told it me. The figure is Faith—a noble and powerful form, sincere and fine. Her bloodstained feet in the light of history need no comment. The sword in her lap we understand but too well. Yet these methods were used in all sincerity. The picture says that. Its message is worthy both of art and faith. It abashes persecution, but with no coarse, cheap, and unsympathetic denunciation. Where both sides persecuted, we, who are still keenly on one, shall better escape the vice by comprehension than by denunciation. Faith has a better word than that, even as it has a better way than privilege, and a better weapon than the sword. Its genius, so long misunderstood, even by itself, is love and service. This was not realised by Romanist or Reformer, except in certain sects, whose descendants are now asked to disown them and tempted to be ashamed of them. History, scientific and sympathetic, tells us that Faith was early poisoned and misled by a false idea, an infection caught from the methods of the world, and foreign to her own true soul. She was seduced by a wily State, but not defiled. The persecutions by the Church were a mistake thrust upon her by the methods of the State when she was too young, with all her vigour, to realise how faithless they were. Vigorous young people of good instincts and even fine aspirations do succumb for a time to the influence of inferior minds and manners whose vices they aggravate by their very vigour, and in a way consecrate by their singleness of devotion. You find zealous, high-minded, unselfish men captured by a political Church idea to-day, and betrayed by it into public conduct towards others which gentlemen would not practise towards each other, to say nothing of what brother owes brother in Christ. So Faith, in her young centuries, was seized by the world ere her own mind was fully formed, and her own genius had found its feet. She was seized by the State idea of force, of persecution. The sword was put into her eager, mighty hand, formed only for the cross. She thought it was the cross, only held by the other end. She thought to use it for Christ's sake and the world's blessing, as she still thinks in quarters that she can use political privilege and the social sword. Many have been her seasons of reflection and doubt. Many such doubts must visit the best minds among those who fight for a political monopoly in religion to-day. Times come when victory disappoints, when the frenzy of the sword is by, when the steel that mowed down men cannot reap the field or carve the food to repair the waste of war or restore the strength for battle. The sword is sheathed for the hour, and laid across the listless knee. And the red feet of battle are bathed and passion cooled in a stream that descends the hillside purer, from nearer heaven, than the crimson-flowing field. Yea, long seasons come when Faith, looking back on the sum total of her policy in history, is filled with disappointment and struck with misgiving about her methods. The sword is at rest—she is sick of the sword. The feet are cooled in the simple water of life that may have slaked the freshly ravished conventicle on such hill or moor as the picture shows. There is leisure for a new revelation to break in upon the still noble if misguided soul, upon Faith, if not upon the Church, on Faith still faithful to God, if blind to the truest Gospel, and cruel to men. Because she has been faithful on the whole in spirit and high in aim, there breaks upon her a new light from her own old word. A reformation is the best reward of old fidelity. A new power swims into her startled ken from the dim horizon of her old truth. It may shatter her old fabric. Vision brings revision. But it builds a new heaven and earth. It may dissolve her old self-confidence, but it opens the glory of a new trust, a new method, a new warfare, a new service, a new humanity. What is this new power?

Mr. Watts's second sketch is larger and completer. It is virtually what may be seen in the Tate Gallery. The same figure sits with her bloody (alas! not bleeding) feet laved in the sweet mountain rill, with its pure and simple water of life. The sword is there on her knee, and the same speculation is in the face. But the idea which smote her inwardly, and broke out through her face, has now received from the artist an outward shape. A female figure is on each side of her. She on the left, with the garland and the harp, singing in one ear of Faith—that is Hope. And her eyes are intent on the second figure to her right, who is whispering into Faith's other ear the startling word which reveals to her her true self. Her hand is gently at the same time putting away the sword neglected now upon the knees of Faith. 'Blessed art thou among women,' says the voice, 'for thou carriest a holier thing and a mightier than thou hast known.' And the promise from without, like any real gospel, stirs the self-rebuke within, 'Thou fool!' Who is this form? Why, who should reveal Faith's soul to herself, and shame her into glory with her own true meaning? Upon whom should Hope's eyes be for ever fixed as her music passes through the listening of Faith? Who should show Faith the more excellent way and antiquate with a word the misguided, rash, intruding methods of the world? Who but Love? The 'truth' and *nisus* of faith is love. Its object and destiny is love. And that is love that is whispering the new-creating, old-destroying word, that forgives and puts the brute sword smiling by, that humbles faith into hopeful repentance, washes from her the blood of horror by the purer stream from a Redeemer's holy, pitiful, broken heart, and gives faith to the world again with a new career of power and a new wealth of subtle blessing to belittle by its greatness all the turgid past.

Mr. Watts has another fine picture, also in the Tate Gallery, representing a tender woman gathering to her arms all the poor children of men. It is an apotheosis of the spirit of philanthropy; and he has entitled it 'Dedicated to all the Churches.' Perhaps the sermon was more needed when the picture was painted than it is now. The lesson has been well learned. And I could wish the inscription removed from the frame where it stands and placed upon the great ideal work I have ventured to expound. It is not the pity that loves down that the churches need now to learn so much as the faith that loves upward and the righteousness that loves the brotherhood around. It is not the love which is natural instinct spiritualised, and which calls in faith in aid, but the love which is supernatural, and grows out of faith as faith comes to itself under the education of grace. The conversion of love by faith is as real as the conversion of faith by love. If love change faith from glory to glory, it is equally true that love itself is changed, by the revelation that faith takes home, from natural pity to supernatural mercy by the Lord the Spirit.

Mr. Watts alone, among all our artists, has an equal power in the tender and the sublime; he almost alone puts brains into his art and paints spiritual thought. By consequence he puzzles the critics, exasperates the dilettanti, and extorts from young ladies of both sexes the distinguished tribute of airy neglect.

Mr. Watts is our only artist who is capable of wrestling with death, and therefore the only one who understands life. It is singular that our sole painter of death is our master in living portraiture. It is not difficult to paint a corpse; it is the triumph of art to paint death. It is easy to paint a man or woman; it is hard to paint life.

This true genius is especially attracted by the majesty, mystery, and mighty interrogative of Death. Years ago he painted Death and Love—Love the cherub borne down by Death irresistible, solemn, sorrowful, benignant, and lighted by a great light from a source unseen. He has in '*Sic Transit*' painted Death and Life. Life is a problem, we are often told. We are not told so often that what makes it the problem is Death. Death is the closing mark which turns Life from an assertion to a question. It is the grand interpellation to the Government of the world. It quenches our dogmatisms in mystery, and makes every man his own chief inquisitor. It quells the glory and wealth of Life in an amazed simplicity which is the standing difficulty of philosophy. One of the chief reasons for regarding it as another fact of Life and not the negation of Life is that, like Love and God, it is only to be understood by experience, and by no wisdom and no tradition of men.

No corpse we ever gaze on in its shroud conveys to us what Art here makes us feel of the majesty of Death in its relation to Life. Actual contact with death breeds sorrow or horror. It needs Art, Thought, or Faith, to fill us with its solemnity.

On a pale tomb lies the dead, completely veiled in a shroud of white, so that the contours alone are seen; and these with fitting mystery are hinted more than seen. The face is not level in repose, but thrown back in helpless question, almost in baffled remonstrance. The mighty mystery and solemn interrogative, I say, of Death.

Who was he, the dead there?

The relics of life in the foreground will tell us. He was a man of power, culture, and success. He had tried many paths and failed in none.

> And we have been on many thousand lines,
> And we have shown, on each, spirit and power;
> But hardly have we, for one little hour,
> Been on our own line, have we been ourselves.

Has he come to himself and found himself in death? Well, did he in life?

The ermine robe huddled on the left tells you that he inherited a lordly place; the laurel crown on the right tells you that he earned no less than he inherited, and added by his deeds to the lustre of the name he received. He came with the ermine, but he went with the laurel. The spear, the gauntlet, and the golden shield tell you that his fame was won in war. The roses scattered among the armour show that he mingled love with war. The peacock feathers in the cuirass point to his taste for the decorations of life. The lute speaks of his musical tastes. The book says that he was not strange to the gentle verse or the ways of meditative lore. And the dark robe with the cockle on it shows that he had his palmer days, his mystic side, his season—perhaps indeed only his fit—of devotion, his presentiment that the wreath of fame was hollow, his fore-feeling of the hour now come when a touch from one light finger throws down all. A high-born man of valour, passion, devotion, taste, and culture—fit to do anything for the State, and do it well; one of life's pets and successes.

> And he lies there in default
> And most innocent revolt.

The life of beauty, prowess, culture, passion, devotion, command, and fame—what does it mean in the face of death? What of all he got, and did, and won, has he taken with him? Has he left it all behind? It is not a case of vulgar wealth and gross getting. It is a trite moralism that the gold must stay when we must go. And that fame fades we have long known. But does it imply in him who earns it anything at all which is able to resist the solvent touch of death? St. Paul makes a fine list of doings not ignoble, but he says, 'If I have not love, I *am* nothing.' These gifts and graces, these high faculties and noble achievements, these loves, these tastes, that intellect, that excellent glory of laudable life in the very perfect gentleman, scholar, courtier—are these of the things that must stay here and not go with the soul into the world unseen? Are these of the Eternal Reality? What is he, what has he, what makes him whatever he is now?

The painter has put along the top of the canvas three brief words with a hint of his intent.

'*What I spent I had.*' He had now lost it.

'*What I saved I lost.*' Thrift is no richer in eternity than the spendthrift. Saving, if it be but hoarding, is losing. Saving is good only if it be the saving of things that can be used, and are used.

'*What I gave I have.*'

'He that saveth his life shall lose it. He that loseth his life shall save it.'

His eternal possession lay in what he laid down. Was it chiefly life? Has he that now?

Is there much sign amid all those symbols of diverse and glorious life that he had given much, that surrender had been the real spirit of his life? There was plenty of culture—but what of the cross?

Death may be solemn in that picture, but the dead is not noble. He is not resting from warfare, but still craving, still imploring, still, with head thrown back, with upcast face and paralysed eagerness, pursuing rather than possessing. Why is something lacking of the nobility of the dead amid the solemnity of death? Because there is lacking in the traces of his fine opulent life any sign that he was ruled by the spirit of giving, of abasement, of truth, that he was much more than a lofty Epicurean or a Stoic of the gentler type. There is no sign of the true cross in life, and so there is still but question and poverty in death.

There is the crown of laurel—where is the crown of thorns? He was, after all, a spiritual Laodicean. 'Thou saidst, I am rich and increased with goods, and have need of nothing; and knewest not that thou wert wretched and miserable and poor and blind and naked.' It was the opulent, cultured, active, eager life that was hollow. Death has just come with the touch of reality, and in a moment shown things as they are. This man may have faced Death on the battlefield, but he had never practised death, till Death surprised him. He gave but little, so in death he has but little—he *is* not much.

A notable sermon to the procession of culture and half-culture that moves through our picture-galleries and takes its pleasure in the least earnest efforts of our soulless, purblind art.

'Desire earnestly the greater gifts. And a still more excellent way show I unto you. . . . Follow after love'—the love that lasts, because it lays down and trusts.

I am happy to know that this exposition of Mr. Watts's '*Sic Transit*' was thought by the great artist both correct and welcome. His picture, entitled 'Woman,' is a scripture much more hard to read. That the public found it so was not doubtful to any one who waited in front of it, and overheard the remarks of the visitors, who stand for a moment bewildered, and frequently move angry away. It is a singular thing this anger of the public with a teacher who puts before them what is not immediately comprehensible. The worship of simplicity is one of the great spiritual dangers of the democracy.

The picture is perfectly correct, like all Mr. Watts does, in colour and in drawing. But, accurate as it is in its technique, it exhibits a skilful and intentional crudity of effect, and it is pervaded by a great and glorious vagueness of poetic suggestion. Let it be said at once that its chief beauty is neither in line, colour, nor proportion, fine as these are. It makes its great appeal to poetic thought. It paints an idea.

Mr. Watts's congenial region is high—where earth and man become the natural sacraments of a vast ideal world, and the concrete utterance of eternal powers which always mean more than they can say, and therefore need the artist's inspiration to complete them and to interpret their message to the soul. He paints not scenes, but principalities and powers that rule the true realism of life. Now, of all the realities which attract the nobler thought of Art, there is none more fascinating, imperious, and profound than Woman. Personal experience and ideal thought combine to give the subject the deepest human interest, and to-day more than ever. It is inevitable, in an age which is at once the most humane, the most social, and the most Christian the world has ever seen, that the position and the meaning of womanhood should engross the attention of men in a degree inferior only to God Himself. We are all aware how true this is in social and political affairs. Woman is awaking out of holy sleep to a still holier day. And what else is meant at heart in these manifold and increasing, and even wearisome, studies from the nude which exercise the artists in one way and the decorous public in another. For the artist especially, and for him in proportion to his greatness, this subject must be a growing spell. What other so combines passion, beauty, and power? The poet is seized by its passion, the painter by its beauty, the thinker by its power. To a poet, artist, and thinker like Mr. Watts, who lives not outside his age, but in it and with it, the subject must appeal with irresistible force. It is Humanity itself in one whole luminous hemisphere—invested with all Man's ideal grandeur, pathos, tenderness, mystery, fertility, and promise. Who can fit Humanity to a mould? Who can paint it in sharp, clear outline? Definition is here destruction. *Determinatio est negatio.* Who with a soul should complain that cloud and darkness are about such a throne.

What we have here is the painter's interpretation of Woman, first, in her vast ideal significance; and second, in her as yet imperfect apprehension of it. It is not a representation of the creation of Woman. Nor is it anything so abstract as womanhood. It is the ideal representation of that half of historic Mankind as it awakes to the consciousness of its own true nature and power. What Mr. Watts has really given us in the language of his art, and using his art but as a language, is the result of his deep reflection and gifted vision on one of the few prime problems of the spiritual age. It is his version of the Woman question as a spiritual question. Twelve years it matured in the painter's studio. For this, if for no other reason, the picture should live as a 'document' for ages to come.

As the figure is over life-size, its suggestions are

ideal. The vagueness which strikes the spectator means, first, that, as in 'a solemn music,' the meaning floats and palpitates in the picture's soul. Mr. Watts is fond of the suggestions that seem to him to *throb and quiver* both in space and in the soul. And it is intended, secondly, to convey the impression of grace and glory amid 'stifled splendour and gloom,' the soul 'moving about in worlds not realised.' Humanity in general, and woman in particular, moves forward in a world of subtle forces, dim possibilities, and rolling powers, which, in this great revealing age, crowd afresh upon our wakening sense. Of all this mighty sum, man is the organ, the word, the passionate epitome. He is the conscious abstract, the condensed and crowning truth of it all; but he is only half-conscious how central and supreme he is. This is especially exemplified in the dim sense which woman as yet has of her true vocation and her great destiny. But she has begun to realise it, though the discovery takes effect at first in many a raw, tentative, and misguided form. The crudity which strikes some in the picture is intended to express this, this bewildered emergence from spiritual chaos. It is part of the art, not the neglect of Art. It helps to make the work a truer expression of the soul of the time.

There is much art, moreover, in the management of the light and shade. In this respect the figure falls into two portions—an upper and a lower. It is on the former that the chief light falls. The intention is to emphasise the upper portion of the body as the seat of the nobler soul. A secondary light falls on the feet to show their firm grasp and tread on earth's realities. The ideal woman is not a bloodless sprite, Shelleyan and ethereal. The intermediate portion is veiled in modest cloud and mystic night, which the tall pure lily, rising to the thighs, invests with a more abundant comeliness. The whole of the lower portion of the figure is associated with woman's actual ordinary charm, her dear great littleness, her tender cares and delicate fears. Her birds are there and her flowers. The crocus-bed on which she treads has the further suggestion of the half-blown springtime of her power and the incipiency of her glory. Her passing smiles and tears are symbolised in the floating rainbow—which, however, swiftly changes like a passage of Wagnerian music, into a suggestion of the demonic evil that flickers about the lower nature, as soon as we observe that its twining beauty takes the malignant form of a serpent. The sweet trivialities, that are as rainbows to cheer, may be made serpents that whisper ruin to the nobler life; the affections that twine about our dearest may become a snare to the soul; and passion may close beautifully round us and take away the heart. The mingled graces, comforts, and pleasures about the lower man may, in all innocence, bar out heaven; and like honey, poppy, and wine, they have ere now medicined men and women to sleep in a common spiritual grave.

All these things are greatened and saved by the upper portion of the figure, as the birds below are transposed into a higher key in the psyche butterfly near the head. If the lower portion of the picture represents the woman of earth and gladness, the upper portion represents her when loss has spiritualised her for us into the heavenly soul she was amid it all. As we look upwards along the figure, George Meredith's words follow our thought: 'A child in pleasure, a woman in pain.' If the feet hold firm to earth, asserting the reality of its joys, and claiming the right of its pleasures, the head is above earthly levels—nay, deep in heaven. Humanity, this female figure tells us, is the real link between heaven and earth. It is in man alone these meet, and he is the true Jacob's ladder and altar of reconciliation. It has been pointed out how the chief light falls on the chest, to accentuate the nobler emotions and spiritualise the heart. But it perplexes some that the head is in cloud, and the face in painful shadow. Why is not the light on the breast continued upward? The woman's power and guiding light is not in brain but in heart. That is one suggestion, and it is true. But it is nearer the painter's mind to remark that the light *is* really continued upward for thought. From the iridescent charm and seduction of the lower world it rises, through the full sunlight on the heart, to the heavenly light, dark with excess, in which the head stands, and through which a flood of glory descends like the tresses of a heavenly self, veiling and consecrating the whole figure in golden rays. This radiance blends with the cloudy masses of golden hair, and two great words meet in our memory: 'The woman is the glory of the man,' and 'If a woman have long hair it is a glory to her, for her hair is given her as a veil.' The expression on the face is adoration and darkling trust, not unmixed with a foretaste of pain, as the woman-soul moves forward from the heaven, which is her birthplace, to be betrayed of man it may be, but at least to serve, to suffer for him, and to greatly die.

> She prayed, and from a happy place
> God's glory smote her on the face.

The attitude of the hands is very beautiful and eloquent of 'sweet renunciations.' The figure is withal most stately, and the whole effect is that mixture of greatness in suggestion, tenderness in expression, and beauty in execution, of which Mr. Watts is such a master.

Tempting vistas of thought open away from this great vision which I do not here pursue. Perhaps the best free comment is Adam's address to Eve in Mrs. Browning's *Drama of Exile.* I will only anticipate the usual charge of reading in a meaning from without by saying that the explanation here given has in substance the highest of all authority.

To the remark that the picture is not at once pleasing it may be conceded that it is not in the style of either Raphael or Tennyson. But these names do not cover the whole area of great Art. Wagner and Browning are not to be ruled out of that realm because they are different. There is great and even immortal art which lacks this prompt and winsome charm, as there are ever memorable faces, lovely not so much in feature as in soul. Mr. Watts may be satisfied to believe that his art, if not superficial, is great, and that it holds of the eternal even if it do not capture with a glance. No more in Art than in Nature is it true that 'He never loved who loved not at first sight.'

HOLMAN HUNT

OR, THE RELIGION OF SPIRITUAL FAITH

I

HIS PROTESTANTISM, ARTISTIC AND RELIGIOUS

IT may seem far-fetched to some, but it will not so appear to a philosophic mind, to say that the possibility of Art depends on a people's idea of God. It will, perhaps, sound more familiar and plausible if I put it differently, and say that Art depends on Religion. But it comes to the same thing, for our Religion depends on our thought of God. One way of thinking about God makes Art impossible; another makes it inevitable. A conception of God like that of the Jews makes Art as impossible as it makes polytheism; a conception of God like the truly Christian makes Art as inevitable as missions. Christian art is indeed the mission of our faith to the paganism of beauty. We may think of God as the One Being sitting apart from the world in supreme and abstract sovereignty—which is the Deist's thought of God—and, in that case, we can have no more Art than Jews, Turks, or last century infidels. And one great reason why the public care so little for Art is because this is still the popular way of thinking about God. He is regarded as the Supernatural merely. He is not a natural God. He is even to a large extent unnatural. And there is something similarly unnatural in the life by which many people think to please Him. There is a gulf cleft between Him and Nature which is fatal to much besides Art and the artistic habit of thinking and feeling. And in like manner there is a gulf set between our Religion and our Imagination, which the former has not wings to cross nor the latter a plummet to sound. For the theologian and the poet the soul seems so often to mean two totally different and uncongenial things—things even incompatible. Our faith does not fascinate and our beauty does not control. The two are too distant and suspicious for either to lend its power to the other for a joint effect. And it all arises from our Anglo-Saxon Theism, so imperfectly Christianised as yet by the principle of Incarnation. It springs from our mechanical and outward view of Revelation. And the breach will never be healed till we acquire the habit of viewing Revelation as an eternal process no less than a historic event, and God as an indwelling Spirit rather than a King whose palace is in the outer suburbs of the world. A distant God, an external God, who from time to time interferes in Nature or the soul, is not a God compatible with Art, nor one very good for piety.

But we are learning the conditions of the Reconciliation. We are coming to think of God, not in this abstract way as a God afar off, but as near and concrete. We are learning to think of Him as the constant ground and breath of Nature, its pervading presence, and its sustaining, quickening spirit. We are coming to think of Him as the living and true God—living, because through Him all life lives; and true, because He is the truth of all things, and the very nature of Nature itself. That is the Christian, though not always the Scriptural, conception of God. He is a God of whom Nature is a constant Incarnation and living Revelation. The Jew certainly believed that God gave revelation, but he did not realise that God *was* revelation. He knew that God spoke from time to time, but he did not know that God was ever speaking, and must ever speak—that the world is His self-utterance, that He is an open-hearted God, that self-revelation is His very nature, and that the whole frame of the world and the soul is tingling with His self-manifestation.

> The spirit-world is never sealed,
> Thy soul is shut, thy heart congealed.

The Jew did not realise, as Christ has taught us to realise, the 'openness' there is about God. Now it is this Christian idea of God as the indwelling ground, thought, and speech of Nature, that makes Art not only possible but inevitable to Christianity. If it be a degradation of God to ascribe to His Eternity human thought or affection, then, of course, really religious Art is not possible. God is too far apart from us and from all that delights us most. But if Christ be not God's degradation, but His revelation, then human nature is of divine significance, and with it Nature is consecrated altogether. It is a mighty sum of things for ever speaking the

Eternal. To interpret that voice of the ever-present God becomes a Christian necessity. And thus we have two things quite inevitable in such a religion. We have Science on the one hand and Art on the other.

If there be no Divine Spirit in Nature, but only a curse upon it, then Art is not possible in any noble way. It will hardly rise above the barbaric or the grotesque. If noble Art could arise in such circumstances, it could neither claim, nor be claimed, to be Christian. No Art is possible to a religion which begins with a text like 'Cursed be the ground.' That is Hebrew, unchristian, untrue—true only in a very one-sided sense; it is a principle that could only issue in such artistic sterility as marks Hebraism in contrast with the Christian religion of a universe already in its principle redeemed. We have in Christianity a power and principle of spirit which 'triumphs in conclusive bliss,' which goes softly back upon creation, and gently pervading all things, draws them into the completeness of its own redeemed being. In the new spirit all things are made new. Nature is seen under no curse. We live on a blessed earth. The only curse upon it is the soul unblest, and only such man is vile.

Art is not Nature, but more than Nature. It is Nature transfused with a certain order of conscious intelligence. A picture is not a patch of Nature, but Nature reflected, coloured, interpreted by a human soul with a piercing, and not merely passive, feeling for Nature. The main thing, therefore, in Art is the quality of the spirit, the genius of the soul that is set to reflect and interpret. The key to Nature is human nature. If the heart regards Nature as either a foe or a foreigner we can have no true Art. If our spirit habitually think of Nature as cursed and God-forsaken, we can have no more Art than Calvinism has left to Scotland. Everything turns on the spiritual state—the spiritual vigour, penetration and hopefulness of man and his creed. The human spirit is the key to Nature, I say. But the key to the human spirit is the Spirit of Christ. The natural man alone supplies no teleology for the nature below man. Nature receives its crown and key only in human nature, but only as that again finds its fulfilment and destiny in the Nature of Christ; and the Nature of Christ is intelligible only by the Nature of God. It is our thought of God that determines our way of looking at Nature, and therefore determines the possibility of Art. Art is not a luxury, not the invention of people with nothing else to occupy them, not the pursuit of a people too frivolous to have any religion. It is a necessity of human nature; it is a necessity of a true, large, humane, divine religion. Every man need not understand Art; but it is indispensable to mankind, if mankind is to rise ever towards the image of God. No religion can be a true religion if it do not encourage a great Art. And Art lies nearer to the nature of religion than Science does. It comes closer to the heart; it speaks the heart's language; and it silently proclaims a practical wisdom, not in abstract truths, but in forms ever memorable and mighty because genial and concrete. It ennobles by other and more effective means than direct instruction. It need not always inform us, or correct our beliefs. It educates otherwise. It exalts, it expands, it purifies us; it brings us nearer, if not to the creed of many Christians, at least to the mind, the stature, the fulness of Christ. It cultivates the harmonies of the soul. It does not reconcile sinful man to God, but it helps to reconcile him with himself. It does not give the unspeakable peace, but it makes a great calm. It places the soul in tune with Nature, even with her own nature, and it disposes to sympathy with a spirit that lives in Nature. Yes, religion must strive to explain Nature and the soul. A great religion reconciles them in the power of the Eternal Spirit. And so a great religion must always, in spite of its pedants, bigots, and dunces, labour onward to a great art, and prepare for the soul an utterance no less lovely than sincere. A great religion brings God so near that our human passions and fates are seen in Him and He in them. They are clothed thus with a great radiance and consecration, which those who are called to the task will be forward to see and set beautifully forth. Art does not exist to reveal Christianity, but it does express it; it rests upon it; it would perish if the distinctive ideas of Christianity were false. Nothing is poorer in Comte's Positivism than his treatment of Art. And there is a Christian art, because there is a distinctive Christian interpretation of the world and the soul. Art is a question of spiritual interpretation, I must keep repeating. It is the interpretation of Nature by Spirit. But before that can be there is one thing needful, the interpretation of Spirit to itself. That is the problem of any religion, but it is the function of Christ's. It was only when Europe's soul became revealed to Europe's self that we reached the greatest art the world has seen. It must ever be so. The greatest art of the past has been Christian art, and Christian art must be the greatest of the future. The greatest spiritual power must be the greatest æsthetic power by a like necessity to that which makes it the great social power—because the spiritual is the power of the completed man.

The great Christian truths are not truths of a church or of a book, but of the human spirit in its very nature and constitution. They are the exposition of that Reason which constitutes the unity of God, man, and nature. They are truths which are at the foundation of Science, Religion, and Art. And Truth is not only true, but beautiful. The soul is so precious because it is so lovely. And Christ as the morally flawless soul is the altogether lovely. The Soul of Christ is not merely a single fine spirit, but it constitutes the ground and living unity of those powers and principles which make great and glorious the entire soul of man. If the human soul be Art's loveliest theme, then the Soul of Christ must be for Art engrossing. The mightiest passion known to the heart is stirred by its relation to Christ. Is this a region of passion from which Art is to be totally detached? The thoughts joined with Christ are the deepest, finest, noblest we know. Is Art not to suggest, to interpret, these in its own way? If Art itself be a deliverance of Nature from her own bondage, and a deliverance by soul, has Art no interest in the deliverance or the deliverer of that soul? If Art be inspired by the principles of Nature's great beauty, shall it have no inspiration from the profounder beauty of the human spirit, nor any power to suggest it? If the truths of the Christian spirit are true, they are splendidly, charmingly, true. Is this the only region of truth's splendour that must go uninterpreted by the ministry of Art? Nay, how much do we not suffer from that parching up or that trimming down of Christian truth which alienates it from those high vital sympathies with which Art dwells? If our truths were less traditions, if they were more principles, and less patterns, more in our intelligence and more in our life, should we not be more willing to see them expressed in our Art, and more keen to mark them when they were? But, for the time being, Christian truth has lost, as truth, its imaginative aspect. Where it is definite it has sunk to orthodoxy, and lost the fascinating radiance of its vital glow. By Agnosticism, even in the name of theology,* it has been emptied of its commanding force over the great Reason which really makes art great. And it seems probable that a great Christian art will never more be possible till the condition of its existence in the Middle Ages is again realised, and we possess a theology which is not only tolerated by the public intelligence, but is welcome for the

* Mansel and his school.

life, commanding for the reason, and fascinating for the imagination of the age.

Starting with the term modern from, say, the thirteenth century, all modern art of the great true sort is really and implicitly Christian. A landscape is Christian, compared with a Greek statue. Paganism is too much afraid of Nature to paint it with our modern and Christian fondness. But within Christian art in this large sense there is a Christian art in the more special sense. Not only is modern art permeated with principles of the Christian imagination, as in Shakespeare and his noble secularity, but much of it is devoted to representing the awe, pathos, and glory of Christian doctrines. We need but instance some of the chief works of the Italian and Flemish masters, like Van Eyck's Adoration of the Slain Lamb. This is Christian art in the truest sense of the word. It is not necessarily Christian art to paint a scene from the New Testament, or from the history of the Church. Before it is true Christian art, such a scene needs to be permeated with Christian feeling, and supported by a soul's grasp of Christian principle. Who could paint the crucifixion aright who had never answered the cross with his heart, never been kindled by it, never been cheered by it in his gloom, and never upheld by it in his weakness? Can he freely paint the cross whom the cross has never freed? The truths and doctrines of Christianity are fit subjects for Art only if they are known to be the secret and glory, not of single souls, nor of sects, nor of churches alone, but of mankind in its greatest, tenderest, holiest heart. True catholicity is an essential condition of great Christian art, and the sects are its ruin. Nonconformity suspects Art, and, as a consequence, Nonconformity can barely hold its own in an age when Art is re-entering social life. Yes, it is possible to paint religion; and not religion only, but theology. The great old painters did it. And our greatest painters to-day come at least very near it. Mr. Watts scarcely escapes it; and Mr. Holman Hunt scarcely tries to escape. Theology handles the principles of the divine soul. And it can be cut off from Art only if there be that fatal severance between the divine soul and the human which has cursed and impoverished our false theologies for so long. Art has nothing directly to do with systematic theology, but it has to do with much more than the religious sentiment. Great religious art cannot flourish in an air in which the need or possibility of a scientific theology is despised. Art surely has to do with those great principles of heart and conscience, those great powers and passions of the soul that are in most tragic, pathetic, or exultant play when they respond to the like in the Soul that fills infinity. Philosophic theology has its own methods of expression. They may be purer, they may in a sense be higher, than that of Art. But the grand passions of the eternal heart, and the solemn principles of the universal soul cannot be quite outside the methods or interests of Art; and Art can express them in a vital, throbbing union with Nature which keeps them close to life, and blends theology with religion in one noble power. Art can not only delight us with an image of what we know, but can also surprise us with a revelation of what we do not know. Art can find in nature not only a power to reflect and express the movements of our own soul, but it finds there a symbolism also, which will without violence bear to be filled with suggestions of the Soul of God, the principles of His heart, the power of His endless life, and the dread mystery of His death. 'All beautiful work,' says Mr. Ruskin, 'has depended on the hope of resurrection.' 'The history of Art after the fall of Greece is that of the obedience and faith of Christianity.'

Christian art need not always be expressly religious. We Protestants say that to be fully Christian we do not need to devote ourselves to what is called the religious life. We are Christian in our vocations no less than in our devotions. But when in Christianity Art does become expressly religious, it must display sincere Christian feeling, and some real faith in Christian principles as the fundamental and crowning principles of human life. And in the highest forms of Christian religious art we shall expect not only a vague supernatural hope, nor a vague committal of the soul to love, but a truly spiritual faith. We shall expect a faith which has passed through question and conjecture to spiritual knowledge, and is not only fired with an aspiration, but assured by a revelation. There is a notion afloat that spiritual means something vague, shadowy, and unsubstantial, and people have even been known to think that one great obstacle to a spiritual faith was a historic religion. They have therefore striven to look away from the Christ of history, or to dissolve Him, instead of transfiguring and looking through Him. They have not thought God artist enough to reveal His heart in concrete human form. And yet they have strangely sought the better guidance in their own individual spirits, and their own far more unsteady and turbid hearts. It is not by ignoring history that we reach the spiritual nature and method of God, who has been teaching men by history above all else. Art must be concrete, and the art of a spiritual faith is one that will be much fascinated by the historic Jesus, and the historic traditions of spiritual thought which strive to explain Him. God is more than merely supernatural, he is actual in things; and our reliance on Him is more than simply hope, it is realisation also. God is spiritual, nay, a spirit. He speaks more plainly and explicitly of His own heart in mankind's spiritual history than in anything we gather from dim intuitions of our own, which reach us from beyond Nature, and enable us to feel little more than that they are above it. We need to know more than what God is not. We are not satisfied to know simply that He is above Nature. We must know what He intrinsically is; that He is spirit; that spirit means, not vagueness, but determinate feature and character; that the greatest of human spirits, the perfectest of souls, the most distinct and impressive of characters, *is*—not bears, but *is*—His revelation; and that His nature is what we mean when we speak of having a spirit-nature of our own. When we know that, we have a bond with God which makes all the art that magnifies humanity divine. And when we know all that is conveyed by spirit, we have not only a supernatural hope but a spiritual faith, which trusts for deeper reasons than that it surmises greatly and intensely admires—because, by the witness of spirit with spirit, it knows. Art which is instinct with the religion of a spiritual, *i.e.* a rational, faith, will always be much occupied with the interpretation, in its own way, of that great history and that great soul which have brought to light the supreme destiny of our spirits, and set us on ground firmer than our own most reverent surmise.

There are men of genius to whom the thought of this age lies nearer than the thought of any age bygone, and to whom Scripture is but a record of receding events, or a treasury of ever-fascinating tales. There are other men, on the contrary, to whom the truths of that book lie nearer than their own thoughts, or the thoughts of any time beside. They live and breathe among such truths. These are the vital principles and the motive forces of life for them; and the Bible, while treated with no superstitious veneration, is yet not only a record of life, but a source of life; not a report nor an effort of men, but a gift and channel of God. This is particularly the case with Mr. Holman Hunt. He seems to paint in the spirit of the old saint-painter, who prayed every time he seated himself at his easel. His art is not only Christian in the complexion, as Mr. Watts's might be, but specifically Christian in character; not only ethically, but doctrinally, spiritually, experimentally Christian. He paints sacred truths and scenes in a spirit lost or forgotten since pre-Reformation times.

No Protestant artist has ever done for Christianity what Holman Hunt has done. He has shown that it is not necessary for an artist, who is also a Christian, to be a Catholic. What Bach did for Protestant music, that Hunt has done for Protestant painting. Artists like Burne Jones and Rossetti may be said to represent rather the Catholic side of the religion of Art. Rossetti, in particular, represents that in Art which corresponds to the Catholic movement in the Church. I do not, of course, mean that he painted Catholicism. He was too realistic, too unconventional in his treatment of sacred subjects, to be welcome to Catholicism. The difference in fresh and original thought between him and the Dusseldorf school, which is so popular among Continental Romanists, is very great. But when I describe Rossetti as expressing the Catholic side of the religion of Art, I mean that he represents the Crucifixion principle rather than the Resurrection, and the subjective rather than the objective side of that. He is dominated by pain, weighed down by sorrow. He is passionate and poetic, but he is unduly arrested by the solemn splendour of life's gloom, and not duly inspired by the mellow radiance of life's renewed glow. He has not gained the victory. He has not risen from the tomb. The melancholy of Italy is always about him; he does not share in the Resurrection spirit of the Teutonic genius. The art of passion got the better in him of the art of reality. Love mastered him at the expense of truth. Love was sustained by its own passion rather than by an eternal moral principle. He does not display the Protestant principle of vigorous truth as he does the Catholic passion of profound love. Consequently, his art is not victorious art. It has passion and intellect, but it has not vigour nor victory. To the English mind at least it strikes foreign. It has not what we understand by a spiritual faith. A spiritual note it has, but not a spiritual faith. It has plenty of soul, but it has not the vigour of will nor the mastery of conscience that mark the Christian *Weltanschauung*.

Now Holman Hunt represents the best that has yet been done by Protestant Christianity in the way of Art. It is Art inspired by the spirit of the Resurrection rather than of the Crucifixion. Mr. Hunt has never painted the Resurrection. Indeed his *subjects*, like the Scapegoat, or the Shadow of Death, lie nearer the great Death than the great Revival. But I am speaking of the *spirit* of his work and treatment. And I say he paints the Cross in the spirit of the Resurrection; whereas Rossetti would have painted the Resurrection in the spirit of the Cross. The one treats Christianity in the Protestant temper, the other in the Catholic. Hunt paints with an exuberant realism and a defiance of tradition which betray the faith that God's Revelation is not the closed appanage of a particular church, but pulsates, always and everywhere, in the world and in man. He refuses to cut off Christian feeling from the world that is around him, and to confine it, like the Catholics, to the personages and events of so-called sacred history. Sacred history sanctifies all history. The sacred person consecrates all men and all manhood. There is nothing utterly dismal, like a Catholic image, even in our worst sorrow. A very acute critic has pointed out as a peculiarity in Mr. Hunt's technique that his 'shadow always means colour as well as darkness. To see the colour in shadow is the last triumph of a great painter.' Now it seems to me that this is a moral quality of Hunt's whole style. It is art which is full, not only of hope, but of faith and forward-looking thoughts. The very darkness of death is made beautiful by a firm faith in the ulterior issues of death. The shadows of life are not stripped of the colours of life. His art paints a Christ that died, nay, rather, that is risen again. No Catholic soul could be more full than Hunt of the doctrine of sacrifice. If you question whether it is possible to paint not only an idea but a doctrine, look at the Scapegoat. But then no Catholic soul could so present the doctrine of sacrifice as the very foundation of all true life inside the Church or out. The Catholic does not represent to us the toil of the overworked man or woman as part of the perennial activity of the cross, nor make all murdered children, whether baptized or not, Holy Innocents of the most genuinely human type. The

Catholic is too prone to dwell on the consolation of the cross, while the Protestant sees in it not that only, but the inspiration of all the renewed life of the future, and the principle of all great life in the past.

Even in Art we can verify the truth so conspicuous in the theories of the two Churches concerning Redemption, that Catholicism has the subjective note of Security, while Protestantism has the objective aim of Certainty. In the one the Soul's first concern is for itself; it is insurance. In the other it is for reality or assurance. And it would not be very difficult, I think, to prove that it is the Protestant spirit in Christianity which has been at the foundation of the best order of pictorial art. Music can perhaps afford to pay less regard to reality, and more exclusive attention to beauty, but painting must begin with that love of truth and that passion for veracity which is the special mark of Protestantism. And if painting is to be the living art of a living age, it must share that belief of true Protestantism in the revelation which proceeds fresh, age after age, from the heart of God's reality in nature or men. Protestantism threw Art upon actuality, it has been said. It made Art humanise itself. It took men's interests away from the heroes, heroines, and politics of the Church, and opened a field of interest and admiration in a larger and more natural area of affairs. It found the present and the future more engrossing, even more beautiful, than the past. But just as Art was long in emerging from the Church of the first millennium, so it has been long in emerging from Protestantism. There were other and more pressing matters for faith to settle. And, indeed, it is only now that the real genius of Protestant Christianity is beginning to take effect in Art. It is but now that the Resurrection spirit which asserted itself in the Reformation is making itself felt in our reformed soul's treatment of Nature. I say the effect of the doctrine of the Resurrection is to consecrate the truth and reality of Nature, to make us realise that we live in a world wholly redeemed and continually rising, that the visible earth is full of divine suggestion, full in every vein of the ceaseless striving after a crown of spiritual perfection, straining in universal evolution after a fuller expression of itself than its own material sphere allows, and waiting in strenuous patience for the relief of utterance in the manifestation of the Sons of God. It is such a manifestation, in one sense, when the artist comes to give Nature an organ for self-expression, and the spirit in Nature a vehicle of self-revelation. The artist shows us how eloquent, how vital, Nature can be in her response to the risen spirit of genius. For him Nature at once 'rests like a picture and acts like a machine.' He shows us that Nature, in her wonderful veracity, her fixity of law, her fluidity of process, her swell of evolution, is rising with Christ; and so rising that she is fit to express the enhanced powers of the Spirit of Europe, as Christ ascends through its growing insight and its enforced obedience to the divine law. The spirit of the Resurrection is the spirit which finds a divine reality and solemn significance, not only in the affairs of the Church, but in the affairs of Nature and the actuality of worldly life, and often more in the latter than in the former.

Against what did Protestantism rise to protest in the region of Art? Was it not against the classicism that overflowed the Church, especially in Italy, from the Renaissance. It rose against the kind of thing which we see in scholastic theology, in Italian architecture, and in English compromises—the grafting of classic forms upon Christian ideas without any real spiritual reconcilement between them. And what was the vice of this classic art? It was ideal in the wrong sense, in the unspiritual, indocile, sense. It aimed in Art, as it had aimed in the Aristotelian philosophy of the mediæval schools, not at studying what God had done, and reading His implanted idea there, but at speculating about what it thought, on the strength of its own idea, its disobedient idea, that God should have done. No, said Protestantism, in substance, God is there self-buried in Nature, and rising continually from the Holy Sepulchre of Nature. Make your pilgrimages to that shrine. Wage your crusades for the mastery and possession, by spiritual knowledge and militant faith, of that sacred land. Come back from tradition to actuality, from church theories to living thought, from dead words to the living conscience and the living Word. God reveals himself in that conscience, that reality, through what men do, and feel, and look like now, no less truly than through what they were years ago. God shows Himself to be above Nature by coming through it, not by going round it; there is no mastery of Nature in that. God is not an abstraction lost in the depths of space and time. He is of all beings the most concrete, most here and now, most interwoven with the passions of men and the courses of things. Do not waste time and strength in thinking what He should do; look what He has done and is doing. It will take all your seeing and thinking power for a very long time to just see that. Do not shape ideal forms in which, if a God appeared, you think He should appear. Recognise that He has appeared once for all, which is an appearance for ever, and mark in what shapes He puts His truth and beauty. Let these be your ideals; paint, interpret, these.

The genius of Protestantism was, therefore, in the direction of that noble and ideal naturalism which flows from the freedom of a spirit reconciled to God, His worship, and His works. Was the classical movement, then, which preceded it, in itself a curse? Surely not. It was called for, its beautiful paganism was demanded, as a protest against the asceticism which had overspread the Church, and cursed nature by its dismal God. What, then, made classicism so dangerous? What made its paganism of more evil effect than its idealism was good? It was the papal sovereignty. It was not classicism that did the mischief, but the fact that it was taken up, not by a spiritual power, but by a degraded hierarchy enthroned in powerful place. The worldliness and vice of the papal court and empire, then in full bloom, laid hold of the congenial paganism in the classic revival. And it turned the classic spirit, which, rightly used, can do such service to a real spiritual religion, into an engine of corruption and untruth. As the connection with an established church has ruined the public reputation of theology, so the connection with an imperial church ruined the influence of Art. Art called for Protestantism as well as did religion and morals. And the foe of Art was neither religion nor the new learning and culture, but the gross, worldly, and vulgarising pomp of a Christianity whose passion was ascendency and empire. Let us beware of a church which fosters the craving for empire, if we have any care for either Religion or Art.

But Luther's Reformation was not the first assertion of the Protestant idea in Christendom. For several centuries before efforts had been made to reform the Church from within; to protest against this enslavement to the empire of the papacy; to recall the Church to spiritual simplicity and natural reality. There was no greater Protestant in his day than the Catholic Dante. And the same period was the age of the great early Italian painters, who were the morning stars of European art. We may find their vast original power profoundly set forth in Browning's poem, 'Old Pictures in Florence.' Browning, as he is one of the first theologians, is also one of the first art-philosophers in England. These early Italian painters were Catholic Protestants. They were mighty realists. Their great and decisive step was a return to the actuality of Nature. They took to painting the men and women they selected to paint just as they were. They gave up the conventional, the frozen, ideal forms of saints and martyrs, and they painted the thoughts and passions of the people as they saw them written in the faces around them. They would 'paint man whatever the issue.' That was the work in Art of the great thirteenth century. It was the origin of Protestant art, of its reverent fidelity, its spiritual veracity, its thirst for truth, its passion for reality, and its inability to enjoy any beauty which had the flavour of carelessness or insincerity. But these artists were only heralds. Their lay work (like that of the great Gothic builders, who were also laymen) received, from the patronage of classicism by the clerical papacy, a blow from which it has taken a long time to recover. After the Renaissance came the Reformation, with its moral, theological, and practical exigencies. And it is only now that the Protestant spirit is in a position to lift its head in Art, and take up again the work which the early Italian and Flemish painters laid down. It should be particularly marked that it is the same continuous and irrepressible spirit which is expressing itself in the two epochs, in the thirteenth century and the nineteenth. It is not merely the latter going back and seizing on the former for an example. We also see now why this great Protestant movement in English Art is called Pre-Raphaelitism. Raphael represents the moment when the conventional classic influence was just mastering and enslaving the simple noble and natural sincerity of the earlier school. Our recent revolt against the remote and paralysing influence of soulless classicism is just the working out on the first possible opportunity of the principles which have been buried for so long under Raphael's splendid but passing empire. And a painter like Holman Hunt reminds us of what history teaches, that the most distinctively Christian art is art based on Protestant principles and the doctrine of the Resurrection. True art is not compatible with Romanism any more than true science, in spite of Mr. Mivart. Pictorial art, at least, is only possible by the same reverent regard for Nature as makes true science possible—a regard which resents the cold tyranny of classic tradition, but corrects the neo-catholic romanticism of the heart by the realities of the eye and the thought.

This return to nature and fact, to accuracy and moral rigour, has doubtless its dangers. In religious Protestantism it has led to an enslaving regard for the letter of Scripture; and in æsthetic Protestantism it has threatened, even in a master like Hunt, to bring in a new bondage of the spirit to the care of detail. We must remember, however, that Pre-Raphaelitism means much more than accuracy of detail in the treatment, just as Protestantism means much more than the closer study of the Bible. Protestantism means the introduction into religion of thought, and especially conscience, or moral thought—the reconcilement of religion, and not its mere conjunction, with living reason and personal responsibility. And the accuracy of Biblical study is urged, not for pedantic reasons, but for the sake of the thought which we would clearly grasp and fondly trace. So the forward Protestantism of Art insisted that painting should be accurate and veracious out of no love for pedantry, which is mere orthodoxy. But it urged that the painter should use fidelity to Nature's letter in order to read the truth on the whole of Nature's lovely thought. What was demanded in a picture was not only accuracy in the treatment but thought in the subject, and the truth of love, not of the letter. Fidelity to the letter was thus saved from becoming idolatry of the letter, and veracity was made a rock, not to crush the freedom of the spirit, but to give it ground on which to stand. It is a common and quite a vulgar error to suppose that this Pre-Raphaelite movement means only, or chiefly, photographic accuracy of detail. That is not its genius. Its genius is to read the large thought in Nature's beauty on the whole. It knows that this cannot be done by careless construction of words or sentences, but just as little can it be done by going as it were into the etymology of every word, or the painting of every fibre and pose. Anybody can do that kind of painting, just as anybody can study the Bible in the grammarian's style, or get up a play of Shakespeare for a University Local Examination. But few can read, by lifelong loving care, the true large thought of Scripture in its subtle veins and shades. And few can interpret Nature with just the amount of precious accuracy needful to establish well the freedom of her larger truth. 'The true work,' says Mr. Ruskin, 'represents all objects exactly as they would appear in nature *in the position and at distances which the arrangement of the picture supposes.* The false work represents them with all their details as if seen through a microscope.'

Now Mr. Holman Hunt, with all his accuracy, belongs, on the whole, not to the race of Bibliolators, but to those who prize the book for the sake of the Word, and the letter because of the spirit and thought it conveys. He selects in Nature as we claim the right to select in Scripture, namely, by the light and sympathy of the same spirit as put Nature and Scripture there. Both Bibles exist for man, not man for either. They rule us; but it is by meeting our needs, fulfilling our mind, and satisfying our conscience, not by coercing our thoughts and repressing our bent. Neither Scripture is mechanical; both are vital and free in their genius, both are solemn and lovely in their lives. If Rossetti corresponds in our earnest Art to the Catholic movement in the earnest Church, Hunt may be said to represent the earnest liberalism of the Church—the Broad-Churchism which still retains its evangelical fervour, and which is the sole hope of Protestantism, or, indeed, Christianity at all. He is the Maurice of painting—with the same moral austerity, the same spiritual splendour, the same uncompromising adherence to unpopular principle, the same terrible uphill struggle, and the same vast influence beyond the pale of any school. And it might further be said that just as Maurice was caught in the thicket of the creeds, his sympathy detached from Bible criticism to the extent almost of Scripturalism, and his arm shortened by the anomaly of an Erastian Establishment, so Hunt has not entirely escaped. He has been straitened by the excess of his realism; and what the Church did to Maurice has perhaps been done by Palestine to Hunt. What the archæology of the creeds did to the theologian, the archæology of the Holy Land seems to have done to the artist. It has engrossed his enthusiasm without always furthering in a proportionate degree the expression of his genius. Both escaped from the bondage of the Bible into a largeness of thought which is the very soul of the Bible. But both came, to some degree, under a new form of bondage which they took for support —the one to the creeds of the church, the other to its cradle. In both this is due to the exaggeration of a sound Protestant principle—a moral tenacity, a historic realism, an appetite for fact which refused to discard either the great labours of the Christian intelligence or the exact circumstances of the Christian world in whatever portion of the past they took up for treatment. But through all and over all in both you have the Christian faith, not parched, secluded, or fetishised, but pervaded, as Rossetti says of one of Hunt's works, with 'the solemn human soul, which seems to vibrate through it *like a bell in a forest.*' What an admirable image! How resonant of that romantic spirit which is the very genius of Christian history! How fragrant of that solemn, subtle, and sympathetic principle which breathes a humane holiness through the stolid egoisms that make history but too like a pine forest, and which tempers the stoical heroisms of our churchly and worldly pagans like a gale of heaven.

Mr. Holman Hunt gave us some time ago an account of the tremendous struggle undergone by the small band of earnest artists known as the Pre-Raphaelites, of whom he is now the chief. It was a movement of reaction and protest against the conventional, unideal, untrue, and feeble spirit of the art around them. The time was one in which the old and conventional classicism had touched its lowest depth, and sunk to the level of the 'mahogany age.' Mere classic attention to artistic form reigned on the one hand, just as in religion there was a superstitious and enslaving devotion to theological form, or orthodoxy. And on the other hand there was in Art an enfeebled and soulless sentiment which was the death of true and noble passion, just as in religion we had, and have, an emasculated pietism sophisticating the moral and manly tone. The Broad movement arose in religion, both outside and inside the Established Church, to protest against the extravagances of orthodoxy and effete evangelicalism. It was a movement at once to correct and expand belief, and to restore to religion the moral and mental verve which pietism had lost. It threw off the bondage of the creeds in the name of the faith, and it asserted for the present truth and reality of the living world a divine place which had been insulted and denied by the 'other-worldliness' of the prosperous and 'eminent' Christians of the day. Just so in Art arose the Pre-Raphaelite movement; and it found in Mr. Ruskin an apostle who combined moral fervour, æsthetic insight, philosophic grasp, and literary power in a way the English world had never seen before. Ruskin, with the great Pre-Raphaelite artists, set to do for painting what the example and influence of Wordsworth had some time before done for poetry. As it was in the sixteenth century, so now, our Reformation is an aspect of our Renaissance. These various movements are all part and parcel of the one great tendency of our day—the return to nature and to conscience, not in a pagan but in a Christian spirit. Nature is sought, but in a way in which she never has been sought before. Science, religion, poetry, and painting seek her, but they seek her with an unexampled power of respecting her, interpreting her, spiritualising without deforming her, and loving her without idolatry. Especially is it felt how indispensable moral conditions are in all the nobler and most successful dealings with Nature. She receives, by association with the conscience, a divinity never assigned to her in old paganism, and is regarded from the viewpoint of what may be called Christian pantheism. She is divine, not merely because God made her, but because God dwells in her; nor only dwells in her, but is in some real sense her life. She is not only to be desired for her beauty, but to be honoured for her truth. Much is to be made of her, but she has much to teach. And her interpretation by Art is really a moral pursuit. Artists form a priesthood, nay, some of them an apostolate. Art has a gospel, a message, news and glad news, of a certain kind. It is deliverance from a spiritual bondage. It is not to release us from thought, but to be the vehicle of true thought and the garment of great praise. Most English art had sunk, when this movement arose, to what in many cases it still remains—mere imitative prettiness, mere pleasure to the eye, as music is thought to be pleasure to the ear. It had no more relation to poetic thought than the exquisite music of Mozart has to the insipid and libertine 'book' of his operas. And just as Wagner arose to insist that great music should be associated with poetry great both in passion and thought, and to supply both as a protest against the over-refined chastity and severe delicacy of Mendelssohn, so the Pre-Raphaelites arose. So they strove to restore manhood to Art, to shock propriety into nobility, to deliver painting from the air of the drawing-room, and restore Art to nature and to religion at once. It was the breaking of the classic spell—the spell, however, of a classicism which was classic far more in form than in spirit. It was a Christian resurrection upon a world of art which was dominated rather by paganism in decay than by classicism in its power. These artists discarded the Latin, the Catholic, idea that Art was simply to indulge and secure the soul; and they infused the Teutonic, the Protestant, idea of demand, instruction, or the certifying of the soul; so that while the form must still please, the thought must instruct and exalt, and the spirit must be fresh and true. For them God and His thought dwelt in outward nature in a way far more after the analogy of His indwelling in human nature than had previously been dreamed. It was not man only, but nature, that Christ had redeemed, and the power which delivered the soul from sense was a power which should also deliver nature from slavery. As religion lay in the redemption of the soul, so Art (like science in its own fashion) lay in the redemption of nature. And the redemption in Christ was the principle and power of both. The deepest influences on the art of our Victorian era have been religious influences. They have come by the application of Christian principles and Protestant faith to the æsthetic side of the human spirit. As Christianity has its art, so Protestantism has its art. And as Christianity rose, by its protest of the cross against the paganism of ancient Greece, to an art such as the world had never seen; so Protestantism, protesting against the paganism of Christian Rome, may be destined, in the strength of its great Resurrection idea, to produce an art as much greater than the mediæval as that was greater than the antique.

Mr. Hunt, in the account he has given us of Pre-Raphaelitism, has much to say in the way of autobiography. And that we may gather how vital to him are the religious principles of a liberal Christianity, how well he understands the broad religious tendencies of his age, and how fit he is to expound them in art, I will adduce two passages in which he makes a sort of confession of his faith. We may mark that his religious mind is not of the uncritical order of Rossetti's, that he has passed through negative stages to his positive rest, that he has fought his way in his religious no less than his æsthetic creed, and that he has handled the theological issues with some of that intellectual stringency with which he has grasped details in his technique.

These are the words in which Mr. Hunt describes the motives which led him to religious subjects. Having stated that in early life he had adopted materialism, he goes on: 'Now I am a freethinker more than when I dubbed myself specially so, because I am free from bondage to incredulous as much as to conventional dictators. There are arguments in materialism itself which are convincing to me of future life, and therefore of future purpose, and of the service of souls made perfect by previous training. I am satisfied that the Father of all has not left us—made as we are with infinite care and thought, with intelligence to understand this, with the carefully stored-up inheritance of all our predecessors in faculties, hopes, and high love, advancing so slowly to the dream of heavenly perfection, from such a remote beginning bewildering in its infinity—to disappear in the black abyss. What an impotent conclusion! For me this would be an aimless mockery! The inheritance that the greatest of the Sons of God has won for us has its welcome in my soul. I want now to carry out my purpose of travel in Palestine, to prove, so far as my painting can, that Christianity is a living faith; that, followed up, new lessons and fresh interests may present themselves by the teaching of art; it was used to teach, not only to divert, in the days when it was at its highest. The mere conventional treatment of the eternal story is altogether doomed. Its claims are too momentous to be trifled with. Adverse criticism is directed against Revelation as a whole, and against the doctrine of the Resurrection as taught by Christ in particular. Such honest and open attacks are less dangerous than the retention of mere disproved and dead adjuncts to its history, retained reverently but unthinkingly by traditionalists. I am not afraid of the full truth, and I wish to help in propagating it. So you will see that I have too many motives of a solemn character joining to induce me to go, and that these cannot be weighed down by considerations of professional prosperity.'

And again, after his stay in Palestine—

'I had increased leisure for reading, and both Biblical and classical Scripture seemed to have unlimited intensification with the life illustrating every epoch of human society around me. I have met many persons and many books, and not a few pictures, bearing testimony that familiarity with the surroundings of holy history has encouraged a lower conception of that history than before. No such effect has it produced on my mind. I am not afraid of looking the matter through and through. I can without loss of reverence allow that the children to whom the

Father's messages were given did use their own faltering lispings, and express themselves with the light of their own age alone; but I recognise through all a divine charge, a Father's adjuration to faith and trust. Brothers and sisters accept the parent's authority; they learn that he is at hand, though the infant lips spoke the word in their own prattling manner. In fulness of time a due interpretation arrives from Him who alone knoweth the end from the beginning. Perhaps, with less opportunity of knowing the real history, the Parisian sentimental travesty of the gospels by Renan, or the romance by Strauss suiting modern intellect, would impress me with some of the respect which so many men have for them. To me their theories present far greater obstacles to faith than the original gospels offer. Is it beside the mark in writing of my professional life to say this? I think not; for I wish always to paint as men are supposed to write—what I believe, although sometimes it may be with playful interpretation.'

HOLMAN HUNT

OR, THE RELIGION OF SPIRITUAL FAITH

SECOND LECTURE

HIS WORKS

I WILL allude only to three pictures by Mr. Hunt —'The Scapegoat,' 'The Shadow of Death,' and 'The Triumph of the Innocents.'

Mr. Hunt paints not only religion, but doctrines, as few preachers can preach them. And when a painter who need not paint doctrine feels himself impelled to paint it, in spite of neglect and challenge alike, it means more, in some respects, than when such exposition is undertaken by one whose professional business it has become.

It is one great doctrine that Mr. Hunt paints throughout these three works. He paints always in the spirit of the Resurrection light and hope, but the particular doctrine that here directly fills his mind is the doctrine of the cross. Two of the pictures deal with the cross in the light of this toiling mortal world—'The Scapegoat' and 'The Shadow of Death'; the third, 'The Triumph of the Innocents,' deals with it in the light of another world, radiant and immortal.

I

First, I will speak of 'The Triumph of the Innocents,' which Mr. Ruskin calls the greatest religious picture of our time. Almost every opinion I have heard in conversation about this painting has been one of distaste. Where it is not unintelligible it is felt to be peculiar. I will leave it to one who, like Mr. Ruskin, has the prophet's right of scornful rebuke, to ask what sympathy there was likely to be with 'The Triumph of the Innocents' in an age or a world where in high quarters the triumph of innocence has become less a faith than a charitable fancy? I will rather remark, in extenuation of the public, that the work is not only charged with thought, but most daring in its defiance of conventionalism. In both these respects it is Browning translated into paint. I have nothing to say of its technical innovations; but the resources of pictorial art are certainly put to a severe strain in being loaded with such a volume of significance. Yet, after all, there is not more symbolism, not more depth or intricacy of meaning, than Art has been compelled successfully to express by several of the great religious painters both in Flemish and Italian schools. The chief difference is this, that these pictures appealed to people who had not been taught to divorce their thought from their religion or their art, and Mr. Hunt confronts an age that has but too well learned this unhappy skill.

The face of the Virgin is described as unpleasing. But have we not been too accustomed to use the Virgin's face to present, not the verisimilitude of Mary of Nazareth, but those ideals of beauty which the ancients in their way expressed in Venus? An earnest and reverent painter like Mr. Hunt does not care to make the mother of the Lord a mere lay figure to be draped with a dream of fair womanhood. Bent on the truth which makes us free, he has turned his thought upon the matter, and he has asked himself what real ground we have for representing Mary as the ideal of female Christian beauty. There is nothing to indicate that in the gospels; what indications there are point only to the homely mother, not to say housewife, who is suggested in 'The Shadow of Death.' Dignity, of course, and sweetness of character we may expect; and these in this face we have, under such a type as Mr. Hunt may have found still existing among the women of Nazareth.

Then complaint is made of the substantiality of the children, as tenants of a spirit world. The notion is here, as it is with so many in matters of thought, that the spiritual must be the hazy. Strangely enough, few people remark on what is one of the most striking charms of the picture, the grouping and the great beauty of these children's faces. To my own mind the full-blooded healthiness of these forms is a deliberate rebuke to our notions of the immortal life. It is the noble realism of this picture which offends our sensuous materialism.

The life beyond life is not ghostly, but spiritual. It is not less substantial, it is more substantial, than the life that is here. The beauty of heaven does not pulse feebler than the beauty of earth. The ethereal is not the eternal. The eternal is neither paler nor thinner than the temporal. We most of us assert our belief in the soul's immortality, and yet I do think we have in the main no higher faith in the vitality of that state than the old pagans had in the filmy shades of the Elysian Fields. The picture is right, and we are wrong. It is this life that is dark and meagre in comparison with another. And, while I am speaking of the children, is it not an exquisite touch of fancy, that happy wonder of the child who, with all his looking, cannot find on his new flesh the wound that slew him, though the shirt is rent still? The world can tear but the garment of the soul. And there may be some childish spirits beginning the life beyond, who are actually disappointed at the loss of an earthly grievance, and puzzled, nay, unsettled, to find how shallow the most poignant and fatal of their old troubles were.

Exception is farther taken to the strange spectacle of a dreamy second river by which these glorified babes dance, and which forms a running accompaniment as it were to the stream which the Holy Family are crossing with the ass. But to the seer's eye is there not a stream by every stream, a reality within every outward symbol, an eternal being within all visible things? It was not the religious spirit which made the man feel

> A primrose by the river's brim
> A yellow primrose was to him,
> And it was nothing more.

The difficulty in this picture is, that the painter is trying to raise us to do what, as an artist and seer, he habitually does—to see with two eyes at once, with the bodily eye and with the soul's; to gain one vision of two worlds; to read one system in two spheres; to behold through the glass the picture, and the water of life within the river of time. The world is a double world, and, whether we be lovers of simplicity or not, we live a double life. The veriest materialist is living two lives. He is performing a conscious part in this world, but he is shaping unconsciously a character which will be all that remains when this material frame shall vanish like a cloud. The singer of the Song of the Shirt represents the sempstress as

> Sewing at once with a double thread
> A shroud as well as a shirt.

It is what we are all doing. Only that for some the shroud is no cerement, but a robe of righteousness and a garment of the eternal spirit. And Art has no higher function, when she can rise to it without over-strain, than this stereoscopic vision of the two worlds. We must not read pictures as if they were specifications. We must not come to a picture like this with our one-eyed worldly wisdom, drawn from a fragmentary and thoughtless experience. We must see the one life not on the flat but in two dimensions at least. We must come bringing an eye trained by special sympathy with the universal experience to behold all things double one against another.

How many of us would be happier, sweeter, and stronger, if we won and kept this vision of our lost ones moving in glory, outside but alongside our darkling hurried way! How many a pilgrimage would be brighter if by us and our dark waters were known to flow the river which makes glad the city of God! How tolerable, how hopeful, would this world be in every way, if within it we had not lost the power to see the movement of another world, to feel in its mortal flow the unearthly spell of the immortal beauty, and trace in its conflict the Lord's controversy! But this is a vision to which we rise, not by the mere experience of life, but by the fellowship of some divine death. In the picture, it is only the Divine Child, born to die, that sees the babes whose death for Him has been their entrance upon life indeed. Undeserved sorrow and the death of the innocent are common things enough, and for the most part depressing enough, shaking to its roots the faith of those who would otherwise not find it hard to believe. But they are things which make the very central issue of Christianity. He who has mastered this mystery has passed within the Christian shrine. The mystery, the glory, the beauty, yes, and the fulness of health and power, in innocent pain and death—that is the very marrow of Christian divinity; and he who has risen to see these things has seen through the first world into the second, and has the power of the life that now is and that which is to come. He has the keys of the invisible world and of death. The cross has for him opened the gates of an abundant and everlasting life.

II

When I come to speak of 'The Scapegoat' (which I do from a reduced replica), it is impossible for me to regard it as a painting merely, and almost as difficult to treat it as no more than the illustration of an idea. There is a certain sacramental value about it, like the awe of death-bed messages, which disposes one rather to meditate than to expound. The technique in the original, I know, has been criticised, and even by Mr. Ruskin. Scarcely a spectator but decides against the colour of these hills, though not one in a thousand ever saw sunset upon porphyry rock, and not one in a million could see it with Mr. Hunt's eye for colour. But are there many who are caught and smitten by the great thought of the work? Nay, it is nothing to them all as they pass by. And it is nothing for one reason, because, while they are keen enough to feel pain, and cry out under it, they have no experience of a speechless curse, and spiritual agony is to them quite unknown. We are busy conquering nature and pushing trade. That is well. We are interested in the alleviation of social ills, the reform of the social order, and the repair of ancient wrong. That is better still. We are more sensitive and sympathetic than ever to the common and palpable forms

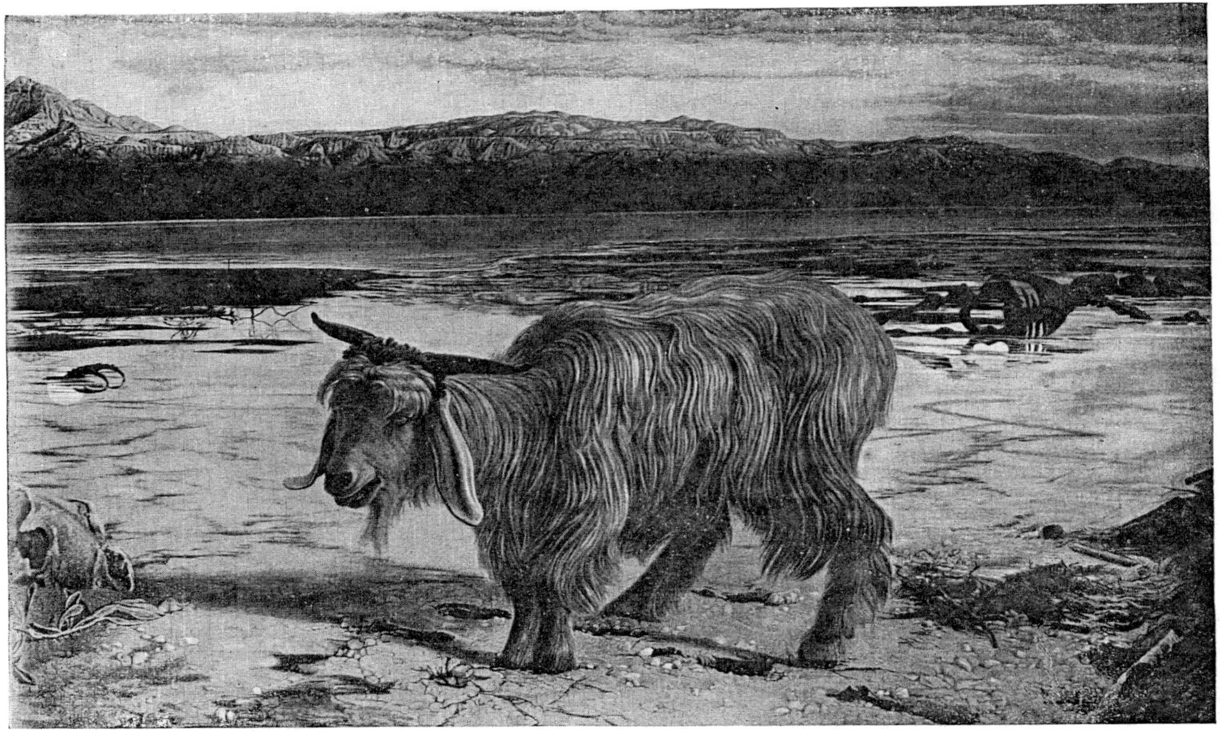

Holman Hunt.

THE SCAPEGOAT.

and spiritual pathos of it all, I cannot in any word tell you. I can but testify to the mysterious art which has conveyed to my soul, by the total effect of the picture, the religious atmosphere of the painter's soul, and made his whole canvas instinct and fragrant with the holy mood. For the highest purposes of religion, symbol is of more value than loftier art, and the animal here is a reverent symbol, not an audacious representation, of the solemn work of Redemption. The very power of a symbol lies in the sublime inadequacy and yet practical effectiveness of its suggestion. And the effect here is largely due to the huge, the pathetic, disparity between the dumb distress of the creature and the divine agony which submits to be hinted thus. The most powerful passion needs for its wakening but the slightest hint which is real at all. An evil word or look may loose the floodgates of unholiness; and an empty little shoe will unman the strongest.

What we have in this picture, if I may venture into its detail, is, first, the glory of nature in its rich hills; second, at its very feet, the curse upon nature, in the Dead Sea and the dying goat; and third, in the rainbow, the redemption from the curse into a heavenly glory and promise above all telling, even by the promise and glory of nature in her flush.

First, you have the beauty of nature and its promise. You have this earth's splendour at its resplendent best, the mountain chain of Abarim coloured like an unearthly world. It is the range upon which Moses died, overlooking the promised land, but not in it; glorious, but not with the glory that excelleth in final rest. It is the hour of sunset and parting light; but there rises full 'the balmy moon of blessed Israel,' type of a light that is coming, and of a radiance, more sombre perhaps, but more searching-subtle in its night than all the arrows of the sun by day.

> Der Tod, der ist die kühle Nacht,
> Das Leben ist der schwüle Tag.

The sky above the hills is sweet and clear, but to the side and the rear there is a gathering gloom like the gloom upon the low slimy waters of the dark Dead Sea beneath.

Just as below the Mount of Transfiguration was the gloomy and frenzied demoniac, baffling the disciples of the Redeemer, so here in shadow, at the very foot of the mountain glory, is the accursed lake and dismal swamp, that covers the ruins of ancient sin, and carries for ever the record of sin's dead level and its bitter end. The reflection of the glowing hills is given back from its moist margin with a ghastly beauty, like the memory of old splendid sins that on his wan life's bitter verge mocks the *roué's* soul in its dull decay. Mark how the very life of vegetation has become contaminated with curse, by the bough in the corner all crusted with pale salt; mark the slimy surface of the water; mark the salt, caked thick upon the long, low shore; mark how horrible this pale stretch of salt is, compared with what would be the unembittered beauty of a like beach of snow; and mark how the blessed promise of the rising moon is marred and turned into ghastly mockery in this cursed land by placing the bleached skull of a goat long perished right in the disc of the moon's reflection upon the damp shore; and mark the still and aching loneliness of this desert edge of the ever unploughed and barren sea. In the miasmal jungle there is death, but there is also teeming life; here there is no life, but total curse, and hard, hopeless blight, as of sins that wither and take away the heart. This is the second death; this is Hell—under the very mountain-throne of God; as a man's damnation underlies the finest possibilities of his high-built soul, and as the pilgrim saw that from the very gate of heaven there was a by-way to hell.

But with all this salt ooze and lifeless waste the curse is not complete, nor the dreariness raised to the agony of utter woe. Some feeling thing must reflect and realise it all in consciousness. It must rise in appeal and prayer to the living God through its reflection in a life. Curse must become lonely agony, and agony pass by innocence into atonement. Another life than the mere glow of nature must redeem the mysterious curse upon nature. The torment of the sensitive soul must deliver the world from its Dead Sea into more than the lost splendour aloft on the hills.

All the economy of Judaism centred in the great Day of Atonement. The moral curse on nature and man was yearly erased by a mystic death and a mystic woe. On the great day, after the priest had gone through some scrupulous ceremonies of cleansing, he stationed himself on the north side of the altar, and two goats exactly alike were brought him. Lots were cast, and one was elected for immediate death and sacrifice by a lot marked 'For Jehovah'; the other was specified for another purpose by a lot marked 'For Azazel.' This goat was taken, a red fillet of wool bound around its horns for distinction's sake, and the high priest, putting both hands upon its head, confessed the sins of the people and transferred them in a symbol to the animal. It was then taken far into the wilderness and let go. The inscription 'For Azazel,' parallel with that 'For Jehovah,' probably is the relic of a time when sacrifice was made to a powerful goat-shaped deity of evil in the early Hebrew days, before monotheism became established. But the idea was a much higher and more significant one when the Jewish ritual came to the perfection of Leviticus after the exile. The goat went out loaded, not with individual guilt, but with the curse of a nation's sin, just as Christ went out bearing, not the *guilt* of sin (for he was pure as the creature was harmless), but the mysterious curse and load of sin as it presses upon the whole world. In the oldest times the goat was supposed to carry the sin and curse back to the great deity that was its author. The Christian thought is that Christ carried the horror and curse of the sin, amid fearful loneliness and agony, into the presence of God by confession full and complete; where the sin, being thus exposed, was purged and burned away in the forgiving love of God who is a consuming fire. Mind after mind, in the solemnised exercise of spiritual imagination, has tried to pierce with sympathy the darkness of Gethsemane, to gauge with amazement the nature of the Saviour's woe, and humbly to bear if it were but the corner of His garment under the load of this curse unspeakable. It is a task too great for human power. Fully to gauge those sorrows would be fully to bear them. Fully to express them would be fully to confess them; the thing no man could do, else the God-man had not come to do it on our behalf. No painter could paint in human features the unutterable horror of this curse and hour. No reverent painter of anything like adequate power would venture to try it. And so this great reverent painter has striven to render the idea by symbol—not by an attempt at expression on a face, but only by the powerful suggestion of a symbol for thought; a symbol far remote indeed from the heart of the reality, yet involved in the action of the reality, as the whole sorrow of the burdened creation is implicated in the redeeming sorrow of Christ. What we have here, then, is a most wonderful and successful symbol, not artificial but natural, not conventional but original, not fanciful but a part of the reality—a symbol with sacramental power to convey the staggering horror of spiritual curse, and the awful strain of the sin-bearing which takes sin away. So powerful is the effect, so masterly the imagination, that we soon cease to see the creature, and what we do see is the invisible load, what we feel is the intolerable burden; what we pity is not the animal, gasping with fatigue, and at the point of death, but it is the despised Life which ached in all its fulness under the world's spiritual load, and was no more able to convey even to His nearest (had they been true) the nature of His pain, than that parched and tottering goat could tell his pain to any were any there to hear. The awful load and the awful loneliness of the Spirit that atones, that is what we see. But he who never had a life's atonement to make knows not how lonely, dreary, and bitter the atoning life must be.

I do not well know how the artist has conveyed the thought in detail, as I said. We mark the trembling forelegs at their last step, the depressed head, the low back, and the outspread hind legs (as if the weakness were no mere sinking of failure, but the pressure of a world of invisible load), the bleeding footprints broken into the caked soil—the record of a long, long journey from Zion and its peace, through a land where 'no man comes nor hath come since the making of the world.' We see the bent and smitten head, the dull dying eye, the parched and gasping mouth. But through and above all we see the soul of the Saviour in the bitter garden, and the sin and the curse upon His lonely broken heart.

And, finally, we see it all enclosed in a rainbow of promise and blessing, laden with colour more mellow, and glory more heavenly, than the sunset upon earth's loveliest hills. There is no pure sorrow but it is covered and beautified by that bow. It is the symbol of the Encircling Father, the triumph of inclusive bliss, beautiful above all the curse, with its blessed arms sanctifying the very agony from which its cherishing presence is hidden, and full of promise for a new heaven and a new earth, wherein dwelleth righteousness and there is curse no more.

III

But was the sorrow of the sin-bearer gathered up and confined within that hour in the garden or that other hour upon the cross? Was not the labour and sorrow of the cross and agony the labour and sorrow of His entire humane and holy life? When we push our inquiry into the nature of the redeeming travail, do we find it with all its mystery utterly inscrutable? Is He then, like His God to the agnostics, a 'black sun'? Has His cross nothing in connection with the sorrow of all good hearts, and the toil of all labouring lives? Have we no key in our own purest conflicts wherewith to unlock the chambers of the Saviour's redeeming soul? Is *our* warfare so alien to *His* great good fight? As we wrestle with nature to redeem her into the feeding of man's body in grain, or the service of his soul in art, is our weariness not some fringe of the great redemptive pain? As we work and pray over human nature, and groan while we lift it to spiritual freedom and divine peace, are we filling up no intelligible and posthumous part of the Redeemer's toil? are we taking no share in His passion? and is our hour of darkness no shadow of His saving cross? How inhuman, then, would so superhuman a Saviour be! How foreign to all our toil would be

His work! How alien to His dying our divinest death! No; the curse which He had upon Him was not inscrutable in the sense which makes it utterly foreign to us. If the Saviour were human, the curse from which he saved was not wholly superhuman. It had a naturalness about it. And here we have its nature shown in the great picture which Manchester may be so proud to possess continually, 'The Shadow of Death.'

I confess (if I may be pardoned the reference) that this picture did not please me when I saw it soon after it was first exhibited. I looked for a great and unmistakable divinity in it, such as doubtless some came expecting, to their disappointment, to find in the Son of Man Himself. I was not offended by the realism of it, but I did not feel that its realism was sufficiently imposing. I think, too, I was misled by some remarks I heard about its representing the dignity of manual work, and I did not perceive the dignity. Perhaps I was thinking too much also of a Christ who must be working out, not Redemption, but the theology of Redemption, dramatising a scheme and personating a part, a Christ always conscious of the fulness of His Godhead, instead of a Christ who, like ourselves, did not always live in the full consciousness of what He really was. I was possessed, perhaps, with the idea that all along Jesus foresaw the exact course of His career, and, even before His public work, had full in view the destiny and the scheme of the cross; having no perplexity as to the line He must take, but only needing to keep Himself by steadfast prayer up to the strength of taking and keeping it to the end.

Those who come to this picture with such notions will not find much in it except to repel. It has no cant in it about the dignity of the artisan. Christ came for another purpose than to lend dignity to a working class. What is here is not work, but toil, labour, too much work; work which leaves the nerves unstrung, the muscles jaded, and the spirits vexed, unsure, and under a curse. Yes, it is the curse of labour that is here, hard labour—not to say penal; labour seen as it is viewed in Genesis, as part of the curse. 'In the sweat of thy face shalt thou eat bread: in toil shalt thou eat of it all the days of thy life.' Is such labour not a part of the curse upon evil? If all men were what they ought to be, would one half of mankind be cursed with over-work, or with the difficulty of getting and keeping work, while the other part is cursed with idleness, or with the difficulty of varying it? The present age has much more to do with the curse of labour than with the dignity of work. Work, before it becomes excessive and laboured, is a pleasure, and has a dignity which it needs no Incarnation to bring home to us. But the great problem set before the redemptive energies of a day like the present arises from the curse that lies upon labour, and the slavery which most work brings upon most men. How far we have yet to go, when you think of the share that men's necessary work has in enslaving their souls, whether it be the work of the money-piler or the toil of those that spin! Work is still mostly felt to have in it more of a curse than a divine dignity, and it will be so felt till, after something like a social revolution, it is regulated and sustained for all men by the redemptive spirit of the work of Christ. When shall that come to give the type and principle of all work? When shall theology be restored to the actuality of life, and in the same hour to life's control?

What we have in this picture is no burly figure over whom the toils of the day pass lightly, and leave the spirits unimpaired. It is a muscular figure, but of fine organisation and nervous sensibility, likely to feel fatigue with more than physical effect. To mention nothing else, look at the left hand—look at the third and fourth fingers. They are closely doubled up, while the first and second are extended. Try to do that, and you will find that you cannot well, unless you use force to dig the points into the hollow of the palm. And you exert that force, in such stretching as is represented here, only as the vehement reaction against intense weariness. It is a clutch, the result of the same spasmodic nervous exhaustion as finds its relief in intense stretching altogether. And there is more of that exhaustion expressed in the position of these two fingers than if they had been represented outspread like the other hand, because it requires more force to keep them down. Yes, what is here is the curse of toil rather than the dignity of work.

And I do not think, farther, there is much of our theology of the Incarnation here present to the conscious mind of the Son of God. Those who look here for any such calm consciousness of what Christendom still believes He was, will be disappointed, not to say shocked. People of an ecclesiastical turn of mind will say, and have said, 'This is a Unitarian Christ.' Well, I do not know Mr. Hunt's views on this point, but I cannot see that the full humanity of Jesus, with the frequent veiling of His Godhead even from Himself, implies the Unitarian position, any more than His true divinity compels you to represent Him with a bright halo, a flowing robe, and a placid face. The Son of God must be a real man. The people of Nazareth found Him such at least. Whatever made the difference in Him was not perceptible by any of the ordinary faculties of men. The intense realism in this picture of Jesus quite corresponds to the realism which offended the Nazarenes. And it is a like realism which offends some as unbeautiful in the face of the Virgin, of which I spoke above. What we have here is not the simpering figure of some popular art, nor the pompous Christ of other such art, nor the hectic idealist of Tolstoi or Munkacsy, nor the sentimentalist of Renan, nor the myth of Strauss. But it is a Christ very simply and sincerely human and serious; on the whole, perhaps, the most truly human Christ that Art has yet given us; whose humanity is not, like that of the representations I have mentioned, incompatible with a real belief in the actuality of the God-man. Art, I have said, in Protestantism humanised itself. It strove for actuality. It would not have an ideal outside realities, but one approving itself through them by a hearty concern in them. It aims not at an abstract, but at a concrete, ideal. It is concrete spirituality. This picture is, in that respect, the greatest Christ that Protestant art has attained to. And if our idea of the God-man is incompatible with such actuality, then it must not hope to be the ruling idea of the Christianity of the future. We need a Saviour who redeems the curse of human toil and sorrow by being in the midst of it, and having it in His own heart. We need a Christianity that shall wrestle with human problems, and work them out into a social salvation. We have had more than enough of a mystic and dreamy salvation which leaves them neither touched nor understood.

I own that what we have here is rather the incipient Saviour, in conflict with the curse of pain and doubt, than the Christ who has attained to the great and crowning conflict with sin. It is the spirit of the artist's age, not indeed wholly to deny the wrestling with sin, but to gather up much arrears of attention which should earlier have been bestowed upon the struggle with pain and doubt. The Christ here represented is taken at a stage of His development before He issued upon His public work, and when there may well enough have been much painful doubt in His mind as to the form of the task imposed by the Father's will. The weariness on His face, and the appeal, arise not only from bodily fatigue, but from that spiritual uncertainty which becomes such an ache, when the jaded frame gives it an opening. We have here our contemporary curse of doubt as well as of labour. But I have already, in speaking of 'The Scapegoat,' given the chief reason why no reverent artist can venture on what so many people desire, who would neither have the sympathy nor the imagination to recognise it if done—I mean the spectacle of the Saviour's acutest struggle with *sin*. The aspect of the awful, godlike conflict with sin, is beyond the limits of human conception or art. We never can have a Christ in Art whose divinity is as unmistakable as His humanity. We have neglected and falsified the humanity in the effort to render such a Christ. Our artistic effort must now, perhaps, be rather to represent the divine Man than the human God. If Art will help us to realise the Man, if imagination will bring near us, and endear to us, and ennoble for us, the passion and presence of His human life, there are other resources which will keep us in the truth as to His Godhead. Meanwhile, it must not be denied or forgotten that we do have here the *dawn* of the conflict with sin no less than with pain or doubt. Both the doubt and the pain spring from the problem of man's curse of evil, and how it must be removed. The sin of His people is part of His load, and its weariness is written in that face of pain and those eyes of prayer.

Let some attention be paid to the title of the picture. It is not the Shadow of the Cross, but the Shadow of Death, and not only of Christ's dying, but of the world's death. If the artist had meant only to paint the curious legend without any profounder thought of the sort I have hinted, he would perhaps have called it the Shadow of the Cross. But we have in this picture also that doubleness of suggestion, that meaning within a meaning, and world within a world, which was so boldly expressed in 'The Triumph of the Innocents.' What the mother of Jesus sees is but the shadow on the wall; what we are intended chiefly to see is the foreshadowing of His death (and so the real nature of it) in His fatigue, His doubt, and His troubled sense of His people's sin. The artist would give us his view of the nature of Christ's death. It was a moral, a spiritual, and therefore not an inhuman, magical, or unintelligible, act. It was, indeed, a prolonged act, a process. It was the obverse of his whole life. It was one in its moral kind with the daily dying which is represented in a single episode here. The destruction of sin is a moral process. The death on the cross was the crowning spiritual act of a long series and process of such acts, which flowed from a moral, not a magical, personality, and which constitute the real spiritual life and work of Christ. He died for us once for all, once, but for ever, by His incessant death unto Himself and to the world. It was an atonement, and an objective one, but it was moral and spiritual in its nature and method. It appeals to the conscience to be understood. It took place under the conditions of character and personality, divine and human. Christ worked out our salvation by working out His own, for His was the soul of humanity. His early conflict, therefore, was the real beginning of His final agony. His last death took its first form in His early dying to all the false and selfish thoughts of Messiahship which were presented to tempt and deflect His purity by the ideas of His nation both present and past. And the conquest of the curse in Gethsemane and on Calvary was of one nature with His painful victory over it in the days of His early purity and doubt and pain.*

* It may interest some if I venture to pursue this train of thought in a note. The sinlessness of Christ was a sinless growth. A perfect life must be a perfect evolution. God's will for life is growth, and Christ completely met it. He grew not *to* God but *in* God. His movement was not towards a spiritual nature, but it was the normal, ideal movement which is the expanding of a spiritual nature in actual life and sinful conditions. He was always perfecting His perfection. He was always learning obedience by the things He suffered; but He learned it completely each time. No lesson had to be twice learned. He met every situation fully as His hour came; He used it rightly, and drew from it all the access of power which it had been ordained by God's wise will to give. It was in the Father's will that the evolutionary method first lay. Character can only arise by moral process, and the perfectness of moral process can only mean that it was normal all along the line, that the supply rose with the rising of the demand. There was always an equally true harmony, but there was not always so deep, rich, and intricate a chord.

Not even God could create a character full blown. It is producible by the soul's moral conflict alone. And the great, the crowning act of a divine character must be all of a piece with the process which reared the character. It must be moral and spiritual. Thus the death of Christ was all of a piece with the spiritual discipline which gave Him power to die, and His last work was but His work in its close. His complete salvation of the world from sin was effected in the completeness of His own personal conquest of it, His own victory over it in an actual passion of experience, and His own entire harmony with the will of God through the deepening history of His spirit's career.

His self was his offering. Only in such sense was his life a sacrifice.

This picture took three years of intense labour, and more than that in accumulated thought, on the part of a man of both genius and piety. There cannot be a line or suggestion in it that is not there for some good if not profound reason. Artists of this stamp do not work at haphazard. And if we are to get the meaning out again, we must not expect to do it in a few minutes. It would be more correct to say that the picture is overloaded with suggestion than that it is devoid of it. We are familiar with the legend. Mary, in an interval of housewifely cares, has come to pay a

What he laid down was his self-will—even the worthy Egotism that makes many men so great. His life was a continuous prayer, a long act of access, obedience, and self-oblation to the Father. Here lay its priestliness. That daily intercourse with God was not something which went on alongside the work of Redemption, or as a preparation for it. It *was* that work. He was priest for others by the same act in which he was priest for Himself, and His priesthood lay in the atoning death of his daily prayer and complete renunciation, as it lay nowhere else when the day came for the shape these took on Calvary.

The work of redemption was the work which made Christ Christ. His vocation gave the law of His personality. It was the continuous, expanding, and complete conquest over sin in a universal soul. And it was performed under the moral conditions of a human conscience, and of that spiritual evolution which, being a law of God's own being, was Christ's native law. The cross is the temptation gathered to its acutest point; the temptation is the cross diffused through life. The cross is the clearest expression of the law of moral growth, the principle of normal human nature, the secret of a man's making by a Creator too faithful to leave His work half done, or human nature complete at the stage of the natural man.

All this is, in very different language, what the picture says simply and suggestively in its own. This human pain, doubt, and prayer is death's own approach, not an adjunct of death, but the act itself on its dark side, and an organic portion of the redemptive work. It is not the presentiment of a crucifixion, but the shadow of death; not a noonday cloud, but the first real shades of night.

visit in His workshop to her dear mystery of a son. With womanly, if not motherly, vanity she does again what doubtless she had often done before. She is not a creature far too bright or good for human nature's daily food. She has the care, the pride, nay, perhaps, the vanities of her position as woman, mother, and housewife; she has possibly her secret worldly ambitions, as she moves among her little set at Nazareth, about the future of her strange and reserved son. She was the last likely to forget the extraordinary forecasts represented by the Magi and their gifts. Often she opened the coffer, and gazed upon the jewels and crowns they left. Often she wondered when they would be required, and marvelled that she saw in the movements of her son no indication of the course to which they pointed. These crowns are, doubtless, painted after strict Oriental patterns, but I do not suppose it is for nothing that the artist has made that one prominent which serves by its spikes to suggest the crown of thorns. Once more, then, Mary has opened the chest, and probably has made some remark which jars upon the deeper mood of Jesus with a worldly tone. It is not difficult to imagine the shape such a remark would take in similar circumstances among ourselves; the somewhat worldly and impatient sigh a widow might breathe, in a moment snatched from household cares, as she handled some heirloom, some goblets, say, witnessing that the family had once held a position which the son gave promise, but too hesitant promise, to restore. Some such remark Mary has just made, when, looking up, she sees a writing on the wall, and a sword pierces her own soul as her words pierced her son's. It is evening. The sun is level in the west, for the shadow of the saw-handle on the opposite wall is almost level with the tool itself. The shadow of Jesus's outstretched figure thus falls full upon the same wall, and especially upon the crossbar of the tool-rack, with a singular suggestion of the attitude with which we are so familiar; and it strikes even Mary with a fearful revulsion of possible meaning as she lifts her eyes from the jewels. Crucifixion could not be unfamiliar in a Roman province, as the reward, too, of failure in any Nationalist enterprise a devoted Jew might lead. Thousands had suffered thus, and recently, in Jerusalem alone. The contrast is very striking between the casket and the cross. And a similar and no less striking contrast is doubtless intended by the gorgeous colouring of the Moabite hills seen through the window to the east. It is the same contrast as we saw marked and brilliant in 'The Scapegoat,' between the mountains of Abarim and the agony of the dreary waste. It is the contrast of nature's splendour and nature's curse; a hint of the untroubled and visible glory so fully resigned for the sake of lifting human nature to an invisible and better glory. Natural beauty and worldly pomp are alike surrendered by Him whose task is not merely to bestow blessing but to redeem from curse, nor only to open the gates of heaven but to destroy the gates of hell.

We should on no account omit to remark that

dramatic unity of the picture to which I have referred. At first glance one does not, perhaps, grasp any connection between the two figures. They seem oblivious of each other. But it is not so. Jesus is wounded (involuntarily) in the house of his friends. It is the action or remark of His mother that has waked the passion in His face, cast the real shadow of death (*i.e.* moral conflict) upon it, and stirred the agonised appeal to the Father in these moist eyes. It is far more than nervous fatigue, far more than hectic enthusiasm, that is written in the passion of that face and form. It is a prelude and moment of *the* Passion. It has in it the burden of moral war, and the strain of solemn spiritual enterprise. This is no olive young Syrian, of singular sweetness and devoutness, but also of dreamy piety and sacred simplicity. It is a Redeemer with human sin for a burden more or less conscious at the root of all His pain and doubt. It is not merely a man in moral earnest, but One whose earnestness mounts to prayer, and, for us at least, is sublimed by the suggestion that His one call is to suffer, His one task to renounce and redeem. You say I am reading this from the gospels into the picture. I say I find it in the dramatic action of the picture and the coherent unity of its thought. I find it in the fact that the expression of the face is one of thoughts stirred by the contrast and irony of these crowns and the ambitions they suggest. And I find it in other careful traits I shall proceed to mention.

'Too brown, decidedly too brown,' I heard a

curate say to a lady behind me as we stood before the picture. But, apart from clerical inspiration, the probability would seem to be with the painter who studied Jewish complexion in Nazareth upon the spot. The general features of the traditional face of Christ have been kept. And as for the perfect sincerity of the work in this face, I can only say that I should judge the weeks of toil which it demanded must also have been a time of profound worship and solemn piety to a spirit like that of the painter. You cannot try to realise the face and soul of Christ with this intensity, and remain a mere artist meanwhile.

The Saviour's head has no conventional halo around it, but with great ingenuity it is placed central against the large open disc pierced in the arch of the window, so that the blue sky forms a halo, and heaven itself is His crowning light. It may also be that the star pierced in another part of the same eastern window is meant to convey, taken with the crowns, a suggestion of the star in the east, still resting here like the abiding seal of heaven upon some real kingship which the Magi and their crowns did but hint. Jesus has raised Himself from His work. Observe the curious form of the trestle, which seems to lack a pair of legs till we mark its peculiar structure, whereby the plank supported is also a support. And here we meet what seems another puzzle. If He has just been using that saw, has He not been using it with His left hand? But you will observe that in the Oriental saw the teeth incline upwards to the hilt, so that the effect is produced rather by the pull than by the thrust. It would require two hands therefore, the workman meanwhile bestriding the plank. Jesus has simply raised Himself to an erect position for change and rest from such laborious work, leaving the tool in the wood, and stepping to one side of it. But these are minor matters. There are certain symbolical features in the picture, deliberate yet not obtrusive, which help us to read in the face and mind of Christ some measure of the thought and shadow of atoning death. We are able to say that we have here no mere fatigue of body, but the agony of a soul brooding on a human curse, feeling that the world was out of joint, and more than surmising that He was born to set it right.

Let me ask you to observe those apples, or rather pomegranates, on the window-sill. What are they there for? Merely to slake occasionally the joiner's thirst? Well, then, that roll of the law beside them; what is that for? To show another kind of refreshment, and a higher, snatched amid His work by this most scriptural soul? Yes, doubtless. But why this pointed proximity of the apples and the roll? Why is that roll not in its place beside the others coiled and put away in the recess under the window-sill? If you carry your eye along that wall, you will traverse a series of three objects nearer and more significant than the beauty of the distant hills —the apples, the open roll of the law, and the shadow of the cross, or, what is the same thing, the suffering figure of Jesus Himself. Is it only my fancy that there is meaning in this, and symbol? Yet, in

'The Light of the World,' Mr. Ruskin points out the apple lying on the ground as marking 'that the entire awakening of the conscience is not merely to committed but to hereditary guilt.' So that this principle of interpretation has good authority, and if the apple means so much in the one picture it may mean no less in the other. The apple, the book, and the cross, mean the series of sin, the law's curse, and redemption. The spray of hyssop in the vase, and the memory of its sprinkling use at the Passover, suggest the same thing. In the figure of Jesus and its shadowed death we are asked to see at once the culmination and the redemption of man's disobedience and the law's curse. And the death-shadow, in this moment of passionate and weary appeal, is cast on His soul no less than on the wall, in a faint foretaste of His death for every man. The parted lips emit as it were by anticipation the cry 'I thirst,' and the melting anguished eyes utter the prayer, 'My God, my God.' The burden that really lies on Him is not His weakness, but human nature's curse; and what fills His soul is a sharp moral conflict stung by the incident of the moment into startling vividness of life. Some word of His mother's, or the sight of the crowns, has revealed to Him with more than usual clearness that that is not His way. I will not go so far as to say the cross, as a form of death, was yet clear in His soul's eye, but one may read in the deprecating appeal of His upward gaze as if He said within, 'Must it then be by the bitter way, and to lift the curse must I bear the curse? My

God, my God.' The shadow of distant death falls at once upon mother and son, suggested by very different lines to each. To her it comes by a vision of fancy, in a sort of miracle; to Him it is psychologically worked out by the swift insight of His labouring soul, the holy logic of His moral thought, and the coherence of a spiritual necessity which it was given him to trace. We are particularly shown that His great agony was not a dull sense of weight and utterly unintelligible curse, as in 'The Scapegoat'; but that it was, if I may say so, rational; that the issues were grasped as moral and personal problems, and fought out in an agony of living thought, growing consciousness, and intelligent choice; not in mere ignorant endurance of suffering, but in the warfare of conscious moral strife round the central issues of the moral reason and of God. It was a condensation of the great central agony of the conscious soul of man in every age. That is the nature of the strife, the death, which, however, is only foreshadowed, only beginning here. This moment is one of the seasons of self-revelation which the temptation narrative figures forth, when the power and glory of a brilliant worldly career were seen in their true dimensions, and put aside by His sense of the sin that needed a deeper cure, and of the will of God that taught a holier.

IV

I SHOULD never have embarked on these lectures but for the prospect of dealing with Mr. Watts, and still more especially with Mr. Holman Hunt. I see the principles of all earnest art, as of all earnest life, running up into the principle of the Cross and Resurrection. I see the spirit of Christ descending, divided into as many tongues of fire as there are fine faculties in man.* I should feel that I had far outrun my knowledge had I ventured on the æsthetic criticism which is the proper province of specialist literature, whether periodical or other. I have found it necessary, indeed, to analyse the pictures, just as the best preaching analyses its text, and even discusses points of its grammar. But it is the thought, and still more the religion pervading the thought, that I have striven to carry home; winged, and made piercing, and fixed by the beauty of impressive imagination. I have treated the artists as teachers, not entertainers; as prophets, and not caterers. Such men come much more to instruct us than to be judged by us. If you say, 'I never saw such a thing in nature,' that is the artist's best justification. If we could see such things we should not need the artist to lead us to see them. If the great, far, spiritual suggestions of nature were palpable to all, the great spiritual interpreters of nature would be superfluous. The

* Visitors to Florence may remember here the great fresco which fills one end of the Spanish chapel in Santa Maria Novella.

artists have not taught me art, because I am no artist; but they have for years taught me to see nature and the soul as I never could have seen them without their aid. They have been eyes to my blindness, and guides to my mazed feet. And they do us no greater service than when they endow us with the power to see in the environs of our daily life new things, and things to be admired and desired. There is a culture of art which leaves us more and more dissatisfied with the surroundings, the duties, and the vexations of our daily life. That is only half culture. True culture makes a man not fastidious, but receptive, and more quick to perceive the beauty that is there than to resent what is not. I can truly say that the effect on me of such pictures, and especially of many landscapes, has been to train and quicken my eye for the shades of beauty and riches of colour round my own neighbourhood during the wealthy summer days. I have felt, since a certain time, a charm I never felt before in the waving of dark green boughs upon white masonry near me; and I could name the picture that woke my eye to that daily grace. I have drawn new pleasure from the hourly sight of red brick dwellings among sweet green trees; and distant, and even dingy walls, pierced with gateways through which comes the glow of the setting sun, have a beauty which I can tell you the painting that made me feel. So it is possible that 'The Triumph of the Innocents' may one day in our sorrow help us to call in the health and beauty of a more innocent world to redress the balance of grief and guilt in this. 'The Scapegoat' may come with a power to cheer and dignify some moments when we feel accursed for God's sake in a desert, and tottering for men's sake in a waste and bitter land. And when flesh and blood find the kingdom of heaven hard; when the spirit agonises as it divinely puts the success of earth away, and, stretching itself upon the tooled rack of the unkind world, finds it a cross; when pain, and doubt, and sin wring from us, in the midst of our labour, sighing, and crying, and a passion of prayer,—then there may come to help us the memory of what an artist can teach us of the Man of Sorrows, and our Shadow of Death will be known to be the end of curse, and the dawn of some true blessing, all undreamed, through us for the world.

RICHARD WAGNER

AND PESSIMISM

I

'The music of the future' is an expression due neither to Wagner himself, nor to a master in the art of nickname. Wagner held that the last word in pure music had been spoken by Beethoven, and that it had not consequently any future corresponding to the excitement gathering about his own name. The phrase which has become so current is one of those hasty blunders into which a literary hack would be apt to fall in translating a new idea in a hurry. Wagner did write a pamphlet with a most succinct account of his work and its meaning, but the title he gave it was 'The Art-work of the Future.' The difference between this and its popular travesty involves the whole significance of Wagner as a thinker and an artist.

The great work to be achieved by Art in the future, Wagner said, is not so much the development of any single art as the reconciliation and organic fusion of the various arts under a single grand idea for the production of one complete æsthetic effect. He would restore on a larger scale that unity of the arts whereby in the great age of Italy, the artist was a man of many crafts, and the painter was often no less famous as poet, sculptor, architect, goldsmith, and even musician. And his own great contribution to this end sprang from the unprecedented fusion in his genius of musical, poetic, and dramatic power. We English are now but beginning to realise how extraordinary, how manifold, Wagner's gifts were. We have not realised how solitary in the history of genius was his combination of various and first-rate endowment. We are, indeed, beginning to admit, with whatever necessary and critical reserves, that in music he must stand among the masters and immortals; and we believe what we are told about his unheard-of but successful demands upon the utmost resources of the stage. But we know nothing, or next to nothing, of his critical work both in music and in the history and genius of dramatic art. We know little of the principles upon which he revolutionised opera, and did for it something like what Bacon did for science, or Cowper and Wordsworth for poetry, by leading, or rather forcing, it back to Nature and Reality. We have no sort of idea, either, of the vast religious thoughts underlying his creative work, or of the religious mission which finally came to dominate his amazing activity. We do not know that he became the most gifted and passionate expositor of that semi-religious philosophy and semi-Christian atheism which is associated with the names of Schopenhauer and Pessimism. Nobody can quite understand Wagner or his spell till he has come to feel the force of so much as is true in Pessimism, and so much as it has of tragic meaning and universal scope. But our great disadvantage for the understanding of Wagner is the absence of any means of becoming acquainted with his splendid poetic power. It is his combination of musical and poetic genius which makes him so solitary in the annals of Art. Even had he been no musician he would have taken a permanent place among dramatists of the stamp represented by Schiller. It is with the idealist Schiller rather than with the 'positive' Goethe that he must be classed. But unfortunately English readers who cannot enjoy German have no means of realising how great Wagner is as a poet. One cannot but regret the amount of time and talent wasted in the production of such versions of the operas as are put into the hands of the English audience. An effort has there been made in which only a genius so like the author's own as Mr. Swinburne could succeed—the effort to reproduce the ancient metres, and even the alliterations, which Wagner uses in so free and masterly a way. And the result is something which only encourages whatever tendency there may be among us to scoff at the new and foreign departure. Mr. Swinburne has already sung his admiration of Wagner's genius. If he would only take in hand, say *Tristan and Isolde*, and give us a translation such as perhaps he alone could give, it would do more for our appreciation of Wagner as a poet than any amount of expository writing. Failing that, surely we might have a readable prose version which should at least not exaggerate the obscurities of the original.

II

PESSIMISM has done what neither Positivism nor Agnosticism has enough human nature to do. It has not only a special and congenial art, but it has produced a great master in Art. If music be its religion, Richard Wagner is the prophet. We have to deal in him with a weightier matter than meets us in the pessimistic poets like Leopardi, or dramatists like Ibsen, or even in such a novelist as Turgenieff. Systematic pessimism could sustain a great master in no other art, probably, but in one with the peculiar characteristics possessed by music. It seems, however, no longer to be seriously denied that in Wagner we have a great master and a genius of the first order. And it is recognised that he is totally different from a mind like Beethoven in having a view of life, a system of the world, an interpretation of history, a *Weltanschauung*, almost a theology. He was not only a musician, but a poet and a thinker. A philosophy, a criticism of life, is embedded in his art, though at first it is but half consciously on the artist's part. He says himself, alluding to the Nibelung dramas, 'In this conception I had unwittingly uttered the truth as to human affairs. All here is tragic from first to last. And the will which sets out to fashion a world according to its wish can attain at the close to nothing more satisfactory than a catastrophe of honourable ruin.' One thinks of Tennyson's Arthur. Latterly, these conceptions were not so unwitting on Wagner's part. After his introduction to the works of Schopenhauer he found in that tragic sage his guide to the philosophy of both Art and Life. He found with delight one who could give clear and rational shape to his own poetic surmise of the world. This influence is very marked in his small treatise on Beethoven. It is apparent, as we shall see, in the moral structure of *Tristan* and of *Parsifal*. And it is unmistakable in a sentence like this from his essay on 'Religion and the State': 'A true knowledge of the world should have taught us from the beginning that the nature of the world is but blindness; that it is not knowledge which induces its motion, but a dark impulse, a blind urging from its own power and force, which creates for itself only so much light and knowledge as it requires for the allaying of the moment's pressing needs.' But his philosophy, however pessimist in its features, was not borrowed from the pessimist philosopher in the first instance; it arose from the contact of the artist's own genius with life. A reader passing from the study of Schopenhauer to that of the great 'Nibelung' tetralogy would find himself in a world familiar down almost to the catchwords of the system. I may quote the untranslatable close of the first poetic version of the *Nibelungenring*. It is omitted in the musical version, only because the artist thought the music sufficiently conveyed its sense—

> Des ew'gen Werdens
> offene Thore
> schliess' ich hinter mir zu.
> Nach dem Wunsch- und wahnlos
> heiligsten Wahlland
> des Weltwerdens Ziel,
> von Wiedergeburt erlöst
> zieht um die Wissende hin.
> Alles Ew'gen
> sel'ges Ende
> wiss't ihr, wie ich's gewann?
> Trauernder Liebe
> tiefstes Leiden
> schloss die Augen mir auf
> enden sah ich die Welt.

Any one familiar with the terminology of Schopenhauer will find in these lines an echo of it which in the circumstances is startling. For when the poem was written, Wagner, we are informed from several quarters, was unacquainted with the works of Schopenhauer, which were only brought under his notice by a friend who had been struck with the resemblance *after* the publication of the *Nibelungenring*. That drama was privately printed as a poem in 1853, and it was not till 1854 that its author sent a copy to Schopenhauer, in a burst of delighted admiration.

The influence of Schopenhauer upon Wagner did not begin till then; but from then it becomes dominant. It appears in his theories of Art; it appears in his ethical views—especially in the Buddhism of his strong vegetarian and anti-vivisection theories; and perhaps, also, in the Ruskin-like impulse given to his social interests, his unmusicianly concern for society as a whole, and his effort to become an agent not only of the noblest delight, but of the profoundest redemption to the soul. He had indeed long pursued his artistic vocation as a national mission and with a patriotic end.* He had long felt that a national music is the highest contribution an artist can make to the music of the world. But he had no sympathy with national militarism, nor was patriotism to him mere national egotism. Especially after the Schopenhauer influence was this the case. He became more concerned in social than political well-being. Dreams were in his mind of a society, or societies, formed by the better spirits among the youth of his country upon this footing:—'We recognise as our basis the fall and corruption of historical humanity as well as the necessity of its regeneration. We believe in the possibility of this regeneration, and we devote ourselves to carrying it out in every way.' But, above all, the influence of the pessimist sage on Wagner appeared in his capacity of tragic artist. A comparison of the *Nibelung* poem with its successors, *Tristan* and *Parsifal*, would make this clear. The development observable in that great tragic series is not a case of the simple explication of an idea, which was itself closed and fixed. We can mark where, after

* His private character does not destroy the truth of this. I know the weakness of Wagner's pecuniary conscience. The *Spectator* in reviewing the first edition of this book ignored the first half of it entirely and printed a contemptuous homily on the point I name as if Turner had no message for the soul, and as if the Church honoured no mendacious saints. Criticism like that surrenders criticism and writes tracts.

the first of the three works named, the powerful influence of Schopenhauer enters and affects the growth of the idea itself. And the change is two-fold. First, a darker and more tragic cloud of fate descends upon human passion and affection. In *Tristan*, earthly and exclusive love appears far more helpless against the terrible and overwhelming background than was the case in the *Nibelungen-ring*. And that poem itself, indeed, is gloomier than the first draft of it (*The Nibelungen*), which does leave us with a prospect, for the lovers, of joy in an immortal world—

> Walhall froh sie begrüssen
> Zu ewiger Wonne vereint.

There is no such suggestion in the *Nibelung* poem. But, for all that, Brunnhilde, as she passes singing rapturously of—

> Love with a light in it,
> Death with a laugh,

is more mistress of the situation than Isolde, and Siegfried is more, as measured against destiny, than is Tristan. There is nothing in the terrible close of *Tristan and Isolde* like the exultation that ends the *Götterdämmerung*—

> Fahr hin Walhall's
> leuchtende Welt!
> Zerfall in Staub
> Deine stolze Burg!
> Leb' wohl, prangende
> Götterpracht!
> Ende in Wonne
> du ewig Geschlecht!
> Zerreisst ihr Nornen
> das Runenseil!

Götterdämmerung
dunkle herauf!
Mir strahlt zur Stunde
Siegfried's Stern;
er ist mir ewig
er ist mir immer
Erb und Eigen
ein und all'
leuchtende Liebe
lachender Tod.

In *Parsifal*, however, human passion is thrust into the background from first to last with an almost monastic severity. And this is because of the second effect of Pessimism on the poet—the growth in him of the idea of Redemption. This is the motive about which moves the whole of the extraordinary work last named. The passion of the natural man which forms the staple of all other operas is here mastered and changed by love of a more ideal, saintly, impersonal, and universal cast. It might even by some be doubted whether the spring of Redemption in *Parsifal* is love in any proper sense of the word, so excessive is its 'detachment.' It would be hard to define the object of it, and to say upon what it is that Parsifal supremely directs the passion which redeems the society of the Grail. Moving though we are amid the poetry of Christian ideas, Christian rites, and Christian phraseology, it is yet hardly possible to describe his devotion as directed either upon a Christ or a God. He works rather under the dreamy inspiration of an idea. He is an inspired idealist, the vehicle of the Supreme *Begriff* to which the Hegelian Left has reduced God, the organ of a stream of tendency which makes, however, for more than righteousness—for Redemption. His lofty passion seems devoid of any such objective point of attachment as love requires in order to remain love. Indeed, in Pessimism altogether love can hardly be the redeeming passion, seeing that it is itself no more than a form, though the finest, of that desire and will to live from which we must be entirely redeemed. It is the last infirmity of noble minds. Wagner once entertained the idea of a drama on 'Jesus of Nazareth.' The self-sacrifice of Jesus seemed to him 'the imperfect expression of that human impulse which urges the individual to rebel against a loveless universe. It is a rebellion which the mere individual can close only by self-destruction, but in this very ruin it announces its true nature to have been to aim not at mere death, but at the negation of the universal lovelessness against which it rose.' He was led, however, to abandon this idea by a remarkable consideration. He thought that the subject would require, for its full effect upon modern conditions, a philosophic adaptation such as he did not then feel in a position to give it. He did not think that human feeling and action, as the mere artist presents them, had a universality commensurate with the universe of fate. Love, of a personal sort, he felt, was narrower than reality—than destiny. It was only Schopenhauer's philosophy, when it came, that seemed to him to supply a principle more adequate. Theories and scruples of this sort would ruin the work of most artists as art. But the enormous power and genius of Wagner bore easily the strain, and *Parsifal* is the result; in which few will venture to say that the æsthetic quality or characterisation is inferior to his earlier and less philosophic feats. What seemed to Wagner defective in Jesus was probably the Saviour's fundamental and quenchless passion for a personality like the Eternal Father. Jesus was unphilosophic in eternalising relations like father and son, which spring from the fatal affection and desire tainting the 'will to be,' and from which, not through which, we must be redeemed. Parsifal's long and dreary preparation for his redeeming task, his Arabia, his temptation in the desert, consists in the lonely *askesis*, or renunciation, in which he roots from his soul the passion even for God, and draws so near to the pure cognition which is the heaven of Pessimism that he has power to lift others to the like release. The closing words of the poem, in which the praise of the brotherhood swells around their new chief, are very significant. Kundry, the saved Magdalen, whose grateful passion follows her saviour, humble, distant, and dumb, is nothing to him, when his work on her is done, and she falls dead and unregarded upon the altar steps, while the jubilant prayer ascends as the final hallelujah of the ransomed host:—

> Heiles höchstes Wunder,
> Erlösung dem Erlöser!
>
> Saving miracle supreme!
> Be redeemed who didst redeem!

'Salvation for the Saviour' is their grateful and crowning aspiration, and they can only pray that in due course he who had delivered them should receive his last promotion to glory, and find his final release from even the noblest, the redemptive, form of the passion of life. Siegfried, in the *Nibelungen-ring*, was a redeemer from the sordid and arbitrary old gods, but against the advance of fate he could do no more than be 'honourably broken.' Brunnhilde's love shone radiant upon it, like the evening star upon a bastion of looming and spreading cloud. It mounts and erases the splendour of Isolde's passion with a tragic darkness all the deeper because since he created Brunnhilde, Wagner had confirmed his Pessimism by the systematic atheology of Schopenhauer. But *Parsifal* resists, conquers, and disappoints this fate by renouncing the passion on which it feeds, because by this time the redemptive idea in the Pessimistic system had risen to dominate the poet's imagination, and in great measure redeem him from Pessimism itself.

III

PESSIMISM, when it is in moral and mental earnest, may be foreign to our crowning Christian instincts and our final Christian faith, but it is not all alien to the secret or the method of Christ. And to the eye which is not misled by the evil associations of a name, there are features in this strange philosophy which raise it almost to a religion having no few points of contact with our own. It is a cry even more than a speculation—a philosophic cry. It is a voice from the laden heart more than a scheme from the vigorous mind. It rises from a burdened world, from a disjointed time, from lands where thought is too much divorced from action, and where the pressure of militarism upon industry co-operates with the ecclesiastical destruction of vital faith to reduce the value, the reasonableness, the sanctity of life. It bears the cross, it sups full of sorrow; but it sees no Resurrection, scarcely hears a Revelation, and trusts no final joy within the heart of things; it is too full of the 'nothingness of the phenomenal world.' It is one side of Christianity, nevertheless, because it is not pure Naturalism, because it is a creed of sorrow, because it distrusts the easy optimism of the merely happy creeds, because it has a heart for the world-pain, something like a sense of sin, and a horizon as large as human fate. It is Christian, furthermore, in that its pessimism is not absolute, misery for it is not final or eternal—we are not in the worst of possible worlds. No world is the very worst which contains the possibility of escape from its ills; and no creed is utterly pessimist which has like this creed the note, the thought, the promise of a Redemption, however inadequate we may deem it. It is Christian in the force with which it insists upon a historic degeneration, a moral Fall, as the obverse of Redemption. Apart from Redemption, Wagner is much more struck with degeneration than with progress in human civilisation when measured by spiritual ideals. 'The deepest foundation of every true religion is to be found in its expression of the world's corruption and the way it points to release from the same. To bear this in upon the dense, natural man requires a superhuman effort, in which respect we discern the sublimest feature of Christianity with its deepest truth for comfort and salvation revealed to the poor in spirit. The founder of Christianity was no sage; He was divine; His doctrine took the shape of voluntary sorrow. To believe in Him meant to follow hard after Him. To hope for Redemption was to seek union with Him. The poor in spirit needed no metaphysical explanation of the world. The knowledge of its sorrow lay open to their heart, and the divine demand was simply that their heart should never be closed.' One is tempted to say in passing that with better metaphysics Wagner would have been not only almost, but altogether, a Christian. Still, let us be just to what his system was. Pessimism may feel the load of earth's sorrow more than the sting of earth's sin. It may not redeem by Love but rather by Will, and not into Love but from it. It may redeem not from evil, but from the crush of suicidal force and the blunder of blind existence; nor into a will regenerate, but into will's cessation and the atrophy of life. It may preach the self-redemption of the race instead of its deliverance by God. Man 'sinks into himself to rise redeemed.' Still it has the note if not the truth of redemption, and of an ethical redemption too. It is a deeper depth than Agnosticism, but it is more hopeful. It is what Agnosticism will become when it has had time to work upon the ultimate aspirations of the heart, when the stoicism that goes with it in

England has collapsed, like the ancient Stoicism, to a despair like that of imperial Rome. It is the deeper dark which precedes the dawn, and a promise, like its Latin counterpart, of a new vision of Redemption and a fresh departure in vital faith. The wail of German Pessimism is a more hopeful though a less sturdy thing than the narcotised indifference of English Agnosticism, because there still beats in it a heart, and there still rises a protest, and by the felt greatness of our misery we still know that we are great. Agnosticism at best but leaves room for a religion; it does not, like Pessimism, demand it. It enthrones the merely regulative element in our knowledge, and chains us to the car of law; but Pessimism opens a little way the nature of reality, if only by the key of Art, and declares it to be a will. It sees 'the greatest of miracles, and calls it Revelation'—revelation being the one idea for which Agnosticism has no room, against which it exists to protest.

Though Schopenhauer's Will is not really will, but a misnomer for the great primal impulse or force, yet it is not utterly inaccessible nor unintelligible, but something which man's will may hold terms with, may encounter, accept, renounce, and, at last, destroy.* Surely that can only be done in

* Schopenhauer's system is anything but satisfactory or coherent on the *Ding an sich*. But the point of moment here is, that with his motto, 'No object without a subject,' he strove to escape from the Kantian isolation of this ultimate reality, and from the hypothesis of an entity known to exist but in its nature unknown. Kant's logic is better than Schopenhauer's; but there may be more truth in the latter's inconsistency, as Hegel shows.

the power of a Will beyond will; 'in whose will,' as Dante says, 'is our peace.' There is some saving play for will among the iron meshes of ubiquitous law, and some counter-will, instead of a Great Unknowable, behind all. One comes to deserts where even Pessimism is an oasis, and we are refreshed to know that anything can be known about the nature of the Supreme Power, or that volition has any bearing at all on reality or on the spirit's final fate. Surely in an age when evolution is treated as an entity, and not only recognised but enthroned as a latter-day Fate, the Christian spirit cannot view with entire coldness a creed which so prunes the egotism of the strongest. Pessimism is a protest against the mere naturalism which has no 'word' to preach deeper than development, and no process to hope for higher than amelioration. Its note is redemption rather than evolution. It quells the passion for self-development by the demand for self-renunciation, and it emphasises conversion even more than education. It calls for a total change, and a return upon the line of natural impulse though against its stream. It would evoke the new man, the man that is ready to die in order to promote the cosmic suicide which is its salvation for the world. And it declares that this power can come of no mere regard to worldly ends or worldly helps, but only from co-operation with a great and universal force, though it be but the grace of a dread, dark God. 'The greatest of miracles,' says Wagner, 'for the natural man, is this conversion of the will and the suspension of natural law it involves. What effects this must be, of necessity, something far above nature and of superhuman power, since union with it is the one thing desired and striven for. Jesus called it to His poor the Kingdom of God, in contrast with the kingdom of the world. And when the weary and heavy laden, the pained and persecuted, the patient and meek, the benefactors of enemies and the lovers of all were called, it was their heavenly Father that called them to Him—the Father, whose Son Jesus was sent to those who were His brothers. We see in this the greatest of miracles, and call it Revelation.' A Fall, Redemption, Conversion, Renunciation, a Cross, and a Regeneration, as conditions of salvation—there is some echo here which might come kindly home to a Christian heart too firmly fixed in its everlasting seat of faith to be intimidated by the negations that lurk behind. Most of our poverty in theological sympathy comes from terror; terror itself is mainly the result of our own insecurity; and we are insecure because we are ignorant, because we know but faintly the real ground of what it is our social fashion to prize deeply. If we become really acquainted with this bogey of atheistic Pessimism, there is a certain spell and grandeur about its vision of doom and its strain of redemption which are sometimes lacking in current Christian conceptions of life or hope. There is a sympathetic quality in its renunciatory ethics which our popular Christianity has not yet learnt. It is a philosophic Jobiad, rising from amid a unique material civilisation in which the soul is captive to the gross and selfish world, as the immortal Hebrew poem rose to set forth 'a Babylonian woe'—the captivity of the people of the soul to the brute forces of a godless empire. It is a Jobiad of disaster, despair, and defiance; but with a true ethical instinct, a dim, fixed consciousness of the one right way, and (must we not hope?) with an impending theophany, as in the Hebrew poem, revealing to current and conventional religion a universe and a destiny grander than its traditional creeds have known. And it is more Christian, perhaps, and profitable, to view these pessimistic systems not as eviscerated Christianity, but as surcharged and yearning Humanity, passionate prayers whose answer is the self-revelation of God, and mighty shadows whose substance is Christ.

IV

WAGNER'S affinity for Pessimism is a phenomenon which suggests much. It sets us to inquire by what independent path the poet divined those views of life and destiny which the sage also formed and systematised. It is an inquiry, indeed, which is suggested by many of the representatives of continental art and thought. They are not borrowers, nor all of them learners, from each other. They are, to a very large extent, independent symptoms of a complicated and serious state of things both in the social relations and the spiritual condition of Europe. Even in robust England, a writer like

George Eliot escapes pessimism by a hope and faith sufficient only to be personal to herself, and which she cannot convey to most of those whose misgiving she can so successfully raise. In Wagner's case several answers to the inquiry occur. His keenness and volume of emotion were combined with an apostolic mission on behalf of the progress of Art. Remarks already made in connection with Rossetti are quite applicable here. Wagner did for music a work parallel to what the Pre-Raphaelites did for painting, and both met with the most embittered opposition, and were brought literally to the verge of starvation in their warfare. Nothing but the most titanic energy and indomitable courage could have come through the struggle. Wagner was a Luther of Art. But conflicts of the kind do not tend to print upon the warriors the most genial view of life, or much admiration for the arrangement of it, in the absence of real, supernatural Christian faith. Again, there is much in life in all ages to force pessimism on one endowed for a tragic artist, as Wagner was. The tragic genius, even in the genial Shakespere, has always felt that there was over man a fate rather than a God. In our own poet, indeed, it is a fate less inhumane than in paganism, with some solemn echo of reconciliation, and some vague promise that our bark sinks but to another sea. But it is fate still. The heroic figure is shown off against it. He or she draws our sympathies away from it, as nothing which reveals a God must ever do. And the tragic fascination lies in the pity and awe of rich and ardent hearts crushed by some sublime, inaccessible, unfeeling, not to say blundering, power. Wagner's tragic genius did not escape from the spell which pessimism always has for such moral sensibility. And in the imaginative aspect of systematic Pessimism there is no small fascination of the sort which gathers about the Pantheism of Spinoza, only more passionate in its gloom, as it is more positive in its attitude to the experiences of life and the history of the heart. There is much grandeur in the spectacle of the dark, blind, labouring will that tumbles in the godless deep, and in 'a grey, void, lampless, deep, unpeopled world' welters big with human fate. And there is no small pathos in the blundering of this power into the fashion of a world of pain and error which it cannot redeem, from which, indeed, it must be redeemed. The most tragic of all philosophies has much to commend it to one of the most tragic of all poets. But it should be remarked that, if Wagner's Fate is less genial than Shakespere's, it is perhaps less omnipotent. In his last work, as we shall see, written after he had come into contact with philosophic Pessimism, he seems to have been profoundly impressed with its idea of redemption. He seizes on that idea with all his poetic and religious passion. He makes more of it than his philosophy could ever have done. And his Parsifal is not only a hero and fate-defier, but something which Shakespere, not having the religious genius, has not—a redeemer. So much may be said, while it is at the same time remembered that it is a redemption, not *to* God, but *from* all the elements which the heart can associate with God. Indeed, like some of the ultra forms of Calvinism published by some anachronist and popular preachers, it appears to be a redemption of God no less than man from a chronic disability which He is Himself powerless to overcome.

But, above all, perhaps, one should remember, in accounting for Wagner's pessimism, the saying of Ruskin about Turner and the pleasure he sometimes took in low colours. It was 'because he had in him the wonder and sorrow concerning life and death which are the inheritance of the Gothic soul from the days of its first sea-kings.' That is the feature of the Teutonic race which emerged in Wagner. It murmurs in the German mystics before the Reformation, sighs in the strain of sadness which runs even through English literature, and protests in the philosophic Pessimism of which we speak. But especially is it the feature of a literature in which Wagner was steeped to the lips, and which he has helped to re-create for our modern mind—the mighty and heroic literature of Teutonic antiquity. It was not, to be sure, its pessimism only that drew Wagner to the Edda. Myth served his purpose for a deeper reason, which he thus explains:—'I was led to select the "Mythos" as the ideal subject-matter for the poet. The myth is that primitive poem of the people which we find at all times taken up and treated anew by the great poets of cultured periods; for in it those conventional forms of human relations, explicable only to abstract reason, almost entirely disappear, and in their place stands that which is always intelligible because it is so purely human, and because of its inimitable concrete form.' These myths Wagner brought into living and unforced connection with modern problems, and with the deep ideal side of modern Christianity. He clothed them in the garb of *the* art which is distinctively modern, ideal, and Christian—Music. And for this purpose he developed to an unparalleled pitch the specially Christian element in music—the element to which colour corresponds in painting—the polyphonic harmony which he describes himself as the invention of the Christian spirit. But at the same time no one can read the Eddas, and certainly no one can study them, without being impressed with the vast and bitter gloom of their mythological world. All and more than all the cruel and dismal climate against which our semi-barbarous forefathers were so scantily protected, all the huge terror of storm and sea, of the long winter and the long nights, all the courage of their reckless hearts, foiled and crushed by the apathy of a pitiless and eccentric Power, are embodied in the sublime and cruel pessimism of the Eddic creed. Passion, daimonic and elemental, stalks large, and by its side illusion goes, shedding a deep pathos on the whole torrent of blood and tangle of thought. Honour, courage, craft, and hate, in men and gods alike, move under blind doom to slaughter and wreck, and love seems only sealed for blight and the blotting out of all. In these poems and legends Wagner took a national pride. He found in them much of the national spirit, and they fitted the nationalism of his art. He revived them, moreover, in a day when the successes of united Germany revived the memory of its forefathers' titanic feats, but when the burden of armaments was grinding into distress whole masses of the population, masses whom the corruption of the creeds had robbed of the support of faith, by making stale or incredible the one Gospel of Redemption. The inward pessimism of the ancient creed returned along with its outward prowess, and together they seemed not quite alien to the situation of the hour. It is in the *Nibelungenring* that Wagner has embodied and resuscitated the heroes of the Edda, and it is there that his pessimism first becomes conspicuous and splendid. When he wrought on the later and more Christian cycle of legends, as in *Tannhäuser* or *Lohengrin*, it was much qualified, even suppressed. And in his closing work, *Parsifal*, we have the two streams flowing together into a pessimism both holier and hopefuller than anything in Schopenhauer, and of a more ethical stamp than is to be found in the *Nibelungenring*.

V

ANOTHER need also sent Wagner to the lucid and apparently logical view of the world offered by Schopenhauer. As his music, growing more tragic, grew more religious, he came to feel the need of something like a theology. His mind was too powerful to permit him to be a mere sentimentalist. He felt the necessity which so many of our leading spirits feel as they recognise that in discarding the theological systems of the universe, they have discarded all system of a profound and quite universal stamp. He felt the need (to the pietist so gratuitous) of an intellectual universe. 'We cannot help remarking,' he says, 'to what moral and spiritual impotence we have sunk for the want of a correct, profound, and all-comprehensive theory of the nature of the world.' Nor can *we* help remarking that we have quite an aching sense of the truth of this observation. Like many another of his countrymen, he was fascinated by the indisputable genius, the admirable and suggestive divination, and the decided style of Schopenhauer, who was as impatient as the public of the laborious and patient calculus of scientific metaphysics whereby alone the great result must be attained. So he continues with more questionable truth — 'Schopenhauer's philosophy must, in every respect, be made the foundation of all further culture, moral and spiritual.' Schopenhauer he regarded as the great deliverer of the world from the 'Judaic idea of God,' which for so many centuries had been suffocating the whole Christian world. The Jewish notion of prohibitory law, the repressive commandment of 'Thou shalt not,' had for the most part only been riveted afresh upon mankind by a Church which professed to be founded on Gospel.

Both philosopher and poet fail to see that the Jewish notion of law is not mere prohibition. It is a notion to which we have as yet only partially attained in our public affairs, and which is the spring of political freedom. The law was for the Jew a 'covenant.' It was not a despotic imposition as in other Oriental lands. It was a treaty. It won its force only by its acceptance by the people. It rested, like Calvin's severest politics, on the consent of the governed. But let that rest. Neither poets nor even philosophers are always quite safe theologians or historians. Let us continue the exposition. The real, positive commandment, the liberating and inspiring element contained in the very idea of the Gospel—namely, Love—had, by the Church especially, been neglected. As early as *Tannhäuser*, Wagner represents the Church as having sunk below the true intuition and stewardship of Christian ideas which are so justly demanded by the soul that they are ministered to it by God over the head of the very Pope. The redeeming power of the Christian commandment had hardly been seriously tried upon history. 'What is our whole civilisation being wrecked upon,' he truly asks, 'but on the want of Love?' 'The lovelessness of the world is its real sorrow.' Caution and mistrust are our earliest and deepest lessons, instead of compassion and the ministries which mitigate or avert our neighbours' pain. The source of this loveless pain is selfish passion — the passion to assert ourselves, to live, to desire, to enjoy. From this desire and passion we must withdraw by the one pure and needful knowledge springing from renunciatory love, to which is revealed the real moral significance of the world. To this gospel there is no such help as 'a wise use' of Schopenhauer. There we learn (in Wagner's words) that 'the only redeeming Christian love is the love which springs from pity, and acts in pity, even to the entire destruction of self-will. In this love, Faith and Hope are fully included. Faith is a consciousness, secure, confirmed beyond doubt by the divinest example, of that moral significance of the world. Hope is the blessed knowledge how impossible it is that such consciousness should be put to shame.' Were the views of the great philosopher's essay on 'The Apparent Want of Purpose in the Fate of the Individual' made really popular (he continues), what a grand meaning would be given to the perverted and common notion of an Eternal Providence! How the despairing would be delivered into a really spiritual idealism from the terrors of the Church and from the flat Atheism of the physicists and chemists! What was to be the great agency for popularising these truths? Art, and, above all, Music, says the philosopher; and with him the artist cordially agrees. He makes a proviso, however—'We must lay our fundamental account for this. All true impulse, and all the power which completely qualifies us to carry out the great Regeneration of the race, can take root only in the deep soil of a genuine religion.'

'When Religion has grown artificial,' he says, with half truth, 'it is for Art to save the kernel of it. Art takes the mythic symbols, which Religion will insist on believing as they stand, and gives them their value as symbols. It sets them forth in ideal fashion, and makes us feel deep-hidden in their heart the truth so unspeakably divine.' These were the agencies to lift the Soul above space and time into the spiritual world, and help it on to pure redemption and peace. This art of religious music was the noblest legacy to us of the Christian Church, teaching mankind a new sense of the Infinite and a new language for its passion to be redeemed. Without stopping to disentangle the truth from the error and rhapsody of such passages, we may remark that no musician—probably no artist of any kind—has ever realised as Wagner did in his own way the moral depth and sting of this need of redemption, in the sense of a total conversion of the soul and deliverance of the race from a universal burden and unspeakable curse. It meant much more than relief from felt pains or disabilities. It was something more universal, spiritual, and solemn than the conquest of certain vices. It was more in the nature of a new creation and a new heart for mankind. 'The most simple and moving of all the confessions which unite us for the common exhibition of our faith, what comes to us from the tragic teachings of great spirits with perennial freshness, and lifts us to a compassionate exaltation, is our sense, in the most various forms, of the need, the passion for Redemption. And we believe we are made partakers in it in that sacred hour when all the shows and forms of the world fall from us in our divining dream. No more, then, are we harassed by the vision of that yawning abyss, those gruesome forms and monsters of the deep, all the sickly misbirths of the self-lacerating Will, which the daylight we call human history presents to us. Pure, peaceable, and making for peace, do we then hear the groaning of the creature, void of fear, and full of hope, all-healing, and redemptive of the world. The Soul of Mankind, joining in this groan, and by it brought to know its high vocation to redeem its whole fellow-sufferer, Nature, soars from the abyss of forms and shows. And, released from the horrible sources of incessant birth and death, the restless Will feels freed from the Self in which it was bound.'

It is doubtful if any artist since the great mediæval painters has worked under such a sense of the redemptive idea as Wagner. I again avoid entering on a serious discussion of the ethical or theological defects of these views. It would be easy to assail pity as a sufficient basis for social morality. Many who are swift to compassion are slow to righteousness. It is one thing to feel deeply a brother's woe, and another to apply the stern self-scrutiny which admits his rights, or the self-control which withholds the instant though useless help. Something else than pity is needed to guide pity, and something more real than an emotion must be the ground of action on the large and beneficent scale. One whole sex which is very prompt to pity is much less amenable to considerations of general justice. Pity ends in philanthropy, which is well, but is far from all, either for the state or the race. It would be no less easy to make the creed of a man like Schopenhauer ridiculous (especially to a public which begins with an amused contempt for the philosophers), by allusions to his personal life. We are not embarked, however, on an estimate of the system, nor on a polemic against it. We are more concerned with the better spirit and true inspiration of these views, with their ideal rather than with their dogmatic aspect, with that which impelled the protest they make rather than with the form such protest assumes. We are tracing the influence of the system on a great genius and artist whose instinct led him to seize rather on its affirmations than its negations, and its aspect of enlargement rather than of depression for human life. Ever since the Reformation we have owed as much to the philosophers and to the men of genius as to the theologians for our amplest and sublimest views of God and destiny. Doubtless a time has dawned when the theologians shall be worthy of theology, and shall learn a new freedom and fascination in serving theology rather than the sects. But while this good time is on the way let us learn wherever strong teaching is to be found, and yield us to the spell of the Lord wherever His Spirit breathes. Art which is saturated with Christian ideas and aspirations cannot be quite outside the kingdom of heaven, even if it misread some of the Christian realities. It may surely be called Christian art which is pervaded by the thought that the world groans, being burdened, that it yearns to a possible and promised deliverance, that its emancipation is by the Eternal Love whose wisdom is the secret of redemptive death. Such a gospel, however incomplete, need not be regarded as utterly hostile to the Christian Cross, in which these things are complete. There is no thought so fascinating, so imperious, so immortal, so essential to either humanity or religion, as this thought of Redemption. The creed of the future will be the creed which shall make it most of a power and a fact. And if Art in its last great scene is dominated by the motive of Redemption, it will combine with a large science, inscribed Reconciliation, to provide a view of life and the world in which the true religion of Salvation shall not feel uneasy or strange.

In his most creative work, it has already been said, Wagner was much more than a Pessimist. With more human nature in his genius than Schopenhauer, he felt more of the part that sin plays in human tragedies, and more of the heart's mastery of fate. He had a holier vision of Redemption, as he had a poet's higher sense of the dignity and sanctity of love. The most unsatisfactory thing in Schopenhauer—in his system as in his life—is his treatment of love. Those gritty chapters in which he deals with that supreme form of the passion to live are quite below the really imaginative power with which the blind, grand, and terrible Force is described as working its tragic blundering way through the tangle of things. And the finer spirit of Hartmann is little more successful. This is a region where the resources of philosophic Pessimism are exhausted and its system shattered on facts. The world of the soul's experience is a world too wide for its shrunk shanks. But it is just here, where the pessimist ends, that the artist begins. Love, in philosophical Pessimism, does not really conquer death. In Wagner it does—if not always in theory yet always like 'King Lear' in the æsthetic effect. The last darkness—and he makes it dark enough—is glorified and warmed by a passion of persistent and all-commanding love, which never lets us go without the sense that salvation hovers about the blackest woe and the most dismal confusion of failure. The dawn of redemption is not far behind the Twilight of the Gods. Even in the Edda, the Götterdämmerung is but the prelude to the return of the nobler gods; and the wreck in Wagner's *Nibelungenring* makes room for the restoration in *Parsifal*. The fall of Walhalla is the collapse of the old apotheosis of lawless power and loveless will. Wotan is blind arbitrary elemental will, will cut off from wisdom or even intelligence. He sinks with his world, as all such systems must. But love is not of his world. Love is the intelligence for whose lack is shattered the brute, blundering will. To Schopenhauer love was but the most powerful form of this blind and doomed will. To Wagner it was the light which gave eyes to will, and redeemed it from its fatal bias and curse. It was not the bloom on the decaying fruit; it was the dawn of a new day, the breath that woke the world to a new hope. The beautiful light which, on the stage, is directed upon Isolde as she sings the song of endless love and its renunciations amid the ruins of all love's delights, is the outward sign of that prophetic halo with which love invests and redeems the world where it perishes. And the last lines of the *Nibelungen-ring* sound like a Scripture, and one reads them over and over and over again with new delight and cheer.

VI

THERE is one point of singular affinity, I have said, between Pessimism and Christianity. It is the way in which each is drawn to the art of Music as specially congenial to its soul and dream.

Music is the art which owes most to Christianity, which is by pre-eminence the æsthetic fruit of Christianity, and which lends itself most readily and universally to Christian uses. 'As Christianity,' says Wagner, 'arose from under the universal civilisation of Rome [and its pessimism], so from the chaos of our modern civilisation [and its pessimism] Music bursts forth; both affirm "our kingdom is not of this world." That is to say—we come from within, you from without; we spring from the essential nature of things, you from their semblance.' Pessimism is the inevitable result of mere phenomenalism, mere externalism, practical or theoretical; and Music and Christianity are so far akin that it is by their inward way that the escape is to be found. It must be a spiritual escape; and it is within us, in the soul's own nature and constitution, that we must find the objective which the outward world cannot give, or gives but to crush us and not to sustain. To look, indeed, for the same effects from an art as from a faith would be worse than unwise. If we are only hampered by outward law or social fashion, Music may open to us a freer world. But it will hardly extract the sting of the world, or heal the soul's wounds when pierced by the world's spear. And if our bondage is yet deeper, if we are crushed by the weight and sin of our own selves, and if we crave some inspiration to give us staying power against self for the large and active life of humanity, we shall have to seek a deeper Redemption and a mightier Saviour than any art. Still, it may be useful to note that the inward Christian faith cleaves with special tenderness to the art most inward in its tone.

But it is also Music that forms the chosen ritual of such religion as Pessimism has. Through Music, says that creed, our will flows directly into reconciliation with the Will which is universal reality, and we grasp the nature of real being which is denied to every kind of perceptive knowledge. In Music our mind does not perceive, our being contemplates, our very soul joins the over-soul, and our individuality is lost for the time. This art is one of the great channels of access which Pessimism has from the soul of man to the vast elemental power which labours in all things, which aches in all conscious being, but which loses its sting in the clairvoyance of æsthetic delight. The other channel, and a greater, is asceticism.

In the system of Schopenhauer the wild egotism of the individual must be trained first to submit itself with all its intelligence to the demands of the Universal Will, and consciously to do what that does unconsciously. Thus we get an Ethic of Renunciation based on compassion for all others who are also under the curse of this self-assertive will to live. But the will to live, which is the ground of all existence, is itself a blunder and a curse, which must be undone, renounced, and destroyed. Suicide is no real renunciation of that will. It is not life but the passion for life that must be destroyed; and suicide may only come from the disappointment, not the extinction, of this self-assertive force. It can be exterminated only by a certain spiritual discipline. And a man should live on to further by every self-denying effort the time when all conscious beings will accept his creed, and agree to *work* the curse of existence out of the race. Hence beyond the ethics of renunciation we have the religion of redemption. It is the hope and discipline towards the hour when the will to live ceases altogether in a man, 'when he has severed the thousand threads of the will which bind us to the world and draw us hither and thither in constant pain under the form of desire, fear, envy, or anger'—in a word, when he has entered the Nirvâna of pure will-less, formless being. Now, according to the æsthetics of Pessimism, it is this state of salvation which we have in purest foretaste in the brief and passing enjoyment of Art. 'True Art,' says Wagner, 'can prosper only on a foundation of true morality, and I find it, indeed, entirely one with true religion.' It is not so much that Art redeems as that it sustains us with the dream and the earnest of redemption. And especially does Pessimism find its religious purposes served by the art of Music. Some of the best things ever said on the philosophy and function of Art in general, and Music in particular, have been said by Schopenhauer. Music copies nothing. It is not an art of imitation. It is not, like a picture, the shadow of a shade, the reflection of phenomena which are themselves but shadows of reality. It is a direct expression of the great underlying will-reality, 'an image of the will itself.' 'It never expresses phenomena, but solely the inner being, the essence of phenomena, the will itself.' It is not an interpretation of ideas. The ideas are themselves but a reflection of reality, and Music stands independently on the same footing. Both approach reality, but from opposite sides and with unequal facility. Music is 'the most direct and immediate objectivation of the will.' It expresses most clearly and truly the inmost nature of things. It answers, as nothing else could, Faust's question, 'Wo fass' ich dich unendliche Natur?' 'The world,' says Schopenhauer, 'is embodied music as well as embodied will.' 'It reveals the most secret sense of scenes or things'—a phrase which we may remember when we come to observe Wagner's use of music less as an end in itself than as a spiritual commentary on the course of dramatic action and thought. Again, 'the composer reveals the inmost and essential being of the world, and expresses the profoundest wisdom in a language his reason does not understand.'

Amongst the movements of thought which have discarded the religions without ceasing to be religious, Pessimism is not alone in finding in Art a cultus to its mind. But it is singular in the supreme position it assigns to Music among the arts, and in the affinity it discovers between the soul of music and its own. The reasons are not far to seek. Pessimism finds in music, with the vague grandeur of its rolling mists, its unsubstantial pageant, and its brief utterance closed at either end by a silence and rounded with a sleep, a fit symbol, and indeed a fragment, of its blind, short, mighty, and tragic world. Schopenhauer describes a symphony of Beethoven's as '*rerum concordia discors,* a true and complete image of the essential nature of the world that rolls on in the boundless complication of countless shapes, and supports itself by constant destruction.' And there is this further reason. No art has such resources as Music for the expression of sorrow. It is the art of pure feeling; and mere feeling, emphasised apart from its object, is mere subjectivity, which is a disease, and constantly gravitates to pain. And when sorrow takes the range and the command of a whole sensitive world, when mankind becomes, in the absence of a real God for its object, the victim of a weary subjectivity and its woe, it seems as if nothing but the great art of pure feeling were adapted to give due utterance to the cosmic ache. In Pessimism feeling has got the better of thought and action, and the basis of morality is compassion. The whole system has more to do with the experience of life in an overcrowded and unbelieving world than with the principles of a Reason which reveals the great ground and goal of life. In Music the relation of thought and feeling is the same. 'Music is a woman,' says Wagner; and feeling is, and must be, the element of it all. In Music, accordingly, Pessimism finds congenial expression, and not only so, but direct access to that irrational Will which is the impulse in all impulse, from the first elemental passions to the noblest hold upon life. In Music, however, this awful Will, or universal *nisus*, emerges with its usual concomitant of pain in abeyance. 'The unutterably tender and heartfelt quality of all music, by virtue of which it touches us—a paradise quite familiar yet ever distant, quite appreciable yet so inexplicable—rests on this, that it reproduces all the emotions of our inmost being, but without actuality and far from its pain.' That is to say, in fine and familiar words, Pessimism, with its laden heart and its Nihilist destiny, takes to music because it is offered there 'a painless sympathy with pain'; because it is a philosophy based upon feeling rather than reason, and upon thought more than concrete action; because its mode of feeling is so Buddhist and subjective that it sympathises rather with pain and failure than with order and joy; and because it finds in music the joy of emotion without its curse, and—shall we add?—its pleasure without its sympathy. How can a pleasure truly humane and sympathetic be had without the price of sorrow which real sympathy must pay in a world like this? It is to be feared that this philosophy of renunciation works round in the end by its atheism to the inevitable moral result of atheism, a refined but no less deadly egotism. Negative ethics and sentimental ethics alike rebound into a very cruel and positive selfishness. The escape into beauty and its ritual of refined emotion detaches the sympathies from unpleasant contact with our brother's need. The Pessimist cultus of beauty goes to war with its *askesis* of philanthropy, its worship with its moral discipline in saintship. Art becomes more of an individual enjoyment than a social bond; æsthetic religion is here, as usual, a selfish religion, with a bias to the morbid, not to say the mean. And redemption without the Redeemer becomes a release, not by love, but from love, from the only thing whose nature and property it is ever to redeem.

VII

DOUBTLESS there is a strong element of pessimism in Christianity, which has received undue emphasis in the old theologies of Manicheanism, and of total depravity. But it is only an element. There is one principle in Christianity which separates it by an impassable gulf from every form of Pessimism as a system of things. And it is this. We can never know things at their worst till we stand where they are at their best. The worst of it is our sin; and that we can never realise till we have got the better of it in Christ, till we have made the best of it in God. It is only as we share the Redemption by Christ that we know what Redemption is. Nor can we know that without gaining thereby a due knowledge of the horror from which we are redeemed. The moral horror of sin is more horrible than the extremes of suffering; and the disorder of it is more dismal than the aimless welter of a world that simply blunders upon mishap. There is much to appal the imagination in the spectacle of a stumbling universe which has hopelessly missed the happy way. There is plenty there to fascinate the genius of tragedy and the morality of compassion. But more terrible than a blundering universe is a will which has taken evil for its good, and more inveterate than ancient error is ingrained sin. And how inveterate it is, and how terrible, can be known to none but Him who has overcome it, and in whom we are more than conquerors. Earth's darkness comes home but to heaven's light. The worst can be realised only by the best. Everything less than the best is the poorer by just so much in the sympathy that makes deep knowledge of man's estate possible. Only from God's height can we sound man's depth; and nothing seems so bad as the thought of what we ought to have been, when we think in the light of what God's grace has made us to be. Earth's darkest shadows are cast in the light of the Lord, but we do not see them till the Lord is our Light. How far we have gone astray we cannot tell till we walk in the living Way. Our great salvation is our worst condemnation. It is a thin and fickle optimism which has not come to its rest by a real conflict with serious pessimism. But it is also a pessimism comparatively superficial which is not viewed from the optimism of an eternal hope. We are not as bad as we might be while we can imagine anything worse. And the imagination for the utmost evil is possible only to Him who is the perfect Good in human shape. This is what Christ claimed to be; and He never was this more truly than when He deprecated a goodness severed from total dependence on God. But it is what the gentle Buddha never claimed, however much his devoted disciples have thrust it upon him. He was but the sweetest prophet of 'the Way.' The Way himself he was not. And this may be the reason for Buddhistic pessimism, as for the new Pessimism of the West. Christianity is not pessimistic, because it has the Holy One of God for its Redeemer, because it measures the world from the side of

Him who by His purity not only pointed the way to destroy sin, but in His self-conquest really destroyed it, and only in destroying it revealed its horror and depth. Buddhism is pessimistic because it has not the conquest but only instructions for it. It is, after all, but an ethical school; and if we have but ethics with which to meet the evil that is in the world, we may readily enough, when we deal with actual life as positively as Schopenhauer did, fall into the despair which identifies evil with existence, and can end the one only by ending the other. But it is a view of Redemption which as it curtails the span belittles the dignity of Humanity, and so reduces its faith in itself as to chill the power of moral effort. Were such the general estimate of life there would not be left in men enough moral grit for the *askesis* required to work out even so poor a salvation. We should be 'half dead to know that we should die.' But we should not have vigour enough to live ourselves quite dead, or deny ourselves back into the negation of existence. It is taken for granted too in this system that sin does not destroy our power over existence, and paralyse in us the very ability to end itself by ending ourselves. But even the pessimist, when he thinks of it, will not credit the sinner with enhanced power over Being, with becoming to an increased extent by his sin the lord of life. Had the power to terminate our existence been a gift of our innocent life, it would have been one of the first gifts for sin to take away; and were we mortal in our ideal state, it would be much more like sin to damn us to the eternal torment of a dread immortality by robbing us of the power of ceasing to be. To be sure, it is not sin but ascetic virtue that is supposed to work the great Nirvâna. But, in the absence of a superhuman Redeemer, what is to feed the vigour for such virtue in a Humanity whose own recuperative power would just be the thing standing in the way of its extinction? And how a world of total blunder can yield a sure method of final bliss it is hard to see—as hard as to think a man redeemable if he is by nature in total depravity. Of the two Calvinisms the old is the better. It crushed man by the holiness of God, but the Holy God was the Deliverer. There may have been an unreconciled dualism in its thought, but there was a practical reconciliation in its effects. It saw a worse world, though not a sorer, than pessimism sees; it felt the guilt more, if it felt the ache less. But it was because it closed all with a greater glory, and looked down upon all from a greater height. It was an exceeding glory which made affliction light and for a moment; but it did not make light of sin. It convicted the world of it, and drove home its exceeding sinfulness. One need be no Calvinist to recognise that it is less Calvin than Paul that speaks there, and Paul as the oracle of Christ.

Pessimism is no true scheme of existence; but it is, perhaps, the truest system of godless existence, and more than Positivism is the positive system befitting a Monism which is realistic but only humane. It is both an inevitable and a valuable protest on the soul's part in an age of unexampled material prosperity, where the greed of happiness is even more eager than the race for wealth. In turning the world into an illusion it has done something to make us realise the real but less sweeping influence of illusion in the education of the world. And it adds a deeper note to the great chord of the Cross, and a new chastening to the glory of its close.

WAGNER'S 'PARSIFAL'

I

Probably no work of Wagner's gives such an overwhelming impression of his many-sided genius as *Parsifal.* Nowhere are we shown in such combination his powers of imposing spectacle, of pure poetry, of philosophic thought, of imaginative passion, of solemn religion, and a dramatic action and characterisation, full of pity, terror, truth, and grandeur. Nothing like *Parsifal,* upon the whole, has been seen, either in art or religion, since the Greek tragedians awed and melted Athens by lyric dramas which were at the same time religious functions. And only once before in the history of Christendom, namely, among the great Italian painters, have Christian ideas (as distinct from doctrines) taken such imperious possession of first-rate art; nor from any art have they ever received such an exposition.

Parsifal is not an opera, but a much more serious matter. Its author would not have it called by that name; nor would he allow it to go upon stages profaned for the most part to the amusement of the natural man and his—wife. Its representation is almost a religious occasion. Great as the art in it is, it is not the mere art that is greatest. The impression is, in the composer's intent, a religious one first of all. We are easily reminded of the Oberammergau spectacle. Both are passion plays, and they cost a pilgrimage apiece. The leading theme of each is Redemption—in the one in historic form, in the other ideal. And at each the true Catholicism may deepen its sense of the Divine Deliverance, and realise with a new hush the tragic awe, pathos, and power of the abiding and searching Cross.

It has been already pointed out how deeply Wagner's genius was imbued with what may be described by the convenient, if somewhat pedantic, term of the theologians as the anthropology of the Cross. It is in *Parsifal* that these ideas have been worked out to the clearest and most religious expression. With the exception of the *Messiah*, perhaps, we have here the greatest Redemption music in the world. It is something beyond what we mean by Passion-Music. And it is more modern, more inward, more psychological than the *Messiah*. It is not more profound than the *Messiah* God-ward, but it is Man-ward. It is not more simple in the great ideal themes. Nothing could be more simple and sublime than a work which adheres so closely as the *Messiah* to the words and thoughts of Scripture. Neither is it more of a marvel in its special art. None admired more than Wagner the contrapuntal grandeur of Handel, or his moving and immortal melody. But *Parsifal* is less theological; and while it loses accordingly in objectivity, and so in power, it is more concrete, searching, humane, and dramatic in its prosecution of the Redemptive idea. It is not so much a message from the delivering God as a representation of deliverance in man's soul. It is the soul singing its own deadly sins, its own mortal agony, and its own regenerate beauty. Wagner sang one side of the truth, 'Work out your own salvation'; Handel sang the other, 'For it is God that worketh in you.'

With the music it is not my province chiefly to deal. I venture, rather, to offer some close account of the poem, its movement, and its idea. It is an undertaking not without risk. Wagner's music is so thoroughly an atmosphere for his thought that to present the thought alone may seem like lifting a fine seaweed from the pool in whose waters only it floated lovely and free. Yet his thought is not mere musical thought. It is not like the soul of a Sonata. It does not lie in such complete solution in the music that verbal expression of it is impossible. Nor is it inseparable from the music, like the moss in an agate. The poem was composed first, and the music came next in strict subordination and commentary. And it may be possible, even in literary form, to present the thought with some pale but not false reflection of the unearthly air that breathes around it on the Bayreuth stage.

It would be interesting (and in any account of Wagner's mind necessary) to trace the development of his ideas through the series of his works, especially in the *Nibelungenring* and *Tristan* to their culmination in *Parsifal.* To some extent this has already been done, and more is not possible here and now.

It may, however, be permitted to recall how the omnipotence of love as a redemption from fate, and of sacrificial renunciation as the deliverance from sin, becomes increasingly the centre and source of Wagner's tragic interest. The love, too, of the central figures undergoes in its nature a detachment and purification which are made perfect and radiant at the close of the series in *Parsifal.* The renunciatory function of love becomes more and more striking in the ascending scale of Siegfried, Tristan, Parsifal, and Kundry. The self-negation which was forced upon the two former is accepted by the two latter. It is Tristan's fate, but it is Parsifal's mission and inspiration. Parsifal represents in reconciliation those forces of love and power which in previous works had been in tragic collision. And it is further notable that, while in *Parsifal* Wagner returns upon the motive of sin, and that redemption from sin, rather than from fate, which played so striking a part in *Tannhäuser*, the release is not in the final drama a mere absolution received from without, but has become a real regeneration worked out through spiritual process within. *Tannhäuser* exhibits an absolution from sin's guilt, but *Parsifal* displays the eradication of its power in human nature.*

* Wagner is held up as the great representative of 'the Christian culture of the German nation.' He is certainly more Christian than either Goethe or Schiller. But it may be as well, even at the risk of repeating from the former essay, to say that one uses the word Christian here in something far short of its complete sense. Wagner is Christian in his ideas but not in his faith. His anthropology is Christian, but his theology is not. His culture, like that of his age and nation, is more Christian than his creed. His is a Christian atheism which is simply an inevitable revolt from some too popular forms of atheistic Christianity.

The legend of the Grail has long had a fascination for the religious side of artistic genius. To Tennyson it appeals on its ethical side. The English wisdom and greatness of Arthur lie in the self-knowledge and self-control with which he refuses to follow the mystic vision and traverse the dread soul-history of those who do. But Arthur, like his race, is spiritually incurious. It is this very soul-history that attracts Wagner. It is a fearful and forbidding road that the knights of the Grail must traverse, and to him who would be their king, and rise above the hero to the saviour, the horror and the glory are alike inevitable and unspeakable. The whole bold uniqueness of *Parsifal* is due to the fact

We have George Eliot described as Christian in the same way, but with, perhaps, less justice. What Pessimism was to Wagner, Positivism was to her. Wagner, however, had all the advantage that Pessimism confers by its sympathy with metaphysics, psychology, and passion, and by its protest (though not antagonism) against mere physical science. It has a larger soul-world. Positivism injured George Eliot's genius by steadily 'wearing' her, as a dog 'wears' a flock, off greener pastures into scientific pedantry. It is a philosophy too meagre, too anti-psychological for the range and quality of her imagination. It has too little of the awful tragic background supplied by Pessimism to the moral imagination. Its sole inspiration is ethical, and its ethics are more scientific than effective, more true than powerful, more sanguine than redemptive. The Pessimist has more heart than the Positivist. His ethics are based on compassion. He is more in tune with the surging passion and dismal failures of the soul. He is more briskly alive to the pathos and tragedy of human life. He is as appalled at the spectacle of disorder as the Positivist is fascinated with the reign of order in human things. He is less political and more spiritual than the Positivist. Some of the great Christian doctrines mean more to him. He starts, like Christianity, from a Fall, and he ends, with Christianity, in a Redemption. Into both these terms he reads ideas more truly Christian than the Positivist. He finds in them more play for his spiritual imagination. His philosophy leads to more searching of heart, and more analysis of spirit. Wagner's close psychological development of passion would have been impossible to that the central figure is set forth not as a hero merely but as a saviour, and the epic of his life is not moral only but imaginatively spiritual, with passages of Christian heart-history that can be uttered by the Christian art of music alone. There is a message for the spirit of Wagner which does not come from either Shakespere or Goethe. He has an echo of reconciliation and a presentiment of unearthly peace which flow from the New Testament and its humilities as surely as Goethe's calm flowed from the stoic self-sufficiencies of Rome and Greece. Philosophic Pessimism is transcended and left behind in the truer inspiration of the artist's genius. He is led by the Spirit out of that wilderness. For no world is the worst possible which

him on the lines of a philosophy which, like Comte's, makes so light of psychology as to deny its scientific possibility. No system which excludes psychology can attract a genius with such mastery of passion as Wagner. It is only some lack of soul that can discard some science of soul. Positivism had begun to pinch George Eliot's genius in her later works, but Pessimism shows no such effect upon Wagner, though he was more deeply committed to his system than she to hers. This may indeed be the very reason for the difference. Wagner may have been sustained by Pessimism as a *system*, while George Eliot was chilled by Positivism as a mere *atmosphere* with a lower temperature than her own. Be that as it may, though his philosophy was as untheistic as hers, its anthropology was of a richer, more ardent, sublime, and imaginative type. The Christian ideas, first shaped by theologians of the heart, were, to him, more fascinating, eloquent, and imperishable. His genius and his heart were Christian in a deeper, warmer sense than was possible to George Eliot with her more jejune creed. The figure of Christ (on which, we have seen, Wagner once sketched a drama), had a fascination for him, and a spiritual meaning, imperfect as we should regard it, which is in striking contrast with the dull dismissal of him from the calendar of Positivist saints. It was by a reaction to realism that Wagner thought to regenerate Art, but it was a realism far more humane, more exalted, and comprehensive, than the empirical realism which calls itself Positivism.

contains even the possibility of Reconciliation and Redemption, and which, indeed, demands them as the crown and goal of the needs, drifts, and passions deepest in life.

It is long since a work of first-class art took its stand upon the almost extinct sense of sin, and made its central motive the idea of Redemption. In poetry, at least, it has not happened since Milton's time. But a comparison between Milton's epic and Wagner's drama of Redemption offers a seductive *aperçu* to which we must here close our eyes. The interval between the two men covers an immense development, and even a revolution, in the human spirit. The precision of Milton's knowledge of the divine hinterland has reverently given way to an intimate and sympathetic acquaintance with the acts and passions of the human soul. Yet Milton it was who inaugurated the new departure. The character of Christ Himself may in one sense be said to have been discovered since the first real effort to read it psychologically was made in 'Paradise Regained.' The decay of the sense of sin within the same period is a striking fact, and not what we should at first expect from a close study of the heart and soul. And it is strong evidence of the theologian's position that neither Humanism with its development of culture and study of goodness, nor Naturalism with its victories of science, is able to reveal the soul's depths to itself in the absence of an increased intimacy with the Spirit of God. Nothing is more remarkable in *Parsifal* than the return to European culture of the sense of sin, the need of forgiveness, and the faith in its possibility. Those that wait for the Lord may take it as an earnest of His second coming to the civilised mind. As the darkest hour is just before the dawn, so the darkest system of philosophy that ever shadowed the western world may be the prelude to a profound Renaissance of spiritual faith. Pessimism, with its soul-hunger, is mere progress and civilisation reduced to an absurdity. Its despair is Naturalism and Agnosticism forced to a logical conclusion. Godlessness at last spells misery. And there is no hope for the world but in the conversion of the egotism on which existing civilisations rest, in that dying to self which has a real meaning only in so far as it means living to God. For Wagner, at the heat and height of his genius, Pessimism is an *überwundener Standpunkt,* and Forgiveness and Redemption give him a new heaven and a new earth by the power and victory of a sinless saviour.

And in this very connection there is one thought of the greatest Christian truth and moment brought home by the psychological treatment of the 'will to save' in Parsifal. It bears on the nature of saving work—of the work of Redemption. The Anselmic theory of satisfaction is now out of date, and has little more than a historic value. With it and its habit of mind have gone also the various substitutionary schemes and commercial transactions into which it has been degraded. They are all more juridical than moral. They fail to satisfy the modern conscience; they fall coldly on our more sympathetic religious intelligence. Nor can the public interest be retained in the metaphysical thesis, which underlay these theories, of the union of the two natures in Christ. Such a thesis may be theologically true or false, but religiously it is ineffective, for the present at least. It is more in the nature of a hypothesis thrown out to explain the fact than a real avenue to the dynamic centre of the fact, or a channel for its blessings. But interest has been increasingly, till it is now intensely, raised in the character and personality of Christ. Milton's seed has grown a tree. No wonder he himself preferred 'Paradise Regained' to 'Paradise Lost.' He did more for the regaining of Paradise than he knew, when he pursued the temptation into the depths of the Saviour's soul, and put us on the way to recover the heaven that is there. It was in that soul and by soul conflict, not by transaction, that the work of Redemption was achieved. It was by no such warfare, or such procedure of heaven's economy as is materialised in 'Paradise Lost.' What Christ did was not to clear from the path obstacles to forgiveness either in man or God. It was not to overthrow an outward enemy encamped in man; and it was not to provide certain prior conditions which should release the mercy of God. Yet it was much more than the announcement, as by a prophet, that God had forgiven or was ready to forgive. If the former view is ecclesiastical, the latter is no more than Socinian. He actualised in human nature, when He actualised in Himself, the forgiving presence of God. God in Him was in human nature, not in a unit of it, and not for a visit, not arranging the terms on which it could be redeemed, or securing the conditions on which we might be saved, but actually redeeming and appropriating it. Christ revealed the Father, not by holding Him up to be seen, but by bearing Him in upon us, leavening us with Him practically and consciously, not metaphysically; and in such a way that henceforth He, the Revealer, should belong to our very existence in this God. The field of Christ's work lay, therefore, in His own spiritual history, among the conditions of spiritual human nature. It was there, in His moral and spiritual energies, that the Redemption was wrought. By no single fact in the Saviour's biography does Christianity stand or fall, but by the Saviour Himself whom the facts reveal, but whom they have also done something to hide. Men wrangle about the historical resurrection till they forget that He rose because He *was* such as death could not hold. He did not become such by rising, nor would any evidence substantiate the resurrection had He been such as we could acquiesce in surrendering to the common irremediable doom. He, and not even His resurrection, is our cardinal Christian fact. The crucifixion was but the externalising of what was really done by the Saviour's spiritual agony in dying to the natural man and living to God, losing His life and so finding it, renouncing the passionate will to live and so realising the will to save, and finding in the personality of the Father the freedom He resigned with His own earthly individualism. He broke by spiritual miracle the chain of the natural will and all its common links and sequences; and so He escaped from the limitation of the race, and from the ignoble pains of self-seeking nature into the power of the Almighty. And as this was a real work and not a dramatic, it follows that it was gone through for Himself, the sinless, no less than for us, the sinful. It engrossed His whole soul, and left no room for the thought (which would, indeed, have been His collapse) that He was acting a part, and that He was doing what for Himself was needless, and only worked out as a means to an end, as an external and impersonal task. His work was no less personal to Himself than representative of us. His sanctification was not a means but an end in itself to Him. Had it been no real end to Him it could be no real end to us.

Redemption, therefore, while it will always remain the miracle of miracles, is not magical, transactional, or external. It is a psychological process within a universal Soul. It was in always truly finding and perfectly keeping the way of God for Himself that Christ opened it for us all. Thus He damned sin in the flesh, in the history of His own human personality. There is no hope for the rehabilitation of evangelical Christianity except upon such lines as these; and they are impressed upon us with all the force of Art by a saviour so inadequate in other points as Parsifal. The work of Redemption had its area in the self-conquest, and the corresponding development of the Saviour's soul. It was pursued under moral conditions as rigid as fine. It was the energy of the universal conscience which was in

Christ. It was a process of the spiritual character, and is to be taken home by us in terms of our own spiritual conflict. And the real birth of the Redeemer, the real Incarnation, is to be found not so much in the mystery of His human parentage as in the history of his own ever-victorious soul. There is the true holy land. It is not Judea, it is not the Church, it is not even the pale of Scripture. There, in the moral personality of Christ, is the sacred soil and fertile field for the rise of better answers to the old problems than have yet been given. These past answers are among the greatest efforts and triumphs of human thought. As theories they are greater and better than anything equally positive existing now. But they are not relevant enough either to the present or the future. They are without influence on the great spiritual products of the time. Still they are living and prophetic. The spirit which inspired them moves still in the mind of man and finishes His work. And, by the same token as made them great, greater things shall we do than the marvels of the past in adjusting for our thought the solemn and subtle relations between God's high Grace and the depths of human sin and woe. Redemption must be driven deeper in upon the thinking soul even if we part with some of the language and associations of Jewish ritual. The psychological redemption in works like *Parsifal*, while doubtless never meant to read a lesson to theologians, is yet one of the most illustrious fruits of that growth in the modern soul from which the scribe truly instructed in the Kingdom will not despise to learn as from God. It is not upon science that the traditional theories of the Gospel chiefly break and fail. It is not upon modern science but on the modern soul. They are not so much in collision with the truth of nature as inadequate to the aspirations of the heart, foreign to the modern conscience, and stale to our new interest in the action of the moral imagination. And if we feel this, and are apt to learn, there is much to be taught us about the Christ of God even by the Godless Christ portrayed in Parsifal by a master of the modern mind so masterly as Wagner.

But the artist's treatment of the Christian ideas is best exhibited, not by analysis of his system, but by a method more akin to his own. One of the most striking features of his genius was the triumphant way in which, starting from an ideal position, he was able, with the true creator's power, to embody it in living action and breathing personalities. His characters are incarnations, they are not simply prophets, or apostles of his ideas. They do not preach their truth as if they were in a religious novel; they embody and show it forth. It was his object to show the idea of Redemption as flowing from the deepest need of the truly human heart. He treats the old legends so as to present 'the fair humanities of old religion' converted, if not to the Christian creed, at least to the Christian spirit and the Christian ideas. It will do him most justice, therefore, if we allow the drama itself to unfold to us his thought and world.

There are in it shocks to our national religious associations and our feeling of religious decorum which are to be got over only by the irresistible effect produced by the complete representation. By the performance of *Parsifal* the soul is raised so far above its habitual level that every valley is exalted, every stumbling-block is absorbed, violence is no more heard in its borders, no demand seems extreme, and no suggestion unholy. No mere exposition of the poem, such as alone is possible here, can expect to destroy the nervousness with which many hear of the Eucharistic feast on the stage, the studied resemblance in the Parsifal of the last act to the traditional appearance of Christ, or the washing of his feet by Kundry and the drying of them with her hair. One can only say, at any risk of censure or ridicule, that the complete experience quite banishes the fears of a partial, and that it is only in one's study beforehand, it is certainly not in the temple-theatre at Bayreuth, that the peril of irreverence can be felt. Those even who have gone there prepared to scoff have remained disposed, at least, to pray. We could suggest no surer means of provoking a distaste for the theatre in general, with the dreary ordinariness of its level of life, than the spectacle of *Parsifal* on the Bayreuth stage. But if exposition cannot do what representation can, it at least does more justice to a genius like Wagner's than any mere analysis.

II

The Grail, in *Lohengrin,* is surrounded by a glamour of knighthood and a haze of mystic heroism. Here, in *Parsifal,* it is the centre of a solemn mystery of faith and love. In *Lohengrin* we are only told of the dim stronghold from which the knights issued on service of the wronged and oppressed. But here, in *Parsifal,* we are taken behind the heroism to that which inspires it. We are plunged in the inmost life of those souls whose heroism was but its outward form. We are admitted to the household and hearth of faith. The noble castle of Montsalvat is situated in the almost inaccessible depths of the mountains of Northern and Gothic Spain. The dim, strait path to it only a destined knight can find and tread. It is the sanctuary of two priceless treasures—the Grail or cup used by our Lord at the Last Supper, and subsequently employed to receive the blood flowing from His pierced side; and the holy spear (symbol of the stinging world) that had inflicted the wound. A vision of angels had brought them to the old King Titurel one blessed night, and it was for their safe keeping and reverential worship that he had built these towers and gorgeous halls. At the date of opening, only one of the treasures is there, and a dreadful sin and grief broods over the holy home. The spear has been lost, and lost thus. Titurel had passed by excessive age into a death-trance, and now lies in a dreamy tomb beneath the shrine of the Grail. The reigning king, Amfortas, is his son, and the sin is his. On the borders of the Grail territory lives a magician, Klingsor, the representative of paganism. He had long ago been refused membership of the holy brotherhood, and had betaken himself for revenge to devilish help, and built a castle as close to Montsalvat as he could. He surrounded it with a garden of delights, stocked with women of diabolic beauty, who from time to time ensnared and ruined one and another of the younger knights. Amfortas had resolved to tolerate this danger no more, and from his mystic Burg rode forth over-confident against the magic stronghold, armed, not with a holy heart, but only with the sacred spear. Alas! he was met by the loveliest and mightiest fiend of all the fatal garden of girls. The spell fell on him, he sank into her arms, and the spear dropped from his hand to be seized on the instant by Klingsor, who was waiting in ambush the success of his infernal plot. Inflicting a malicious wound on the King's side, Klingsor vanished with his prey. The King's retinue rushed in at his harrowing cry, but too late to do more than carry him off, protected by their shields from the weapons of Klingsor's host of apostate knights. The spear at the opening of the play is in Klingsor's hands. It gives him renewed power against the good, and he is sanguine that the Grail itself with its sanctuary will now soon fall into his hands. Meantime the King's wound is incurable by anything except a touch of the spear that had smitten him (*una eademque manus vulnus opemque tulit*), and his bodily pain is but a type of his spiritual agony and fever of remorse. His cry is the cry of Humanity, his wound is the sting of its perennial sin, and the spear is the world-power so potent to curse or to bless, according to him who wields it.

In Wagner's manner, this preliminary history is narrated by Gurnemanz, the chief of the knights, shortly after the play begins.

The lights in the theatre go gently down, a deep hush falls on the house, the strings wail out the exquisitely sweet and pathetic bars that open the overture, and before a few minutes are over we are caught up in the spirit to a new world of mystic sorrow, passion, and faith. This overture is a great symphony. There are movements in it that thrill strings in our soul rarely touched by any art, and not touched often in the emotional experience even of the very good. The awful, tender, triumphant woe of saviour-souls pierced by the spear of the world's passion and the world's sin—the crucifixion of a Christ, prolonged and renewed in the hearts of sinful men—the shadow spread upon faithful hearts the world over by one man's disobedience—the grief and the glory of a whole redeemed world—these things vibrate, sob, and triumph round us in this unearthly realm.

> For a' the bluid that's shed upon earth
> Rins through the streams o' that countrie.

The curtain rises on a lovely scene. The centre

of the stage is a piece of rocky floor in the midst of a shady wood, dim but not gloomy. It is in the precincts of Montsalvat. To the left mounts the path to the Castle; to the right it sinks towards a lake which is sparkling in the rear. Day is breaking. The chief knight, Gurnemanz, a vigorous, iron-grey figure, is asleep with two youthful squires. The motive of the Grail suddenly sounds out on trumpets from the unseen castle, and the men awake and kneel in silent prayer. At its close two heralds appear, and announce the approach of the royal litter carrying the sick King to his bath in the holy lake. A new medicine he had tried has been fruitless. 'Fools,' says Gurnemanz:

> 'Fools we were to hope for easement
> Where a cure alone can ease.'

The words are accompanied by what may be called the Messianic-motive or the promise of a saviour. The cure, we are musically informed, is on the way in the saviour who is commissioned to redeem.

At this moment the squires catch sight of a wild female figure coming towards them on horseback, they can hardly say whether on earth or air. It is Kundry. Let her be marked well—a strange being, half light, half darkness, serving sometimes the Grail, sometimes Klingsor, the victim of a terrible magic power which binds her if it cannot hold her, the home of a legion of devils, torn between good instincts and evil bondage, with an alternate passion for redemption and destruction, the type of womankind at its worst and its best, as Amfortas is the type of sin-torn man. The history of Kundry's redemption, the stormy process of her soul's development and deliverance is one whole side and sex of universal history, and is something not excelled in any literature. Kundry, dismounting, hurries forward, wild in mien and clothing. She is girdled high on the waist with serpent skins. Her long black hair hangs matted about her tawny face. Her piercing dark eyes can blaze like coals, but are mostly fixed and dull. It is her mood of service now. She runs up to Gurnemanz with a small flask, which she has brought from Arabia, with a balsam for the King. She is tired and sullen, will answer no questions, and flings herself impetuously on the ground. At this moment the King enters, groaning, on the litter, which is accordingly set down for his ease. The music here has a hint of the Eucharistic-motive blending with the notes of the King's pain, whereby the sorrow of the saviour is placed in hopeful conjunction with the woe of human sin. The glory of the dawn overpowers for a little Amfortas's misery, and soothes him after a wretched night. The radiance of the woodland morning is expressed by the orchestra in a movement of extreme beauty, blended of peaceful floating airs, the grace of waving trees, and all the colours of dewy flowers. Conversing with Gurnemanz, Amfortas, in the failure of all medicine for his diseased mind, falls back for comfort upon an old word of gospel promise and Messianic hope. For once, since his sin, in the fever of his agony and the fervour of prayer, he lay prostrate before the half-harried shrine, and implored some sign of a deliverance to come, when suddenly a holy glow was shed from the Grail, a blessed vision stood before him, and the clear words came to him thus:

> Through Pity wise
> The sinless Fool—
> Wait, I have chosen *Him*
> For my tool.

This is the promise of the saviour. As a musical motive it is one of the most conspicuous in the work. We mark here too a first trace of the ethics of Schopenhauer—pity as the spring of moral excellence and saving power, or a morality based on compassion. And it will be part of our business to observe how, when the destined saviour appears, his education for his final work is the education of this virtue. His wisdom comes by the deepening of his power of sympathy with sin and sorrow. Wagner, like Schopenhauer, was in strong revolt against the heartless wisdom which flows from mere outward observation, and which has received so undue a consecration in the joint worship of science and success. 'We worship action,' he says in a prose tract, 'and sing our peans to the most universal conqueror, but we will hear nothing of the sorrows of Humanity. But with the Redeemer in our hearts we feel that it is not their actions, but their sorrows that bring near us the men of the past, and make them worthy of our remembrance. Our sympathy belongs then to the vanquished, not to the victorious hero. Whatever our own peace of conscience may be, everywhere and always (from the giant forces of Nature to the worm of the dust) we must come to feel the awful tragedy involved in the existence of this world, and daily we shall have to turn our gaze as a last sublime refuge to the Redeemer on the Cross.'

The Cross, and no self-satisfied goodness, as the ground and measure and hope of the world! There is something far from foreign to the Christian ear in that. Nor is it strange to us to be told that the world's Christ is the world's fool, or the world's wisdom folly at the last for the ends that are best.

Upon this promise the King falls back, as a despairing Psalmist of old retired upon the Messianic hope, as weary mankind, racked with evil, falls helpless back on the Word of God. But Gurnemanz, who is a 'plain man,' is a little sceptical about visions and their promise, and he invites the King to be practical, and try the flask that Kundry has brought. Amfortas recognises her as the serviceable maid who had before now been of use to the fraternity of the Grail, but as nothing more. It is otherwise with Kundry. His thanks deepen the restlessness with which the sight of Amfortas had affected her. She repudiates them with something like horror. She is so full of self-hate and self-contempt that she will not bear to be told she is of service to any. 'I never do good—I want to be left alone.' But there is a more specific ground for her horror at the thanks of Amfortas, and one known to her alone. Kundry in one of her seasons of possession had been the agent used by Klingsor to seduce the spear from the King.

The King drinks the potion and is borne along to his bath in the lake, leaving Gurnemanz, the squires, and Kundry behind. These squires feel an inexplicable aversion and suspicion towards Kundry, who meets it with anything but conciliation. Her part is taken against their taunts and charges by Gurnemanz, who points out that she cannot be so bad, seeing that she is ready enough to serve the brotherhood. They reply with the awkward suggestion that she might be sent after the lost spear. This leads to the whole narration by Gurnemanz of the story with which we began; the tale being accompanied by considerable agitation on the part of Kundry, who still lies prone on the bank where she had thrown herself, with her head buried in the moss, or occasionally propped surlily on her elbows.

Just as Gurnemanz has told the story of the King's vision and the words of promise, a breath of the swan-motive in *Lohengrin* is heard from the orchestra, followed by a sudden uproar in the direction of the lake. A wild swan flutters across the scene, falls, struggles, and dies. The stage is quickly filled with an angry crowd, some of whom pick up the bird and bring it gently forward, while others drag in a handsome youth who is half dazed by the commotion. The orchestra tells us by his appropriate motive that this is Parsifal. The swan had been sailing about the lake to the delight of the King, who deemed it a good omen, when it was suddenly pierced by an arrow which it was easy to identify as one of those in the quiver of the simple and seemly youth. 'Shot it?' Yes, he had shot it. He 'shoots anything on the wing.' Gurnemanz then takes him in hand, and administers a touching and effective rebuke. He dwells on the sanctity of the animals in that holy region, and enlarges on the pathos of the beautiful creature thus robbed of life, and the wanton destructiveness that could bring such a cruel thing to pass. Parsifal meanwhile becomes a little ashamed of himself, and as the reproaches of Gurnemanz work upon his guileless heart, he becomes quite overwhelmed, snaps his bow in two, and, pleading ignorance, flings his quiver away.

We note here, first, that reverence for life which is so prominent in both ancient Buddhism and its modern and occidental form of Pessimism. Wagner's own fondness for animals was very great, and he was theoretically, at least, a vegetarian. One aspect of his fascination by the Eucharist was the fact that it seemed to him the consecration of such a vegetable diet as, if it were more common, would much reduce the suffering, to say nothing of the sin of men. And we remark, secondly, that this is the first lesson Parsifal receives in that discipline of pity which is to lift him out of the natural into the spiritual man. Parsifal in this stage is the natural man at his best and noblest, the finest image of the earthly, but innocent only, hardly pure, for he has not yet known good by evil, and his health and childish thoughtlessness have precluded much knowledge of pain. He represents the ideal childhood of the race. And we cannot help the suggestion and comparison of the like incident in the 'Ancient Mariner,' and its moral uses there.

Interrogated about himself, Parsifal seems fool enough. He knows nothing of his father, of who sent him that way, of his home, or of his name. We recall King Arthur, in 'The Idylls':—

> His coming and his going no man knows,
> From the great deep to the great deep he goes.

He only remembers he had a mother—Herzeleide (Heartache, another eloquent Schopenhauerism)—and that they lived a roaming life by forest and field. Gurnemanz recognises a nobility about the youth, and feels an attraction to him of which he is but half aware, when Kundry, who has been eyeing Parsifal with prophetic aversion, interposes sharply with a contemptuous narrative of several other facts which, in her eccentric wanderings, she had gathered about him. His father had fallen in battle, and to preserve him from a like end his 'fool of a mother' had reared him in the wilderness away from men. This jogs Parsifal's own memory or his attention, and he recalls how he followed a passing troop of dazzling knights away across the world, without being able to overtake them, and without a thought of the mother he had so gaily left behind. Kundry knows still more, and she throws him into a state of frightful excitement by the news that his mother is dead, and that she died of a broken heart caused by his desertion, and that she saw her die. He springs passionately at Kundry's throat, and her life is only saved by the interference of Gurnemanz, who has again to censure the reckless violence of his fine savage. From violence Parsifal subsides into a fit of stunned abstraction, and then into trembling. His second lesson in Pity is being read to him, and this time with an added bitterness of remorse for what his thoughtlessness had done to the one being he so unconsciously loved. Pain is opening up life to him, and kindling manhood as no happiness could. He has not sinned, wittingly at least, yet how he suffers! He is on the point of fainting when he is caught by Gurnemanz, while Kundry, womanlike, forgetting her assault, hurries to the spring and brings water to sprinkle his face. She quickly subsides, however, into her sullen self-contempt when the knight praises her for thus overcoming evil with good. She will not be called good—'I never do good; I would only be at rest,' she fretfully cries. She retires morosely and slowly behind the two other figures, and is slipping away into the bush. But watch her—something is coming over her, and she knows what it is but too well. Most piteous is her deep shuddering cry for rest, rest, sleep, sleep—if she could but for ever sleep. Her hour is come, and the power of darkness. The devil is waking within her better self. A redeemer has dawned in Parsifal, and she is required by the evil spirit whose business it is to ruin by hellish love the apostles of the heavenly. She utters a dull cry. She shivers. Her arms fall, her head sinks, and she staggers a few steps on. 'Powerless struggle! The time has come!—sleep—sleep—I *must.*' She slips to the ground behind a bush, and vanishes from the rest of the act. It is most touching to see this strange, and far from heartless being, just as her womanliness asserts itself through all her sin, seized by a power of wickedness she has lost power to resist, and dragged into hell with her hand upon the very latch of heaven. But sinful woman is neither utterly feeble nor utterly bad. And to a heart 'in which the Redeemer dwells,' there is, beyond her wicked witchery, another and tenderer spell, not unholy, round the great world-Magdalen who has shared and borne the sins of so many an age—and borne them in sad disproportion to her share.

Gurnemanz has been too much occupied with Parsifal to pay attention to the behaviour of Kundry, usually strange. He is more and more interested in the youth. He feels that Parsifal has no common origin, and may have no common destiny. The promise of the 'guileless fool' haunts even his sceptical ears. (Your 'plain man' is always sceptical at bottom.) It occurs to him that he will put the boy to a great test. He will bring him as a spectator to the great divine event now impending, to the solemn ceremony and sacrament of the Grail in Montsalvat. 'What is the Grail?' says Parsifal. 'That,' replies Gurnemanz, 'is not to be told. If thou art elect for its service thou shalt not fail to know. I think I have read thee aright. To this Grail there is no earthly path, and none can go to it but those whom itself leads.' We are instantly made to feel that we are on the threshold of a mystic land, at the portals of the spiritual. We enter a region where progress is not by speed of foot, and things are heard by no hearing of the ear, where our questions about 'Where' and 'When' are answered by a blessed and timeless smile. 'For,' says Wagner, in a prose work, quoting from Schopenhauer, 'Peace, rest, and blessedness dwell only there where there is neither "Where" nor "When."' Time, as in the Apocalypse, is no longer, and space is no more. Each of the two men puts an arm round the other. Yes, they feel the Grail wills that this new soul approach it. They begin to step gently out in the direction of the Burg. And at the moment, by a singular panoramic stage effect, the scenery begins to move. The world and its fashion passes away. 'I scarcely step, and yet I seem so far,' says the astonished Parsifal. 'Thou seest, my son,' replies Gurnemanz, with grave affection, 'time turns here to space.' Slowly, from right to left, as the light fades into almost entire darkness, the wood moves away; a door opens in the rock and receives the pilgrims from our sight; we catch glimpses of them faintly among ascending corridors hewn in the gaunt rock; antres vast and magical pillars glide by, their outline hardly seen; the darkness deepens; the situation is most solemn. It is a transformation scene, only in spirit-land instead of fairy-land. But it is in the musical commentary that we must seek the complete effect. The scene is accompanied by what is known as the *Verwandlungs-Musik.* It is a procession through a region weird and wild, dark and difficult, full of risk, bewilderment, labour, and pain, as if it were the world stumbling out of the dark unconscious into the tragic sorrow of divine life and thought. The music moves in painful dissonance up and down, as if following the steps of a soul bemazed among the ragged rocks, and dumbfoundered in the crisis of a new birth in a sinful world. Even this holy land has a curse on it and woe. The dark shadow of the King's sin, and the echo of his pain fall upon the precincts of his house. It is toilsome enough for any soul to rise to its spiritual life, and we agonise at that strait gate. But for Parsifal the darkness, labour, and pain around the shrine are deepened by the sin that has defiled its holiness, and filled its air with moral bewilderment and royal woe.

At last the great bells of Montsalvat are heard pealing in majestic music from afar. Nearer and nearer they come, and long-drawn trumpet notes float in with the Eucharist strain. A lofty and vaulted hall glimmers through the dark. The light slowly rises, and its beauty is .gently revealed. Noble pillars and arches carry the octagonal walls up into a lofty dome, from which alone the light streams down amid waves of waxing music. In the centre is a veiled shrine, and round it two long, semicircular tables, covered with white, and set out with chalices. Parsifal and Gurnemanz emerge on this scene at the side, and there remain. At the rear on each hand a door opens, and from the right the Knights of the Grail enter in long and stately procession, with a peculiar, solemn step. Amid the music of noble hymns of grief and faith, slowly they file round and arrange themselves at the board. For his grand faith-motive here Wagner utilises a German chorale. The bells swell, the Grail-motive rings out, the Saviour's sorrow blends with the strain of Amfortas's woe, the music seems to rise into the dome, the orchestra ceases, and boys' voices alone from a height unseen echo the sweetly solemn words of faith and invitation, 'Take, eat.' A few beautifully managed bars of the faith-motive are made to suggest the sweep and beat of wings, as if the Holy Ghost descended, like a dove, unseen, to fill the house where they are sitting. From the left door in the rear now enters the litter of the sick King, followed by a band of beautiful boys bearing the covered treasure of the Grail, which is reverently set upon the central shrine, while the King is deposited on a couch behind. It is his function to uncover the Grail and dispense the sacred elements for the spiritual refreshment of the fraternity. There is a long pause and silence, broken at last by the weird voice of the trance-laid Titurel from beneath the shrine, like a word from the grave, an impulse from his past, or the voice of the hereditary conscience, calling on

Amfortas to proceed to his office. The miserable man shrinks, and the voice calls him again. Again he shrinks and refuses the task. Why? The significant Kundry-motive sounds from the orchestra to tell us, while the King gives vent to the passionate agony of the defiled priest who, with his hands unclean and shattered heart, must dispense the peace, the purity, and the healing of the world. The tragic power of this character is overwhelming. And what an old story it is. *Es ist eine alte Geschichte, doch bleibt sie immer neu.* 'What is the pain of a wound,' he cries; 'what is the torrent of remorse, compared to the hell of being cursed to this office? I, the sole sinner, am the sole intercessor here, and the sole dispenser of the spirit's blessing and the holiness of the cross. Is there any woe like the abuse of grace? I long unutterably for that consolation from which I yet shrink with horror unspeakable.* In my heart wells up the holy

* We remember Newman's lines in the 'Dream of Gerontius'—

> It is the face of the Incarnate God
> Shall smite thee with that keen and subtle pain;
> And yet the memory which it leaves will be
> A sovereign febrifuge to heal the wound;
> And yet withal it will the wound provoke,
> And aggravate and widen it the more.
> Then wilt thou feel that thou hast sinned
> As never thou didst feel; and wilt desire
> To slink away, and hide thee from His sight;
> And yet wilt have a longing aye to dwell
> Within the beauty of His countenance.
> And these two pains, so counter and so keen,—
> The longing for Him when thou seest Him not;
> The shame of self at thought of seeing Him,—
> Will be thy veriest, sharpest purgatory.

blood of life, and I am pierced with the pain of the blessedest joy. Then to meet that surges again the blood of passion, the concupiscence of sin. [Here sounds the Kundry-motive.] And in the clash of these currents I am ground to dust. The blood flows from my wound. Ah! how unlike the redeeming blood that flowed from His! From the spring of desire flows the hot and bloody stream of sin. [Mark here the influence of a Buddhistic Pessimism.] Mercy! Mercy! Thou all-merciful! for no penitence can lay my pangs.' In the orchestra the motive of the magician swallows up the Grail-motive, and the laughter of the bewitched and evil Kundry is heard between as the King sinks fainting on his couch.

From the dome the Messianic promise is immediately sung by the voices of the boys, and the knights take up the comfort of the hope. Titurel again calls. The boys as angels echo the divine invitation, 'Take, eat.' Amfortas slowly rises, and bends in rapt devotion over the Grail, which the attendant pages have uncovered. A gloom fills the hall, and then a blinding light falls from above on the Grail, which begins to glow in a dark and deepening red. Amfortas, with ecstatic face, raises it in his hands, and waves it solemnly to and fro. All have fallen on their knees and adore. Presently the light fades from the Grail, the gloom from the hall. The chalices are filled with wine by the pages, and bread set beside each, after which all sit down to the holy meal amid hymns renewed and jubilant bells.

Where, meanwhile, are Gurnemanz and Parsifal? Gurnemanz, at the beginning of the ceremony, had left the youth at the side, and taken his place at the head of the knights. Parsifal stands with his back to the audience, an amazed spectator of the whole scene. Though he does not speak a word, and nothing but his back is seen, he attracts nearly as much of our attention as the great spectacle itself. It is an utter and riveting mystery to him. It holds him, but it awakens little or nothing in kind. He is not yet capable of spiritual understanding. Only once he seems much agitated, and clutches at his heart. His natural sympathy is called forth by the evident suffering of Amfortas in his terrible conflict of passion and faith. As the knights sit down to the meal Gurnemanz beckons him to come and partake, but he makes no response. He only feels an impulse, too vague to follow, to do something to rescue the sufferer from his invisible foe. A chivalrous compassion urges him, but utter bewilderment holds him. He is fixed, dumb, overwhelmed; impressed, but unintelligent. The rock has been struck, but only stunned; the water does not yet flow; though deep below his consciousness hidden channels have been dimly stirred, and in the darkness a something moved and crept at the sight of sin and the suggestion of salvation. This is Parsifal's third lesson of pity.

At the close of the meal the knights embrace, and retire in the same grave fashion as they came. The King and the Grail are removed amid the echoes of stately faith and joy. Gurnemanz, impatient and angry, advancing to Parsifal, asks if he knows what he has seen. Parsifal, still grasping at his heart, cannot utter a word, only shakes his head. His *motive* as saviour palpitates in the orchestra, as if to indicate that the reply was not completely true, and that the redeemer had just quickened within the natural man. But Gurnemanz loses all patience. He is one of those robust Christians whose insight bears no proportion to their loyalty, and who make the most lamentable mistakes in spiritual judgment. His disappointment is very great. 'A fool is just what thou art. Out with thee. Leave swans alone, and, gooseherd, look for geese.' And he bundles him out at a small door. The moment he is gone, Gurnemanz is arrested by the Messiah strain of the Sinless Fool, which peals from the dome above. He wanders reflectively after the royal train; and the curtain falls on the first act.

III

WE are cast in the second act from heaven to hell. From the hall and sanctuary of the Grail we are transferred to the magic hold of Klingsor and its devilry. The overture is a piece of fearsome work. The harsh and unholy Klingsor-motive is in full blast, mingled with the strain of the misery of Amfortas, which together represent the captive agony of the human soul to the spell of evil. Again and again sounds the dreadful laugh of

Kundry in the full frenzy of her demoniacal possession, and inspired with the hellish jubilance of despair over the ruin and mockery of all things good and pure. As the Klingsor-motive rushes down three octaves of hell-harrowing incantation, the curtain rises, and displays the magician in a chamber within his castle tower gazing intently into a mirror amid the apparatus of necromantic art. He knows the hour has come when he must win or lose all. He knows the spiritual mission of Parsifal far better than Parsifal himself. Every resource must be strained to ruin this saviour. He must be plied with temptations almost superhuman. Sense must be rallied against soul. His noblest instincts must be seized, turned, and made to rend him. He is not like the larger-minded Jesus to be exposed to the temptations of empire. He has no social or political instincts in the tissue of his natural soul. But all the curses that lie possible in woman's love, as mother or other, must be conjured upon him, and he must be beset with all the perils incident to a soul naturally religious. Klingsor has seen Parsifal's expulsion by Gurnemanz with that keenness of eye in which the devil often excels the church. Wandering an outcast from the house of God, the youth (as so often) is drawn to the temple of Satan, and now Klingsor by his magic mirror sees him approach in the high spirits of his still unconquered *naïveté*. The wizard sets to work. He rises, goes to the edge of an abyss which opens in the floor, lights some charm which covers the pit with livid smoke, returns to his seat, and calls with mysterious gestures towards the abyss. It is Kundry, whom we have already seen overpowered by his arts, it is Kundry that he will force to his presence and purpose—Kundry, the perennial principle of deadly, worldly womankind—Kundry, who once as Herodias, had laughed at Christ stumbling under His cross, and had ever since been haunted by His look, cursed with hellish laughter, incapable of tears, and driven by the curse anew to evil every time she seeks to turn to good. She figures among the Scandinavian Walkyries as Gundryggja; she is the nameless with many names, 'the primeval she-devil, the Rose of Hell.' It is this Kundry the magician conjures to his sight and help. No less a devil's angel can cope with the coming angel of light. Amid the blue smoke the veiled figure of Kundry rises, magnificently clad. Slowly, most reluctantly, she emerges from the abyss, for she is not yet wholly under the spell. The instinct to save is still feebly struggling with the passion to destroy. She is not half awake, and her moans have a horror of spiritual desolation in them which we carry long in our ears. They become, shortly, howls from the very soul of damnation, and then die into a whisper of impotence. Klingsor deepens her agony by taunting her with being ready and on the spot as another victim draws near. She writhes under the curse, she defies her master, she declares he cannot hold her. No, he replies, but he can bind her so long as to use her. And the power he has over her is because he is invincible to her witchery of beauty.

He is so heartless, so purely devilish, so full of the arid fury of evil and enthusiasm of inhumanity, that she cannot tempt him. 'Yes!' he says; 'and he who frees thee must withstand thee, too.' Whoever should resist her, not by insensibility to love, but by a diviner love with the power to renounce, the same should redeem her. Resisted from below, she was conquered and bound; resisted from above, she was conquered and redeemed. 'Try the youth who is coming,' says Klingsor with a sneer, and a covert allusion to Amfortas. And the poor sorceress wails again to think that the very King had proved himself as weak as all the rest, and become involved in the curse which anointed her to destroy. Her reiterated passion for salvation on the very brink and mission of damnation is a most touching thing. Parsifal by this time is in the precincts of the castle, laying about him at the apostate knights in Klingsor's service, who resent his intrusion. The magician himself has mounted the battlements, where he can look down on the fray outside and on Kundry within. He gleefully describes the scrimmage to her, while she is slowly mastered by the continued working of his spell. Her devilish laugh becomes more frequent, and her wail of regret dies away. Finally, she vanishes downwards with another howl, and tower and wizard sink slowly through the ground, while a gorgeous scene rises in their place. We gaze on a garden of the hugest and most garish flowers, in the gaudy glory of luscious colour and golden light. On the wall far in the rear stands Parsifal, his powerful frame as simply clad as we saw him last, and looking down upon the scene after his tussle in vigorous and childlike delight. Girls troop in, artfully dressed like huge flowers, in a state of the utmost commotion at the loss or wounds of their knights during the fray. At the sight of him they are terrified, but he soon reassures them, and steps down among them—a great boy who has found new playmates. They surround him and quarrel for him. They hang about him and caress him. The loveliest of slow waltzes accompanies their seductive efforts, till at last Parsifal, finding them as troublesome as so many flies, and no more dangerous, sends them irritably about their business, and turns to go. At that moment a rich voice arrests him: 'Parsifal—stay!' He had no name, but now he remembers to have heard that word upon his mother's lips. Mark how the pure love of his mother makes a soil for the seductress to work upon. Something in her voice, too, arrests him. This is none of the common tribe that had been so powerless even to tempt him. It is deep calling unto deep. It is a being on a scale like his own. He is tried by his peer. Kundry is no child, and now she thrusts Parsifal into his destined manhood, just as, at a later point, she helps him to realise his vocation as saviour. It is beautiful from this point onwards to mark how she is associated with his development. Meant only for his ruin, she works him an otherwise impossible good. For is she not in the hands of that wicked but ever-chagrined spirit—*der stets das Böse will und stets das Gute schafft?*

Parsifal feels as if in a dream. A new force has laid hold of his careless, boyish naturalism. He looks shyly in the direction of the voice. The bushes part and reveal, reclining on a couch of flowers, a woman of the sweetest and most royal beauty. It is Kundry—metamorphosed, resplendent, on the very crest of her demoniac inspiration, clean forgetful of her serving hour and her better dream. We have seen her in her misery and collapse. It is now her hour of Satanic glory and fatal glow. This is Kundry, the seductress; woman, the deadly, the 'sweet and bitter in a breath,' *das ewig Weibliche,* on its fatal side. What is from this point to be marked is the masterly psychology of passion with which the artist following her regeneration makes her pass from the devil to the true woman, and from that to the woman forgiven, redeemed, and sainted. Love unholy and pitiless passes into a passion womanly and humane. But that is not enough. It does not go beyond a transfigured egotism. It must go on and develop into the selfless passion of renouncing and atoning servitude which is the heaven of the soul. Kundry is redeemed, but by a way she knew not, to a heaven she never sought—nay, which she resents and resists as keenly as ever she craved salvation. Indeed, it might be urged as a blemish in the play that we are more seized, held, and melted by Kundry than even by Parsifal, by the redeemed than by the redeemer.

They enter speech. She tells him the meaning of his name, Parsifal, 'the guileless fool.' This is but a symbolic way of describing how woman reveals to him his true self, manhood, and mission. With winsome sweetness she tells him the story of his mother and her death, and simulates a sympathy which draws him nearer and nearer her feet. A soul like his can be tempted only by good, assailed only through its nobility, and ruined by its best affections. Kundry knows her business with great hearts. The sorrow of Herzeleide, which comes floating up from the orchestra, breathes through the artful tale. Made for the schooling of pity, Parsifal is beside himself with grief, but it is a grief in which compassion is blended with remorse. A destined saviour cannot be taught by pity alone. He must conquer in a more moral conflict, a conflict with guilt; and to redeem from sorrow, more than sorrow must be overcome. In a passion of self-reproach Parsifal, who has been gradually and unconsciously approaching Kundry, at length falls with a torrent of self-accusation at her feet. The charm works well. Kundry bends over him full of the sweetest sympathy, caresses his brow, and puts her arm around his neck. But Parsifal can only bewail his error and his mother. Kundry takes another step and a most careful one—never leaving the foothold she has won in Parsifal's filial love. 'Penitence is atonement enough,' she plausibly says. 'There is a passionate love which thy mother poured on thy father. It is not withheld from thee. Nay, it is her blessing left to thee, and I am its executor'—

> Take her legacy of bliss,
> Take it now in love's—first—kiss.

She stoops over his face and fixes a long kiss upon his lips.

One tense moment for the poison to work, and then Parsifal springs to his feet, and rushes from her with every sign of extreme horror. His whole demeanour is changed. In frightful agitation he grasps at his heart as if he would pluck out a raging pain. At last he has waked to moral consciousness. Love—woman—has called consciousness into life. He has found himself. A perfect insurrection riots in his soul. The slow and gentle discipline of sentiment is over. He is taken from Pity's school by a more imperious teacher sent from Heaven. He wakes to the first consciousness that upon him is laid a mission which is passing the love of woman, and which is not to enjoy, but to sorrow, atone, and redeem. We hear the motive of the saviour's grief mingled with the woe of Amfortas, and the Kundry-motive struggling with both. The fountains of Parsifal's great deep are broken up. The waters that darkly crept at the foundations of his soul as he gazed smitten but only stunned upon the agony of Amfortas, now burst to the light. Vision streams upon him of the meaning of moral pain and spiritual saving woe. The first word he utters is 'Amfortas.' It is a lost soul, and a soul lost thus, that is his first thought under his first kiss. Sin has touched him, and the wound that burned in the heart of the king now burns sympathetically in his own. The world's sin and sorrow is becoming, by the very power of his purity, his own. Clear vision he has none, but the ache, terror, and spell of the new life, which is divine death, wrestle in his soul. But, alas! what wakes his soul wakes also his heart. The springs of his own natural passion are unloosed. The passion to redeem has to push its way through a boiling flood of earthly desire, roused and released. 'This is no wound like the wound I saw bleed. It is my heart's heart that burns. This terrible craving! This thirst that coerces my every sense! This torment of panting, longing love.' It is Wagner's, it is Europe's, fierce conflict of sense and soul. Then his voice sinks stricken and low. He is back in spirit in the hall of the Grail. The scene, till now a memory, becomes a presence. The Grail music, from below, interprets his mood to us. He sees again the rapt gaze fixed on the chalice, and the holy blood aglow. Its meaning opens to him. Reminiscence grows Revelation. The spirit is bringing things to his remembrance. The joy of Redemption he perceives trembling soft and divine in every soul. In his own heart only the ache will not yield. There rings in his ears (as on ours from the orchestra) the strain of the Saviour's wail over the defiled sanctuary, 'Save me from guilty hands.' Now we get a clearer glimpse of what passed dimly in his heart as he stood and gazed on the miserable king. He felt a vague motion, which he did not then realise as a divine call, to deliver the brotherhood from their load and curse. Now he scourges himself because he did not follow the instinct up, but fled like a fool back to the life of a child. He falls on his knees crying to the Saviour for forgiveness.

And Kundry? Kundry rises with Parsifal to the situation. As his agitation rages, she gazes on him amazed and terrified. Quickly, and too truly, she knows she has lost him. Yes, she has lost him as a victim, but may she not gain him in a better way? A wild new hope is born in her. The seductress is foiled, but the woman dawns. She has met one who can resist her from above, not as Klingsor, from beneath. Surely, then, her redemption draws nigh. The desire to ruin gives way to the passion to win. She is no more the wizard's tool. She is again the woman waiting to be saved, and now with salvation for not only a longing but a hope. She enters on her second stage as she feels for Parsifal a love none had ever inspired her with before. It is the story of Traviata, but how noble, how divine in its Teutonic, as compared with its Romance treatment. The whole width of the moral world lies between Sarah Bernhardt's *Dame aux Camélias* and Fräulein Malten's *Kundry*, as the last act of Parsifal will show.

She is more eager to win him now than ever, because more sincerely passionate. This is no innocent, she feels. This is a man clothed with royalty, if not hedged with some divinity. She draws timidly near him. She beseeches his grace. She is more winning, more dangerous, because more natural and earnest than ever. She glides across the width of the stage to where Parsifal kneels regardless of her presence. She lavishes on him caresses which we now feel more pathetic than hateful. Parsifal stares at her blankly. She stirs in him a deeper abstraction because she causes a new and deeper vision of inward revelation. Of kingly build, he has spiritual divination of a king's bane. He recognises in her the witch who ruined Amfortas. To every caress he only replies, 'Yes, it was thus she smiled, she bent, she languished on him, and kissed his soul away.' She kisses Parsifal again, and again recalled, he springs to his feet, flings her from him, and bids her leave him for ever. The moans of Amfortas reach us from the instruments. The splendid passion of this scene is not surpassed in art. Kundry's speech, in reply, would tax any actress, and, indeed, Wagner's drama, so far from being written for particular actors, has to manufacture its own. She taunts him; she cowers to him; she would move the pity of a stone by her double prayer for love and redemption. 'Redeemer art thou! and wilt thou redeem all but me? O, how I have waited for thee! From eternity I have waited. None have waited like me. Woman waits for redemption in me. If thou knewest my curse, steeled ever by new laughter to new woe! I laughed at HIM once, and His look is my curse. From world to world I seek Him. I think sometimes I have found that heavenly glance again, but again my curse and my laughter return, and I make another sinner fall. Weep I cannot, only cry and rage, deluded ever in the night. At last a redeemer has come to me. Let me weep but for an hour on thy bosom. Then be I outcast from God or man I will be purged and redeemed in thee.' If Kundry cannot weep for herself, we can weep for her here.

'Love is enough,' she would say, with a thin

semi-pagan school of our own. Wagner knows better. 'We were together damned eternally,' says Parsifal, 'if for one hour I forgot my mission in thine arms.' Nothing can save them but a divine sternness on his part which has to become harshness in the end. Mark how the temptation passes from his filial affection to play now on that very pity in him which was his first discipline from heaven. He has to turn round upon his own past pieties, even on the pity in which his better self began. And he takes up his saving work by becoming the preacher to Kundry of the one true way. 'Not by such love cometh thy salvation.'

> 'The solace which shall end thy woe
> From that woe's spring can never flow,
> Salvation never on thee fall
> Till that spring close for good and all.'

The spring, that is, of passion and the desire to possess. The love of passion and possession is not the redeeming love. There is here a suggestion of the Buddhist and Pessimist doctrine of the extinction of sorrow by the extinction of desire. Such metaphysics are disputable. But the moral truth in these lines is not disputable. Such sin as Kundry's cannot be expiated by any purities of earthly love, however blessed these may be for those who have not sinned in the similitude of her transgression. Deadly love is not atoned by love legitimate, and the love of a man and woman can redeem the soul of neither, much as it may mend the life. The defiled love of earth is to be cleansed only by the unearthly love of heaven, by the divine love, whose happiness is complete devotion to one who is no exclusive possession, and by the purity of service which looks for nothing again. The next act will show us what this means.

Parsifal knows the way, but he knows not as yet the redeemer. Clouds and darkness are still about his soul. 'Another must be thy redeemer,' he cries, 'and others than thou wait his appearing.' He is thinking of the knights. 'But how to know him. O this curse of illusion and error about all salvation!' And with the doubt rises the earthly longings and seductions again. The soul-emotions are turbid with the 'blood-emotions.' The stream of his consecration is tainted with his red human earth, and like Amfortas, like Augustine, he is the victim of a divided being and a fever of holy war.

> 'O this night of world-illusion,
> Weal and woe in dire confusion,
> Heavenly yearnings, thirsts for hell.'

Kundry pursues him with the tenacity which is fast becoming the recklessness of despair. 'Did my kiss open for thee a world? Take my embrace and become its god.' Then, with a woman's bitterness, 'Oh, yes, redeem the world, become its god, and for that leave me for ever damned!' 'No; I offer redemption also to thee.' 'Let me love thee then.' 'Love and redemption thou shalt have—only show me the way to Amfortas.' Kundry breaks into fury. 'What! shall it ever be mankind first—this man, too, of all others—and me last?' She is beside herself. She relapses into hellish laughter over those she has damned. 'Never. And thou shalt never find this way. Ha! struck with his own spear, Christ's spear, that Christ's curse gave me power to win!' Then in a flash to the other pole. 'Pity! Pity! One hour be mine, and I *will* show thee the way.' This is dreadful to see and hear; what must it be to act? She makes to embrace him. He dashes her from him. She is now mad and blind. She shrieks to Klingsor and all his angels for help, and she curses Parsifal to endless mazes of error on the paths that lead him from her. Klingsor suddenly appears, and bars Parsifal's exit with the sacred spear. The girls return and gather to Kundry—again one of themselves. The wizard hurls the spear at Parsifal, and lo! it stops in the air and quivers harmless over his head. He seizes it with rapture, and makes with it the sign of the cross. The castle and its master sink in ruins through the yawning earth. The girls collapse like withered flowers of passion past, and the garden turns to a desert. Kundry falls to the ground, and Parsifal departs by the background as he came, turning only to call to Kundry, who raises her head for a last, dumb, desperate look. 'Thou knowest where thou shalt see me again.'

IV

THE overture to the third act is as dreary as the last was dreadful. It is a long desert twilight. It is a musical picture of the most forlorn doubt; of the maze, the struggle, the labour, and sorrow of Parsifal in his *preparatio evangelica.* It is the fearful pit and miry clay. All at first is lonely, hopeless, and dismal. It is 'desolation deified.' It is a 'grey, void, lampless, deep, unpeopled world.' Echoes of Kundry's curse mingle in conflict with the strains of the Grail. She had power, not, indeed, to master him, but still to condemn him to this. After the surrender in which he put the cup of joy away, he is now in the love-lorn chaos of a world not realised, seeking for a goal he is still far from finding, amid a dark and spectral travail of spirit which music alone has the power to interpret. The motive of the spear and the strain of promise sound as battle-cries in the grim good fight.

The curtain rises on a scene in the precincts of the Grail. A long time has elapsed. The temptation in the last scene was not a brief episode in Parsifal's life, but the symbol of prolonged warfare, and the overture covers years of 'Arabia.' It is spring, and Good Friday. The open corner of a wood is before us, with a lovely meadow rising to the rear. On the right is a fountain; on the left a hermit's hut. It is early morning, and a fresh, dewy radiance is over all. The sweet, cool light and the small wild flowers are in exquisite contrast with the fever of the blazing garden in the last scene. Gurnemanz, now white and failing, clad only in the shirt of the knights without their robe, is the hermit of the hut. He issues and listens. He has heard a moan. Again it comes. He makes for the thicket, parts the bushes, and discovers the well-known but long lost Kundry in a state of semi-consciousness. He drags her out, sets her on the bank, and uses every means to recall her to life. 'Wake, wake, spring is here.' So it is; the spring of a sweeter summer than the old knight knew. At last she wakes. She is attired as in the first act, but much paler. Her long hair streams over her coarse brown robe, and the fierceness is departed from her face and eyes. Long she stares at Gurnemanz. Then suddenly she recollects herself, and begins to arrange her clothes and hair. It is her first little sign of an infinite change to true womanhood. The sullen spirit has gone. Humility, too humble to know it is humble, has taken the place of self-contempt. Service has become a second nature, not a freak. Without speaking a word she rises, and goes quite naturally about the first menial offices she can find. She enters the hut and re-issues with a pitcher to draw water. Her gait is gentle, languid, even crushed. Gurnemanz gazes after her with an amazement interpreted by the triolets in the bass. 'What, no word of thanks?' She bends her head gently, and utters long and low the words, 'Service! Service!' It is the old sweet voice, but it has a new sweetness too. The motive that sounds from the orchestra is the same that marked her in the best moments of her previous life near the Grail, as when she brought the balsam for the King.

We have already seen Parsifal performing with his back alone for half an act. That was nothing to what we must now mark. Kundry does not utter another sound throughout the rest of this great act, and yet she is the central figure in it. We cannot see the rest sometimes for her and the tears she draws from us. It is all done by pure acting, and the poet's power of situation. The greatest voices of the German operatic stage must consent to be entirely silent in the crowning act, and produce their overwhelming effect by gesture and expression alone. And Wagner has persuaded the greatest artists the German stage can produce to do it, to do it with all their hearts, and to become greater artists than ever in doing it. He discovered Fräulein Malten to herself for one.

Gurnemanz grows more and more amazed as Kundry moves about in her quiet and *distrait* way. What has done this? Is it the influence of the holy day — the charm which moves with such melting melody in the accompaniment to all this scene? Waiting for her pitcher to fill, Kundry becomes suddenly interested in something in the wood. She beckons Gurnemanz to come and look, and then, her interest gone again, she retires with the water to the hut, and occupies herself with its arrangement. No incidents of the day can keep her curiosity long alive, for her whole life is now one unearthly event. We may compare here Browning's Lazarus in the 'Epistle of Karshish.' A strange figure approaches, enters, and moves dreamily past Gurnemanz, who stands aside puzzled and lets him slowly pass. He is clad from head to heel in black armour. His helmet is closed, his spear dropped, his head sunk on his breast, and he drags weariness in every step. He reaches a small hillock where he sits down by the spring. Who is this that cometh from Edom? In the orchestra we hear the Parsifal-motive mingling with that dreary wilderness-strain which opened the overture. Gurnemanz stares, approaches, and asks if he can serve the stranger by showing him the way. The figure does not even salute, but gently and sadly shakes his head, at which Gurnemanz takes the liberty to tell him he is on holy ground, where men are not wont to come in armour. Does he not know what day it is? The figure shakes his head again. 'What a heathen! It is Good Friday.' The head sinks deeper than ever. 'Down with thy weapons,' continues Gurnemanz, 'on His day who, weaponless, shed His holy blood for the world.' After a brief silence the figure slowly rises, thrusts the butt of his spear into the ground, lays sword, helmet, and shield reverently beside it, gently kneels before the head of the spear, and is lost in silent adoration of it. Gurnemanz gazes with sudden and growing agitation. Kundry issues from the hut, and he beckons her to his side. It *is* he. It is Parsifal. Gurnemanz's excitement becomes intense. 'Yes, it is the fool I thrust out of doors. And it is—the spear.' Kundry has recognised him too, but her memories of him are of a different cast. At last then they meet again. She turns her face away, and creeps to the rear of the stage, where she stands by the hut looking away from both men over the shining meadow and its flowers. Parsifal rises from prayer, looks round and recognises Gurnemanz, who is beside himself at the greeting. 'Whence comest thou?' he says. 'From the paths of coil and woe I come. Are they here at end? Or is this a new illusion, and am I wandering still? All is changed.' 'Whom seekest thou?' 'Him whose woes I once saw with a fool's eyes. I feel as if I were chosen to bring him weal. But alas! a curse haunts me still.' But his mission is not even yet clear to him or sure. The wound of a godless, womanless, wandering world is still open; the agony of lover's enunciation still mutters in his soul; spectral fightings and fears still beset his spiritual way. And he is the type of many pure ones who would do good, but know not how in this dissolving age, who find the way of salvation beset with illusions the most thickly of all. 'I am cursed never to find the way to save, to wander in trackless error and incessant war. I wellnigh despair. Why with such reverence have I kept this lance? For what have I ever refused to lift it in my own defence? Unconsecrate, how could I wield the holy thing? I bring it home. It is the sacred spear.' Gurnemanz is in solemn ecstasy. The redeemer has come at last. Parsifal is not sure of this, but the old knight is. But one step remains for Parsifal to take, and it is his last. To complete the sense of saviourhood he requires only that the faith of others in him should seal his call. Let him be believed in by only one, and he can be sure of himself. Till now, called as he was and anointed of heaven, he could do no great work because none were found to believe in him, and no human sympathy lighted his way. Now in the faith of Gurnemanz, and still more, perhaps, as we shall see, in that of Kundry, he finds himself. For the second time Kundry does him that service. As for her, while Parsifal speaks of the curse and the night, she shrinks still further out of sight. She slips unobserved into the hut, and we can only see her outline upon its window, as she continues to gaze upon the peaceful mead. Perhaps her presence was still sinister upon Parsifal. At any rate, her withdrawal has a studied coincidence with Gurnemanz's next words. 'Thy curse is gone,' he cries; 'if curse it was, it has gone. Thou art near the Grail. Its knights await thee. O what misery has been ours! How we need thee! The King, more desperate than ever, refuses to uncover the Grail and dispense our souls' food. If he look not on the life-giving Grail he thinks he may die, and death is his one desire. Our knightly power is sick and dying. We have neither courage nor aspiration, and we wander aimless, weak, and pale. Titurel is dead, and here in solitude I wait the call to follow him.' Parsifal's misery returns at this account. He accuses himself and his cowardice, and seems slipping back into the desert of soul from which he came. Chosen for redemption, yet the last path of deliverance seems to him now closed, since things in Montsalvat are so hopeless. Kundry has gathered courage from his self-reproach to come to the door of the hut and lift her eyes to him. He does not see her. He totters, and Gurnemanz, catching him in his arms, carries him to the edge of the holy well, and lays him on the moss. Kundry hurries out with a basin and water to revive him, while in the band her stormy motive passes into her motive of service. It is her first chance of real service, the first time she seems really needed; and it is, therefore, like a sword-thrust when Gurnemanz motions her back, and damps her new eagerness into the utter resignation of her habitual mien. She wanders bent and slow to the hut again. But it is no rebuff. Gurnemanz, too, has a mission now—the mission of the Baptist. 'Our sacred well must sprinkle him. A great work waits him, and a holy, and the dust of error must be washed and blessed away.' Kundry, encouraged, returns, and devoutly helps to divest Parsifal of his remaining armour. With what tender awe she handles cuirass, greaves, and shoes! As Parsifal half reclines in his white robe there is a studied resemblance in his features and mien to the traditional representation of Christ. It is deeply affecting, as Kundry, on her knees, in an abstraction of passionate reverence, proceeds to bathe his feet from the spring. She stoops as if to kiss them if she dared; but she never ventures to lift her eyes to his face. The scene is too solemn to be sentimental. 'All is quiet, happy, and suppressed.' The music throughout combines the holiness of the Grail and the peace of Resurrection with the tender grace of the spring. Wearily Parsifal inquires if he shall be taken to Amfortas to-day. Amfortas first again! But that is nothing to Kundry now. She is not at her deliverer's head, but to be at his feet is too much honour for her. While Gurnemanz replies that all awaits them at Montsalvat, and to-day is the funeral of Titurel, which he is about to attend, the glance of Parsifal falls for the first time on Kundry with a quick, pleased wonder; and at the same moment we hear in the orchestra a peculiar movement which occurred once before as Kundry described to Parsifal the glance upon her of the eye of Christ. Through Parsifal the Saviour has looked on her again, and not now to curse, but to bless and release. But the wonder of Parsifal is not simply caused by the sight of Kundry. It is also due to the new sense of what Kundry's devotion is rousing within himself. To even her is it given, as it may have been given to her prototype of old, not only to gladden, but even to certify in some degree her saviour's soul. If ever Christ rejoiced in spirit, realised to Himself His saving vocation, and was refreshed to go on His redeeming way, surely He must have so felt when such women knelt to Him, when they kissed His feet, and departed ecstatic, humbled, and forgiven.

In the presence of Kundry and Gurnemanz Parsifal's last doubt vanishes. He rises to his high calling. A solemn certainty fills his soul, and the radiance of it passes into his face. It is hardly possible to believe that this noble and joyful figure is the same as he who but a little while ago entered from the desert and its temptations, scarcely saved.

Of such power it is that we should be believed in. Such virtue enters us, and such added being, in the act that we are beloved. What respect is to the upright, what admiration is to the hero, that are faith and love to the saviour kind.

With a grave gentleness and a royal kindness he associates the prodigal woman with her elder brother, the knight, and gives them an equal share in the ministry of his consecration. Addressing first Kundry, then Gurnemanz, he says, 'Thou hast washed my feet, now let my friend sprinkle my head.' Wagner selects as eternally and ideally significant only the two (Protestant) sacraments. We have seen his treatment of the Eucharist. Here we have consecration by Baptism, with all its suggestions of refreshment and purity. Gurnemanz takes water from the spring, and sprinkles it on Parsifal's head, blessing him into purity by the pure, and loosing the very last chains and stains of the world's sin. Kundry meanwhile, still kneeling in busy rapture, has pulled from her bosom a golden vial, and slowly poured its unguent upon his feet. As slowly and as gravely she gathers her long black hair from her shoulders, and like one in a dream dries with it the ointment away. Up till now Parsifal has been reclining on the bank where he had been laid; but the influence of Kundry's worship in helping him to full possession of himself is shown by his rising here to a sitting position, and extending his hand in benediction and acknowledgment. It is a somewhat perilous situation. Any but first-rate art would be in danger of lapsing into sentiment, to the vulgarising and collapse of all. But Wagner is safe, and his feeling is sound. There is no effusiveness anywhere. All is strong and chaste, even holy. The spiritual atmosphere is 'Touch-me-not,' even when contact comes. The passionate reserves of unselfish passion and the deep modesties of profound religion have no small share in the ineffable impression we here feel. Gently still, for we are in the believing world that makes not haste, Parsifal takes the vial from her hand with a tender radiance deeper than a smile, and, handing it to Gurnemanz, at last proclaims himself the old knight's suzerain and the heir of the Grail. 'Dost thou anoint my feet, too?' he says to Kundry; 'then let Titurel's comrade anoint my head, that to-day he may hail me as king.'

We may mark how both the official functions of Gurnemanz upon his head, by water and by oil, are suggested and anticipated by the loving instinct of the abased Kundry at his feet. Hers is the woman's function of initiating by suggestion rather than by performance. The post of humility is really the post of honour, and love like hers is the divining love that in the long-run moves and leads the sterner world. The Parsifal-motive sounds from the orchestra, passing into union with the Messiah strain and that of the Grail, as Gurnemanz in exaltation anoints Parsifal and salutes him. More radiant than ever, and more grave, Parsifal turns to perform the first act of his reign. It is not now Amfortas first, it is at length Kundry—who seeks but to be last, and less than nothing. As the glorified

Christ appeared first to Mary, so Parsifal's first business is with Kundry. The strains of faith and of the Grail stream up from the instruments as he gazes on her face upturned at last; and as her head quickly droops he baptizes her with water from the well. Once he nearly killed her, and she gave him a cup of cold water in reply. Now he returns it with heavenly interest, and it nearly kills her again. Her old self it does finally kill. It kills utterly her curse. 'Take thy baptism, and believe in the redeemer.' The pity he sternly refused to Kundry as her lover he freely bestows as her saviour, and her redemption is complete. And the sign of it is this. She sinks on her face, not stunned now, but overwhelmed, shaken to the very depths of her great being. She weeps passionately whose curse had been laughter, and her sobs are now the only possible expression of her supernatural joy.

It is a new world and a redeemed. The glory of spring is now the glory of resurrection. The landscape itself becomes sacramental. How sweet the world sleeps when passion's fitful fever is by! How cool is reality, how fevered and false is the illusion of selfish desire! How fresh is our last best truth! How various is the great simplicity! How manifold of life is the shining meadow and its deep green flowery peace! Yes, the last peace is green, not grey; and it is not loud, but deep. Spring, resurrection, chaste, sane, satisfying joy, sober certainty, and tender peace,—such things as these speak to us in the exquisite orchestral number which now begins, and expresses the spiritual atmosphere to which all have come. It is a great 'pastoral symphony' as has been said. Parsifal lifts his head and gazes, entranced, upon forest and field. He never saw nature like this. In his youth even it was not so gladsome as now. The desert rejoices and blossoms. Gardens are gaudy and wild compared with the cultured grace of nature redeemed—the same, but not the same. 'Marvellous flowers,' he says, 'once I saw, which clamoured about me high as my head. Never saw I blossom or bough so gentle, so tender, as this. None ever shone with such fragrant, child-like, grace; none ever spoke to me with such frankness of love.' The contrast, of course, is with the magic garden of sin. 'Yes,' replies Gurnemanz, 'it is the Good Friday magic. Nay, sink not, mourn not, weep not. Here sinners' tears are turned to holy dew. Here every creature glories in a world redeemed. The Crucified we see not on His cross, we see His redeemed among men. The very flowers feel that they are trodden lightlier or not at all, and nature celebrates its Innocents' Day.'

The magic air invades the soul of the prostrate Kundry. It is no longer passion's hour, but peace has become a passion. Redemption even is not now a prayer but a great calm, a reality ever to abide. She slowly gathers her sobbing form and lifts her bared head. She is still at Parsifal's feet. With streaming eyes she gazes in his face. Is something lacking yet? Her look is still a speechless prayer, and the orchestra gives it wings. Does she quite know what she wants? Perhaps not. But something in her tells her she lacks the last touch of the redemptive spring. 'There is no sin,' says the *Imitation*, 'but shall have its torment in kind.' Shall forgiveness also be in any sense in terms of the offence? Parsifal understands.

> I saw some fade who laughed on me;
> Crave they Redemption now like thee?
> But thy tears, too, are healing dew.
> Thou weepest! See, the world smiles new.

And he slowly stoops and puts his lips to her brow, as in other scenes she had done to him. It is the holy kiss of Scripture; the last seal of forgiveness; the sweet, modest, human sacrament in its most sacred use. And the lovely motive of the flowery mead tells us that the tears of sinners restored are part of the Eternal Beauty as surely as the pure dew upon the field. Much high-flown nonsense is talked by the younger devotees of Wagner and Pessimism about the redemptive mission of Art. The master's genius is far truer and deeper than the disciples' interpretation of it; and it may be asked of their ardent unwisdom if it was Art that redeemed Kundry.

But much must yet be done. The conquest of sin is not yet complete, and its sting is still aching in the world. Solemn bells begin to strike upon our ear from the holy Burg, and amid the Easter joy there intrudes the remembrance of the spiritual famine and anarchy among the knights. These have culminated in the death of Titurel for lack of refreshment from the long-closed Grail. ''Tis noon,' says Gurnemanz, 'and it is the hour.' The motive of Parsifal sounds out, only to pass into the weird Transformation music which in the first act expounded to us the solemn fear that girds the sanctuary. Gurnemanz and Kundry invest Parsifal with the mail and mantle of the knights. The scene begins slowly to change and pass in the same mystic way as in the first act, only now in the contrary direction, from left to right. Parsifal grasps reverently the spear and follows Gurnemanz, Kundry following him 'afar off.' The wood vanishes as the gloom descends. Portals open in massive rocks, and gradually the three are lost to sight. The mournful bells sound nearer and nearer. We perceive dim corridors traversed by figures in funereal guise. And at last the light rises again upon the hall of the Grail as we saw it before, only now without the tables. In the gloom a train of knights slowly moves from the rear on the right, bearing the coffin of the dead Titurel. From the left emerges a second train, bearing in front the covered Grail, and behind it on his litter the sick Amfortas. The two trains move forward to meet each other in the central foreground, then turn and carry their respective burdens back to the centre of the stage, where the bier is laid on a catafalque, the Grail on the altar behind, and behind that the King Amfortas. The trains as they advance address each other in antiphon. 'We carry the Grail. What carry ye?' 'We carry Titurel.' 'What aileth him?' 'The burden of age slew him, as the vision of the Grail was denied him.' 'Who denied it?' 'That sinner whom ye escort.' 'We escort him to-day once more to perform his office for the last time.' 'Woe and warning! We warn thee to thy task.' With this the bier and the King are both deposited, and the knights are gathered round, restless and threatening. Amfortas takes up the 'woe.' 'Yes, woe to me. Will ye not slay me?' Then he bursts into a torrent of remorseful appeal to his now sainted father. 'I brought death to thee; O thou who art now in the Saviour's glorious presence, pray that His blood unveiled, as it brings life's blessing to these knights, may bring to me the blessing of death. So only can my wound and poison die.' The knights with still more menace press upon him the unveiling of the Grail. He grows desperate. He refuses. He rises frantic from his couch. He rushes down the steps among the appalled and yielding brotherhood. He tears open the bosom of his mantle. He prays them to strike and bring him his end. 'Slay the sinner, and of itself the Grail will then beam upon you.'

By this time Parsifal, Gurnemanz, and Kundry have entered unperceived among the knights. The great moment has come. Parsifal steps forward, raises the spear, and with its point touches the King's side, exclaiming—

One only weapon serves the hour,
The spear that smote to heal has power.

The King's frenzy passes into ecstasy; he totters, and is caught by Gurnemanz. 'Be whole,' continues Parsifal; 'be purified, atoned, for I will take thine office. Blessed be thy woe. It gave the shrinking fool pity, supreme power, and the might of purest knowledge. I bring you back the sacred spear.' Parsifal holds it aloft, and they gaze raptly upon its point, which begins to glow an awful red. 'O miracle! It closed thy wound, and now I see flowing from it the holy blood, yearning to rejoin its spring there in the depths of the Grail. Unveil the Grail. It shall be closed no more.' The shrine is opened by the boys. Parsifal takes the cup, elevates it, and kneels before it in dumb devotion. It glows in his hands. A flood of light flows from above upon the whole company. Titurel, restored for a moment to life, rises from his bier to bless the solemn hour. A dove descends, and hovers above Parsifal, who waves the Grail gently over the bowed heads from the altar steps. Amfortas and Gurnemanz kneel and revere Parsifal, while the whole assembly, in a tone of subdued triumph and joy, sing, to the sound of harpers harping upon their harps, and in the strain of the Fool-motive, now glorified as a Saviour-motive—

> Miracle of Grace supreme!
> Be redeemed who didst redeem.

And what of Kundry? She is that dark figure, softly going, who follows Parsifal like his shadow, yet remote, without lifting her eyes from his form. Unregarded, she moves slowly and timidly towards the altar steps, up which she creeps the most unworthy and most dear of all. Amid the tumult of worship she lies prone in adoration, and as the joy and glory is at its height she turns over and dies, with the glory pouring upon her upturned face and the throne of the opened heaven in her eyes. Is she extinct, as the sad philosophers would teach? Believe it who can.

As the strain of praise rises from deep men's voices through the youths to the boys in the dome, there floats down on the softest pinions of sound the great faith-motive. Worlds seem opening upon worlds. Bliss unspeakable is uttered in the music which alone can tell it. The motive of the Grail prolongs the solemn tale, and upon its notes the redeemed come to themselves again with singing and great joy upon their heads, and sorrow and sighing flee away.

It is needless to dwell upon the shortcomings of a work like this if placed in any rivalry with the Christian Redemption. Parsifal is no more the world's Messiah than Deronda. It is neither as the founder nor the prophet of a new religion that Wagner will live. He is an artist with a message for the soul; but it is not for artists to bring the soul's redemption. When it comes, it comes by no godless Messiah. But if too little stress has been laid by the Church upon Christ's conquest of man's sin in His own spiritual history; if His life-long temptation and victory have been neglected as the real work of Redemption; if Christian people have been too easily satisfied to have such a work done for them instead of repeated in them; if the Christian conflict has been too un-moral, too legal, fanciful, or sentimental, and if it has thus been severed from the great Art of the spiritual imagination, we may gladly submit to be recalled to one neglected truth of Scripture by an artist and thinker who is not singular, but the hierophant of God's Spirit of the age.

The effect upon the world of such a work as this must become extraordinary as it becomes more and more known. But without indulging in forecast we are free to marvel at such a product from amidst a people who are reported to have left religion behind, and to have fallen into a scientific paganism and a military materialism. We are free to dwell upon this witness to the indestructible vitality of the great Christian needs in the soul, and the invincible might of the great Christian ideas in the world. And we are free, perhaps, to look forward to such a restoration of belief as shall make Christ not only Saviour of the complex and vexed modern spirit, but the Deliverer from that sin which is still the torment and dead-weight of the race. It is the sin of sex that is becoming more than intemperance the fatal sin of modern life. And the new development of the old gospel of Love will probably have to arrive through its application to the impurity of society and its conflict with the degradation of love. The great Redemption is a redemption of Man, of both sexes alike. And it must be a Redemption chiefly from that sin in which they are one flesh to the purity in which they are one spirit. It is most hopeful that the last great work of the thinking nation should be the utterance of man's need for Redemption as his deepest passion. It is most hopeful that it should be the need for Redemption from that sin which more than any other destroys society and makes a true Socialism impossible. The passion of sex is the deepest passion of the race, except the passion to be delivered in God from the abuse of passion. It is that abuse which most threatens the social future. It is with that abuse that the Gospel of the future of Europe must wrestle. And it is in the conflict with such abuse and sin that the most potent resource, the most awful solemnity, and the most ineffable tenderness of the Gospel, will emerge. The Art of the present forecasts the Religion of the future; but it is Religion and not Art that must fight the battles of the future, and lead us by spiritual conflict with the wild beasts of passion, and the dark phantoms of error, to the moral way, and the paths of righteousness, and the gates of freedom and joy.